WILLIAM ELKIN MUSIC
SERVICES
Station Road Ind. Estate
SALHOUSE · NORWICH
NR13 6NY   ENGLAND

MUSIC in ENGLAND

1885–1920

Overleaf: Sir Edward Elgar

MUSIC in ENGLAND
1885 – 1920
as recounted in Hazell's Annual

edited with illustrations, introduction,
and index
by
LEWIS FOREMAN

Thames Publishing
London
1994

ISBN 0 905210 32 8

The annual reviews of music from *Hazell's* which are reproduced here originally appeared over a period of 36 years, and while every effort has been made to maintain a consistent print quality, inevitably there is some variation from year to year, owing to the considerable variation in quality of the originals.

ACKNOWLEDGEMENTS

My chief debts are to my wife, Susan, and to my publisher, John Bishop, for their long patience and detailed assistance in the preparation of this book. Susan's labours to get my typescript index into the Macrex computer program and subsequently corrected were considerable and immeasurably lightened the load in the pre-publication period. A very wide selection of copies of *Hazell's* were consulted from a variety of libraries, and it is no longer possible to identify which came from where – thank you librarians, everywhere! The pictures are all taken from my own collection, largely from picture postcards, though a few are from other contemporary sources. Finally I am very grateful to Stephen Lloyd, who read the introduction at a late stage and raised a number of points; any errors that remain are my own.

LEWIS FOREMAN
21 January 1994

Printed by Hobbs the Printers of Southampton

CONTENTS

ILLUSTRATIONS

HAZELL'S 1885–1920

As there is no entry for the year 1915 the editor has compiled one from contemporary press notices. Although p.v. appears after a number of names throughout this compilation, the articles to which they refer are not reprinted here.

Sir Hubert Parry

Sir Arthur Sullivan

Sir A C Mackenzie

Sir Charles Stanford

The Revival of
Victorian and Edwardian Music

Hazell's Annual first appeared in 1886, in direct competition with *Whitaker's Almanack*, as *Hazell's Annual Cyclopedia*. It dropped the last word of the title after three years' publication, and in 1917 was relaunched as *The New Hazell Annual and Almanack*. It ceased publication with the 1922 edition. A valuable feature of each issue was its two- or three-page survey of the previous year's musical events in London, with brief notes on the main provincial festivals; and thus, by extracting these annual surveys of the musical scene, we can assemble a continuous chronological summary of the period from 1885 to 1920 inclusive, excluding 1915, when no musical review was published. (The final issue also contained no article on music.)

It is an oft-quoted maxim, and in my experience a true one, that the most assiduous user of any reference book is its originator. Certainly the compilation which follows has been assembled in the first place for the convenience of the editor. It is most useful to be able to survey the main events in a particular field over a run of years. Particularly as *Hazell's Annual* is to be found in so few libraries, it is hoped that by extracting the annual musical reviews and assembling them as a coherent sequence, with the important additions of an entry for 1915 (assembled by the editor from commentary in *The Musical Times* and *The Times* newspaper), a detailed index of names and places, and a wide selection of contemporary illustrations, it will become not only more generally available, but will have a much enhanced value to students of British music of this fascinating period.

One should emphasise the place of the index in making this mass of names and forgotten composers accessible to the user. In this period there are many musical journals but few adequate indexes to individual titles, and virtually nothing to the whole literature or even part of it. So tracing names and dates from the sequence I offer here may well provide a key for research elsewhere.

Although the author or authors of the *Hazell's* surveys obviously only presented the then contemporary assessment of the music as it was when first played, at the very least we are given an *aide-mémoire* to once celebrated scores, and provided with a guide in planning the reassessment of the British music of the late Victorian and Edwardian periods in performance. Now that the investigation and assessment of Elgar and his music is virtually completed, the spadework has also been done for turning the lens on those who were his contemporaries during all parts of his life.

After hearing the music in question, a valuable clue to the spirit of a period is to see good contemporary portraits of those involved, and of the places where the music was played. Fortunately the rise of the picture postcard is almost exactly contemporary with our history, and so there are splendid photographs available from postcards of the time. A good collection of these postcards is still comparatively easy to assemble, and they are almost an essential source for any writer about the music of the late nineteenth and early twentieth centuries, and one surprisingly little exploited by authors or their publishers. Many British composers and performing artists who appear here are also illustrated, as well as many celebrated foreign musicians whose visits to the UK are documented by *Hazell's* surveys.

The ultimate focus of all musical research is performance, and even if there were no other reason, these pages are of interest in bringing to our notice works and composers once popular but who have subsequently been forgotten. To what extent should the works chronicled here, and in particular those that were first heard before the First World War, be revived in modern times? Rejecting the temptation prevalent 20 years ago to indulge in the wholesale condemnation of the British music of this period, unheard, are we able to come even to an interim assessment based on recent performances? Certainly we are *beginning* to be able to do so, and this is an appropriate place, in particular, briefly to review our present understanding of the music of Parry, Mackenzie, Stanford, Cowen, Coleridge-Taylor and Bantock in the light of modern performances, and a rapidly expanding catalogue of CD recordings. Revivals of this music have certainly been gathering momentum, and there is now a sufficiently large body of recent aural experience to provide a strong feeling for where the swans – and the geese – may be found. Elgar[1] has been given a very good crack of the whip over the last few years, and so we may exclude him from this particular survey. Excluded, too, are the more familiar composers of the 'British musical renaissance', including Bridge, Vaughan Williams and Holst, who begin to loom large in the second half of this chronology, for they, too, have been discussed elsewhere, whereas the 'big' names of the late Victorian and Edwardian periods had, until very recently, not been considered *from first-hand experience* for many years.

The names of Sir Charles Hubert Hastings Parry (1848–1918) and Sir Charles Villiers Stanford (1852–1924) dominate the British music of the late nineteenth century. Their influential positions as respectively Director and Professor of Composition at the Royal College of Music over many years (both were associated with the College from 1883 to their deaths) mean that, if nothing else, they have held an almost unassailable historical position through the achievement of their pupils. Yet they both wrote an enormous amount of music. In each case this music was of surprisingly variable quality, and neither composer can be judged on the basis of just one or two works. It is really only in the last few years that they are beginning to be properly evaluated *in performance*, and in particular the recent excellent recordings of many forgotten scores have brought to light some remarkably fine works.

Performance of the violin concertos of Mackenzie and Coleridge-Taylor, and the revival in the USA, and subsequent CD recording, of the Mass in D by Ethel Smyth remind us of the sheer volume of unknown music (and unknown composers!) of the late Victorian period deserving evaluation. Smyth's Mass in D, though the stuff of legend, has not been often performed. First played in 1893 under Barnby, it was not heard again until Boult gave it in Birmingham in 1924. The present-day revival started with a performance in Minneapolis on 4 May 1980 conducted by Philip Brunelle and it subsequently had two or three performances in the UK, including one at Charterhouse School Chapel, and was then revived by the BBC in December 1985 and broadcast on 6 April 1986 and repeated on 22 July 1988. Later came the Virgin Classics recording conducted by Philip Brunelle[2] and most recently a blistering performance at

---

[1] For a discussion of the revival of Elgar's choral music see my article 'The Revival of Elgar's Choral Music', *Musical Opinion*, Feb 1975, pp239–40, 243.

[2] Dame Ethel Smyth: Mass in D; Mrs Waters' aria from *The Boatswain's Mate*; *The March of the Women*. The Plymouth Music Series/Philip Brunelle, VIRGIN VC 7 91188-2.

London's Queen Elizabeth Hall conducted by Odaline de la Martinez.[3] Without performances we cannot fully understand the period, or the British music of the twentieth century which grew from it. Only then will Parry, Stanford and the others be seen in their proper context.

PARRY

Parry was never completely forgotten, even when his reputation was at its lowest ebb, for that highly characteristic score *Blest Pair of Sirens* (Vaughan Williams said: 'the finest musical work that has come out of these islands') has always been popular with choirs and has continued to be played. Also, Parry's hymn-tunes, headed by 'Jerusalem' and including such favourites as 'Wesley', 'Repton' and 'Rustington', are deeply implanted in the broader public's musical awareness. Sir Adrian Boult, a lifelong champion of Parry, always attempted to keep examples of the music before the public and to the end of his life he performed a number of scores, some of which he recorded. (It is interesting to note that when Boult wanted to include the late symphonic poem *From Death to Life* on his last LP, performing materials could not be procured and he had to substitute a second recording of the better known *Symphonic Variations*: a typical and unfortunate problem, in this instance since rectified, in the path of anyone trying to revive such a long-unplayed score.) Unfortunately, Boult's championship of Parry's orchestral music on disc came rather late in his career, and it is arguable that in his performance of the Fifth Symphony, for example, he was no longer fully capable of catching the fire and passion implicit in it, qualities which need to be underlined for the music to be properly reappraised.

Critical opinion is divided as to which of Parry's long procession of choral works deserve to live, and which are unlikely to be worth revival in the 1990s and beyond. Certainly that old standby of bashing through the vocal score at the piano can be unexpectedly misleading in the case of Parry, just as it was even more misleading before Elgar's earlier choral music was revived and found to be far better than many had expected. In fact, Parry's orchestration, although perhaps somewhat plain – in his later years he shrank from colour for colour's sake – is a vital component for the full appreciation of his music.

Apart from the organ music and the celebrated *a capella Songs of Farewell*, which have become more widely sung again, there is a rapidly growing representation of the orchestral music revived on disc,[4] and the Chandos series of CDs[5] in particular, certainly make a substantial case for Parry as a significant figure in the

[3] On 11 April 1993. The programme also included the first performance for 100 years of Smyth's striking overture *Anthony and Cleopatra*.

[4] On LP: *Concertstück* for orchestra, *Elegy for Brahms, An English Suite* for strings, *Lady Radnor's Suite, Overture to an Unwritten Tragedy*, Symphonic Variations and the Third and Fifth Symphonies. Subsequently Lyrita repackaged their Boult recordings of Parry onto one CD (*An English* and *Lady Radnor's Suites, Overture to an Unwritten Tragedy*, Symphonic Variations, and the glorious *Bridal March* written in 1883 for Aristophanes' *The Birds*, on SRCD 220).

[5] No one, even in their wildest flights of fancy, can have ever expected to see a boxed set of the complete Parry symphonies. Not only is this available from Chandos (CHAN 9120–22), a tremendous achievement, together with the Symphonic Variations, *Elegy for Brahms* and *From Death to Life* (the last two if the symphonies are purchased separately), but also three extended choral works, *The Soul's Ransom, The Lotos Eaters* and *Invocation to Music*, all funded by the Vaughan Williams Trust.

history of British music. If the Second, Third and Fourth Symphonies as revived by Matthias Bamert had been available earlier, no serious critic could have been tempted to the ludicrous proposition that no significant English symphonies preceded Elgar. However, it may well be to the revival of Parry's choral music that we must look for an assessment of his final place in the nation's musical heart.

Not surprisingly it was Vaughan Williams' own Leith Hill Music Festival that gave consistent support to Parry's choral works over the years. Apart from many performances of *Blest Pair of Sirens*, Leith Hill revived *Job* and scenes from *Judith* during the Second World War, and later tackled the *Ode on St Cecilia's Day* (1950), *The Glories of Our Blood and State* (1957) and *Ode to Music* (1958), the last two not otherwise heard since Parry's lifetime.

This revival has been a very gradual affair, and as well as Sir Adrian's contribution, performances have come from less celebrated, though no less committed, conductors. Since the Second World War eighteen of Parry's choral works have been revived — *Job; The Glories of Our Blood and State; Ode to Music; I Was Glad; De Profundis; Coronation Te Deum* (1911); *Voces Clamantium; Ode on St Cecilia's Day; The Soul's Ransom; Prometheus Unbound; Invocation to Music; Beyond These Voices There is Peace; England; The Lotos Eaters; The Pied Piper of Hamelin; Hear My Words, Ye People; Ode on the Nativity* and *Eton*. Perhaps *Job* is the most contentious of these. It was the subject of vilification by George Bernard Shaw which has tended to stick, especially among those who have never heard the music performed. Sir Adrian gave it three times on the BBC between the Parry Centenary in 1948, and 1970, and spoke very highly of it, a championship which was echoed by Vaughan Williams. However, it must be admitted that in performance one has a certain sympathy for what Shaw meant, and one can see how some recent critics probably heard the 1970 broadcast and have applied their criticisms of that score, by extension, to the rest of Parry's choral music. What *Job* lacks is dramatic drive. It is in too 'safe' an idiom for its subject, yet in memorable melody and stirring and imposing chorus work it demonstrates many of Parry's strengths, which perhaps are best heard in shorter works. Certainly one can see from *Job* why its successor, the larger-scale *King Saul*, is probably not likely to succeed today, though well received by *Hazell's* in 1894. As to *Job's* predecessor, the oratorio *Judith*, also well received in the pages that follow, it is difficult to know whether it would stand revival — possibly Parry's own published abridgement would be worth a trial by an enterprising choral society. The impact of *I was glad* at the Coronation in 1953 has made it a favourite short score either with organ accompaniment or with orchestra. Boult revived the 12-part *De Profundis* in a broadcast in the late 1950s, and in the 1960s an isolated broadcast of the 1911 *Coronation Te Deum* (with organ) was heard. Both are interesting and worthwhile scores, though perhaps lacking the greater moments of which Parry was capable.

Present interest has centred on a number of revivals which began in the late 1970s. One of the best was the splendid *Voces Clamantium* revived with organ by Jonathan Rennert at St Michael's, Cornhill (and recorded by him on ANTI 2503), and with orchestra by the Kensington Symphony Orchestra and Choir conducted by Leslie Head, a comparison which overwhelmingly underlines the importance of the orchestra in Parry's choral works. Given with just organ they lose much of their grandeur and idiosyncratic colouring. Parry described this 22-minute setting of words from the Book of Isaiah as a motet. Written for the Three Choirs Festival at Hereford in 1903, it typifies the call to humanity that echoes through all his later choral

The climax of Parry's *Voices Clamantium*, taken from the Novello vocal score.

music. Mackenzie, Parry's opposite number at the Royal Academy of Music, referred to 'that purposeful sequence of appeals for brotherhood among the peoples' which began with this score and ended with the comparatively familiar *Songs of Farewell*.

The anthem *Hear my Words, ye People*, written for Salisbury Cathedral in 1894, was featured in the 300th Anniversary Service of the Festival of the Sons of the Clergy in St Paul's Cathedral on 16 May 1978 in an orchestration by Richard Barnes.

It has since been recorded by the choir of St George's Chapel, Windsor, with organ accompaniment (Hyperion CDA 66273).[6]

Robert Tucker, whose Broadheath Singers' annual concert (once at Slough, but for many years now at Eton) has revived many worthwhile forgotten scores by Victorian and Edwardian composers, has given what is probably the most valuable of the Parry revivals so far: the *Ode on St Cecilia's Day* of 1889. This is a 45-minute, five-movement cantata with soprano and baritone soloists. Tucker has also programmed the much shorter 'ode' for Eton College to words by Swinburne, called just *Eton* (1891) but very much more than a school song, and concluding with a broad, wide-spanning marching tune which almost rivals the splendid setting of 'O man, look upward where the skies are clear' that ends *Voces Clamantium* so memorably.

The renaissance of British music in the first half of the twentieth century is said to date from the first performance of Parry's *Prometheus Unbound* in 1880. The BBC marked the centenary of this event by reviving Parry's score before an invited audience at the Henry Wood Hall in London. This was an historic occasion, and certainly few present at that performance had ever expected to have the opportunity to hear a performance of Parry's epoch-making score. However, although *Prometheus* must have appeared revolutionary to its first audience, the revival (which was conducted by Vernon Handley) underlined the fact that in 1880 the 32-year-old Parry had still not fully assimilated his models, and his personal style would not emerge at its most characteristic for another five years or so. Nevertheless, it was a valuable effort by the BBC, allowing, as it did, the modern audience to gain a considerable insight into so historically important a score, which still offers many felicities on its own account.

Invocation to Music, Parry's collaboration with the poet Robert Bridges for a work to mark the bicentenary in 1895 of Purcell's death, remained unheard for many years: like so many of these scores, just another brown Novello vocal score on the junk trays outside second-hand music shops. Its revival by Denys Darlow with the Tilford and Bath Bach choirs at Bath Abbey in April 1988 revealed a work of some grandeur, crowned by haunting settings of Bridges' magnificent Dirge: 'Man born of desire' and 'Rejoice ye dead' – words more familiar from Holst's better-known *Choral Fantasia* of 1930. This is Parry at the peak of his powers and when the soprano, the personification of sorrow, soars on Parry's radiant invention, echoed by the chorus, we know we face a composer of permanent value who can speak to all. As Bridges wrote: 'the identification of music with the religious (or whatever you call it) spirit, ... corresponds with the aspirations at the bottom of the social movements of our time'.[7] When Chandos came to record it (CHAN 9025) in 1992, Anne Dawson and Arthur Davies replaced Lorna Anderson and Charles Daniels as the soprano and tenor soloists, but Brian Rayner Cook preserved his Bath interpretation on the CD recording. The story of its composition is told by Jeremy Dibble in his pioneering study of Parry, during which he quotes Bridges' original concept of the work as '... a celebration of the beauties of nature, a contemplation of the mysteries of death, including a lament (in this context on the premature death of Purcell himself) and a choral dirge for the dead artist, thereafter passing into triumph, joy, and dance ...'.[8]

---

[6] Performing materials from Cathedral Music, Maudlin House, Westhampnett, Chichester PO180PB.
[7] Letter Robert Bridges to Parry, 16 Oct. 1894, quoted in Jeremy Dibble's *C Hubert H Parry: his life and music*, Oxford, Clarendon Press, 1992, p 323.
[8] Ibid.

Even Parry's contemporaries tended to refer to the choral works he wrote after the death of Queen Victoria as uneven, excusing the composer on grounds of over-work. Four of these scores have been revived, one appearing on LP and another on CD. They are *The Pied Piper of Hamelin* (1905), *The Soul's Ransom* (1906), *Beyond These Voices There is Peace* (1908) and the *Ode on the Nativity* (1912), and it can be reported that none need excuses. Although Parry did write some uneven works during the Edwardian period, there are undoubtedly several other worthwhile scores awaiting adventurous pioneering choral societies. *The Pied Piper of Hamelin*, revived at the Brighton Festival in 1985, is enjoyable but proved not to be in the main stream of Parry's choral style. The *Ode on the Nativity* first reappeared in a BBC broadcast on Radio 3 in 1976. It was heard again in public at the Royal College of Music, an interpretation that was later recorded (on Lyrita SRCS 125), though with the London Philharmonic Orchestra in place of the RCM First Orchestra who had played at the concert. This is an immediately attractive score, setting Dunbar's well-known poem in an unbroken half-hour span, which encompasses a delightfully pastoral orchestral introduction, an affecting solo soprano and vigorous choral writing. Orchestrally, too, it is notable for the luminous scoring, with masterful touches of colour in characteristic vein.

The Soul's Ransom had probably not been heard since its first performance in 1907, and new performing materials and vocal scores had to be produced for its revival at Haddo House, near Aberdeen, in May 1981. It was subsequently given in London, in October 1983, by the BBC Club Choir and Orchestra conducted by Ronald Corp, and at the Bach Choir's memorable all-Parry Concert in June 1985 sponsored by the Vaughan Williams Trust. Matthias Bamert's fine CD recording for Chandos presents the work in its best possible light. This is an imposing and memorable score, which Bernard Benoliel in the programme note for the 1983 performance characterised as 'the link work between *The Dream of Gerontius* and the *Sea Symphony*'. Yet it does not have quite the memorable invention of some other Parry choral works, and its championship at the expense of alternative revivals may yet be seen to be misplaced.

Both Parry and Stanford produced works in which they appear to pre-echo scores by their juniors but which on closer investigation prove to have been written subsequent to the younger man's work. Certainly Stanford in his Fifth *Irish Rhapsody* was taking his cue from Vaughan Williams rather than the reverse, and although Elgar was undoubtedly fundamentally influenced by Parry, Parry's most superficially Elgarian moment, in the 'Sarabande' of his *English Suite*, was written long after any similar piece by Elgar. In each case a touching, if probably unconscious, tribute.

MACKENZIE

Sir Alexander Campbell Mackenzie (1847–1935) (the knighthood came in 1895) clearly wrote in an idiom – perhaps one should say idioms – which his contem-porary audiences found attractive, yet his reputation barely survived the Great War, though he lived on for another 17 years. A number of orchestral scores have recently been revived and these have revealed an engaging body of work, but one without a common style. Mackenzie adopted the idioms current in his young manhood and always remained a Victorian composer by technique and by temperament. While it is not likely that one will hear an unknown piece and immediately recognise it to be by him, for he never achieved a recognisable personal style, he nevertheless wrote a number of works that deserve to live at least on the fringes of the repertoire.

In the prelude to his opera *Colomba* he writes a splendid 'lollipop' in the style of Gounod, complete with a glorious string tune, while in the Violin Concerto he underlines that he is a student of Raff, and in the *Scottish Piano Concerto* his treatment of Scottish folk elements bears comparison with Max Bruch in his *Scottish Fantasia*. Mackenzie's music may well be evoked for a modern audience unfamiliar with it, by reference to the Bruch. In the tone poems, such as the 'orchestral ballad' *La Belle Dame sans Merci*, which was sympathetically presented by the Royal Academy of Music in May 1984, Mackenzie writes pleasingly for the orchestra. From time to time the BBC have presented the occasional work by Mackenzie, usually with regional orchestras, and the three *Scottish Rhapsodies*, the overture *Cricket on the Hearth* (once recorded on LP) and the overture *Youth, Sport and Loyalty* reveal his ability to write likeable if unoriginal orchestral music, though music seemingly without the grasp of a symphonic intellect of stature.

Investigation of the operas has revealed a similar situation – a varied idiom, tuneful and attractive, but ultimately probably difficult to bring off on the stage today. Here – and even more in his voluminous choral music – we need to hear some of the better extracts performed with orchestra to enable us really to come to grips with them. In his day the choral music – *The Rose of Sharon* and *The Dream of Jubal* in particular – were popular, and the student needs to take account of them. The unexpected revival of the late, 70-minute cantata *The Sun God's Return* by the Royal Scottish National Orchestra, conducted by Christopher Bell, in October 1993 underlined that Mackenzie certainly wrote worthwhile music requiring our assessment today. First performed in Cardiff in 1910, where the work received a hostile press, it was heard again in Sheffield and (in 1911) in Vienna, where the press were kind, before passing into oblivion for 82 years. The work reveals influences of Wagner and Elgar.

STANFORD

Possibly Sir Charles Villiers Stanford is the most noticeably uneven of the establishment names of the late Victorian period. At his best he is superb, and is the composer of much of the music of his generation that is likely to last – the opera most capable of revival (*Much Ado About Nothing* – hear an extended extract from Act I on the Opera Viva recording, see footnote 24 on page 23), the choral masterpiece (the *Requiem*), many of the finest songs, and probably the concerto of greatest stature (and there are some very worthwhile Victorian concerti by British composers) in his *Down Among the Dead Men* variations for piano and orchestra. When one then remembers the influence of Stanford in respect of Anglican church music, his was a considerable overall achievement.

Drawing, as he does, on Irish folksong in many of his works, it was perhaps easier for him to coin a personal style; yet on occasion he will be found to incline more towards Mackenzie's cultural orientation than Parry's. A very large corpus of orchestral, and choral and orchestral music, by Stanford remains to be heard again, and among those works which have been revived the *Requiem*, for example, clearly owes more to Verdi than to Brahms, and includes one passage that is frankly Wagnerian. But for its memorable invention and its dramatic pacing the *Requiem* is a gripping work and one of the finest of the Victorian period. Stanford wrote his extended *Requiem* in memory of Lord Leighton, the Victorian painter and sculptor whose extreme delicacy of finish and vivid use of colour appealed to a wide audience in his day, especially in classical subjects such as 'The Garden of the Hesperides', and who died in 1896. As Verdi reacted to Manzoni's death so did Stanford to Leighton's.

The orchestral full score (Boosey, 1897) of Stanford's Requiem *at the climax of the 'Lacrimosa'. (Courtesy Boosey & Hawkes.)*

It is interesting to note the features of Stanford's style that constantly recur throughout the *Requiem* and are evident from the very beginning. In particular his use of brass figures which are continually repeated; the extended sequences of accompanimental figures higher in the texture; and his blended treatment of the orchestral fabric, which also means that when he allows one colour suddenly to shine out – say trumpets, or violins playing the top line – the effect is immediately striking. What is also intriguing about this score are the several momentary turns of phrase or gesture that antedate similar usage in his pupils, particularly Holst and Vaughan Williams.

The heart of the *Requiem* is the mighty 'Sequence' (*Dies irae, Rex tremendae, Recordare, Confutatis maledictis, Lacrimosa* and *Pie Jesu*). It opens most unusually with soft but urgent mutterings of 'Dies irae' from the men, and rises to a powerful climax at 'tuba mirum'. A notable effect is the repeated descending quaver motif in the bass (33 times on its first appearance) at 'Judex ergo' that reminds us how one of Stanford's pupils was Gustav Holst. When the words 'Rex tremendae' are introduced by the soprano soloist, Stanford underlines his personal involvement in the work by his marking 'con grande espressione ed apassionato'.

The pivot of the 'Sequence' comes with the tenor soloist's extended 'Juste judex' (*andante maestoso*), and then the contralto and soprano soloists launch the passionately chromatic vocal lines of the 'Lacrimosa', which rises to a thrilling and wide-spanning climax; the cymbal clashes here are all the more effective for Stanford having used very little percussion earlier in the score – in accordance with his well-known dictum that it is effective in inverse proportion to its frequency of use.

This is a work that maintained some currency right up to the 1950s, being conducted on more than one occasion by Sir Malcolm Sargent, and once by Sir Thomas Beecham (BBC Symphony Orchestra at Maida Vale Studios on 11 October 1951). For over 25 years it then went unplayed until revived by the BBC in October 1978, conducted by John Poole, and subsequently by the Kensington Symphony Orchestra and Choir conducted by Leslie Head at Southwark Cathedral in February 1981

Stanford's extended six-movement *Te Deum* is perhaps more overtly Victorian than the *Requiem* in its stylistic orientation, yet it was heard twice in the 1980s. It was first revived by the Broadheath Singers at Slough, and later in the Queen Elizabeth Hall, where it was presented by the Chelsea Harmonic Society conducted by Edward de Rivera, in the same (very long) programme as the *Requiem*. It again proved rewarding, but it was clear that for an audience of the 1980s the *Requiem* is the better work.

Stanford's more popular works, such as the vivid *Songs of the Sea* and *Songs of the Fleet*, once they were recorded on LP (they were previously also favourites on 78s) had a considerable following, as would a number of others in the same popular style were they to be made available. The revival of the tuneful 26-minute cantata *The Revenge*, once a mainstay of public school concerts, by the Walton and Oaklands Choral Society in 1988 and later the same year by the Broadheath Singers, underlined that it would certainly appeal to the same audience who enjoys Coleridge-Taylor's *Hiawatha's Wedding Feast*, and there are a good many other similar short scores, of which only the stage-Irish *Phaudrig Crohoore*, revived by the BBC, and the vivid *Battle of the Baltic*, revived by the Broadheath Singers, have been heard recently.

Stanford's 56-minute setting of the *Stabat Mater* was completed in March 1906 and first performed at the Leeds Festival of 1907. By this date, when not only Elgar's three great choral works but also part one of Bantock's *Omar Khayyam* had all been heard, Stanford's 'symphonic cantata' may have appeared a little dated. Nevertheless, it was for a time recognised as one of his best works and was performed reasonably frequently. It had not been performed for several decades, however, when it was revived by the Milton Abbey Music Festival on 30 August 1987 in the splendid setting of the Abbey Church at Milton Abbey School, Dorset, under the sympathetic baton of Richard Hall. The work breaks into five movements, two of which are orchestral. After a dramatic and extended symphonic prelude the words 'Stabat Mater' are presented in a setting of gathering elaboration with the solo soprano at first singing unaccompanied but soon involving all four soli and then the chorus. The music is dramatic as well as lyrical, but again, if he has models at all, Stanford is looking to Italy rather than Germany.

Stanford's surviving canon has been expanded by the discovery of various works believed either lost or not previously listed. The delightful *Serenade*, Op 95, for nonet — almost a sinfonietta — was revived by a student group at the Royal College of Music in March 1987 and was soon recorded by Hyperion (CDA 66291), coupled with Parry's early Nonet in Bb: they make a delightful programme. Totally unknown was the *Concert Piece* 'for Organ Solo with an accompaniment of brass, drums and strings' dating from April 1921 before it was recorded by Chandos (CHAN 8861).

The achievement of Stanford's orchestral music has been brought into focus by the splendid Chandos series of CDs[9] presenting all seven symphonies, six *Irish Rhapsodies* and three concerti — for clarinet, piano (No 2), and *Down Among the Dead Men*, also for piano and orchestra. The *Irish Rhapsodies* in particular are vivid settings of traditional Irish tunes, symphonic in scale and immediately attractive in their orchestral dress. Now that all six are available, they make a strong case for being regarded as among Stanford's greatest — and most characteristic — achievements.

COWEN

Of all the composers considered here, Sir Frederic Hymen Cowen (1852–1935) underwent a more dramatic fall in reputation in the last quarter-century of his career than any of the others. Stanford and Parry both died as acclaimed and famous composers, Mackenzie certainly outlived his period (both Mackenzie and Cowen died in 1935, that is a year after the three most famous composers of the succeeding generation — Elgar, Delius and Holst). Only Cowen, who in his day had been one of the most celebrated of British composers, and possibly the highest paid conductor, suffered so complete a reversal.

We have no recent experience of Cowen's many choral works, whose promotion in Victorian times is so successfully documented in *Hazell's*, and even tracing copies of the published vocal scores is far from easy today. The revival of an excerpt from the early opera *Pauline* by Opera Viva in 1983 (recorded on Opera Viva), while revealing a charming light style, was ultimately of little consequence and gave no clue to the manner of his more Wagnerian operas, such as *Thorgrim*, well received by *Hazell's* (but ridiculed by George Bernard Shaw) in 1890.

Vivid, fluent and tuneful, Cowen must have seemed a striking new force in his

---

[9] CHAN 9049: Symphony No 1 in Bb major and *Irish Rhapsody No 2*; CHAN 8991: Symphony No 2, *Elegiac* and Clarinet Concerto; CHAN 8545: Symphony No 3, *Irish* and *Irish Rhapsody No 5*; CHAN 8884: Symphony No 4, *Irish Rhapsody No 6* and *Oedipus Rex* Prelude; CHAN 8581: Symphony No 5, *L'Allegro Ed I Pensieroso* and *Irish Rhapsody No 4*; CHAN 8627: Symphony No 6, *In Memoriam G F Watts* and *Irish Rhapsody No 1*; CHAN 8861: Symphony No 7, *Irish Rhapsody No 3* and Concert Piece for Organ and Orchestra.

day, appealing to a wide public. Yet our only recent clue to Cowen's achievement is not a promising one. This is a recording of historic reissues of Cowen's music, almost all of it in a lighter style (RRE 190). Certainly the overture *The Butterfly's Ball* was long popular and has occasionally appeared in the BBC's lighter programmes. But it reminds us of the greatest puzzle of all, for although in his day Cowen was the first – and at the time most popular – modern British symphonist, today his six symphonies have sunk almost without trace. Only the third, the *Scandinavian*, which made him an important composer at 30, has now been issued on CD (Marco Polo 8.223273). Colourful and lyrical, it and its successors, the *Welsh* (the fourth), the un-named fifth and the *Idyllic* sixth, were celebrated in the closing years of Victoria's reign. Performing materials of numbers three to five are still available from Novello, and a recording of the *Welsh Symphony* by the City of Hull Youth Orchestra conducted by Geoffrey Heald-Smith was made in the mid-1980s, although it has never been issued.

SYMPHONIES

The unprecedented expansion in the composition of symphonies by British composers during our period was not fully reflected in the accounts in *Hazell*'s. While the period was crowned by the symphonies of Elgar, and the first two of Vaughan Williams, the curious fact is that veneration for Beethoven and, later, Schumann and Brahms had suggested to preceding generations that the time of the symphony had passed. As George Bernard Shaw remarked in 1888 after a performance of Stanford's *Irish Symphony*, 'the symphony, as a musical form, is stone dead. Some such structure as that used by Liszt in his symphonic poems would have been admirably suited to Mr Stanford's fantasie on Irish airs'.[10] Yet with the perspective of hindsight we can see that it was a time when composers wishing to make the big personal statement found the symphony the ideal canvas. After all, Mahler was even then working in Vienna, and particularly in the reign of King Edward VII the number and complexity of symphonies grew.

Parry characterised Brahms' symphonies, which he found 'extraordinarily successful', by saying that 'they reproduce the austerest and noblest form of art in the strongest and healthiest way'.[11] Earlier, when only the first two Brahms symphonies were known, he had written: 'It is not likely that many will be able to follow Brahms in his severe and uncompromising methods; but he himself has shown more than any one how elastic the old principles may yet be made ... though we can hardly hope that even the greatest composers of the future will surpass the symphonic triumphs of the past'.[12]

At this time (1889) Parry, having mentioned Sir Julius Benedict as a composer who had 'given the world examples in earnest style and full of vigour and good workmanship', and the Sullivan symphony, 'which had such marks of excellence', picked Stanford's *Elegiac Symphony* for its 'excellent workmanship, vivacity of ideas, and fluency of development combine to establish it as an admirable example of its class'.[13] A pity that Parry's championship should be the prelude for the work remaining unheard for over 90 years. He also mentioned the *Scandinavian Symphony* of Cowen as 'original and picturesque in thought and treatment'.

[10] *Pall Mall Gazette*, 15 May 1888.
[11] *Grove's Dictionary of Music and Musicians*, 3rd ed., Vol V, Macmillan, 1928, p 235.
[12] *Grove's Dictionary of Music and Musicians*, 1st ed., Vol IV, Macmillan, 1889, p 42.
[13] Ibid.

The orchestral full score of Cowen's Symphony No 4 (The Welsh) in Bb minor (Novello, Ewer & Co., 1885). (Courtesy Novello & Co.)

14

But to consider Parry himself for a moment, it is difficult to realise how challenging a work such as Parry's First Symphony of 1882 may have appeared at first. August Manns, after giving the work its first performance at Crystal Palace, remarked that it was 'a very difficult work ... [but] some music is awfully difficult to master'.[14]

The divide came with Elgar's First Symphony, and with the blaze of that great marching score many admirable but lesser works were shrivelled by comparison. Elgar's second was not so well received in the Coronation season of 1911, and new modes of thought were heralded by the distinctive style of Vaughan Williams' *A London Symphony*, a score looking to France rather than Germany for its harmonic ancestry, yet showing a different facet of a distinctive national style.

In the last of Balfour Gardiner's celebrated series of concerts at Queen's Hall, on 18 March 1913, Gardiner conducted Frederic Austin's Symphony in E major, accompanied by a programme note by the composer challenging what he felt to be the contemporary 'comparative neglect of the symphony'. This is a view with which we must sympathise at the time when the Diaghilev ballet was making much of the running in new music. Austin added: 'The charge that most modern composers would bring against it would perhaps be its lack of flexibility, its cumbersome and tautological structure ... the more intellectually daring composers seem to have felt that the only way of insisting upon the real nature and origin of music was to break away from a form that increasingly became the property of the professor ... Thus was born the symphonic poem ...'.[15] Not only the form of the symphony would change and develop but also it would absorb programmatic elements which would ensure its future. Austin's symphony exemplified this approach. He continued in another programme note: 'The formal scheme differs considerably from that usually employed, recapitulations and the usual sections of statement and development being dispensed with. A structural method very largely used is that of a continuous development from a germinal idea.[16]

During the First World War, Bantock's *Hebridean Symphony*, completed in 1916[17] and first performed in Glasgow that year, made a considerable impact. In one movement, it has been felt by many to be more tone-poem than symphony, and has had to wait for Vernon Handley's superb recording by Hyperion (CDA 66450) and even more his public performance at London's Royal Festival Hall on 11 May 1993, to be taken seriously, Anthony Payne noting how its 'single movement, cogently structured, links episode to episode with considerable symphonic craft'.[18] Superb and convincing in every way, Handley's championship made clear that the one or two effects that are doubtful when heard in a recording (notably the repeated trumpets towards the end) become triumphantly successful when heard under a sympathetic conductor in the wide space of a large concert hall, and moreover especially well heard in as clean and analytical an acoustic as that of the Festival Hall.

Now that Stanford and Parry are known and even Cowen is beginning to show above the horizon, we need to ask ourselves what other British symphonists there were at the turn of the century, and a list of symphonies by British composers produced during our period by the Bournemouth Municipal Orchestra under Dan Godfrey shows a surprising number of unfamiliar names and gives a vivid snapshot of varied activity, with not only a variety of local composers being performed but also a higher percentage of women composers than one might expect, although only one composed a symphony and hence is listed here.

[14] Dibble, *op cit*, p 201. [15] Queen's Hall programme, 18 March 1913.
[16] Queen's Hall programme, 20 November 1913. [17] The piano score sketch is dated 20 June 1915.
[18] *The Independent*, 14 May 1993, p 15.

BRITISH SYMPHONIES[19]

Performed at symphony, classical and musical festival concerts, Bournemouth, from 1895 to 1921.

fp   first performance
+   composer conducting; the remainder, unless otherwise stated, conducted by [Sir] Dan Godfrey.

ALBERT, Eugene d' (1864–1932, Scottish-born, German)
Symphony in F
   7.12.99

BAINTON, Edgar L (1880–1956)
Symphony No 1 in B flat *A Phantasy of Life and Progress*
   15.10.03 fp +

BANTOCK, Sir Granville (1868–1946)
Hebridean Symphony
   31.3.21   6.10.21   (and 5 times more)

BARCLAY, Arthur (1869–1943)
Symphony in C minor
   22.11.00 +

BELL, W H (1873–1946)
Symphony *Walt Whitman*
   21.4.02 (first complete perf.) +

BENNETT, W Sterndale (1816–1875)
Symphony in G minor

20.2.96	30.4.96	17.12.96	8.4.97	23.12.01	21.12.03	9.1.05	7.5.06
23.11.08	21.11.10	29.4.12	20.4.16				

BRIDGE, Joseph (1853–1929)
Symphony No 3 in F
   26.11.03 +

BRYSON, Ernest (1867–1942)
Symphony No 1 in D major
   1.2.12   cond. Dr J Lyon

BURTON, T Arthur [Organist St Peter's, Bournemouth]
Symphony No 1 in E major
   6.3.99 fp
Symphony No 2 in E minor
   16.3.03 +
Symphony No 3 *Variations*
   10.11.05 +
Symphony No 4
   13.11.11 fp +

CARSE, A von Ahn [later known as Adam Carse] (1878–1958)
Symphony No 1
   22.11.06 +
Symphony No 2 in G minor
   27.1.10 +   26.1.11 +

CLIFFE, Frederick (1857–1931)
Symphony No 1 in C minor

13.2.02 +	20.10.02	27.10.04	15.2.06	29.4.07	9.1.08	13.1.10	22.11.17

Symphony No 2 in E minor
   13.11.02 +

---

[19] I must thank Stephen Lloyd for his generosity in allowing me to extract this list from his unpublished catalogue of Bournemouth performances.

16

COLERIDGE-TAYLOR, Samuel (1875–1912)
Symphony in A minor
    30.4.00 (first complete perf.)

COWEN, Sir Frederic H (1852–1935)
Symphony No 3 *Scandinavian*
    15.3.00   1.3.06 +   18.2.09 +   15.5.11 [...]Scherzo only, Crystal Palace]
Symphony No 4 *Welsh*
    4.1.97   5.3.03 +
Symphony No 6 *Idyllic*
    25.4.01 +   3.3.10 +

ELGAR, Sir Edward (1857–1934)
Symphony No 1
    27.2.09   17.4.09   9.10.13   21.10.20
Symphony No 2
    9.3.12 +   18.4.12   10.2.21   28.4.21 +

GERMAN, Sir Edward (1862–1936)
Symphony No 1 in E minor (1890)
    25.1.06 +
Symphony No 2 in A minor (1893)
    21.1.04 + (and 4 times more)

GLADSTONE, F E (1845–1928)
Symphony in G
    27.11.99   26.1.20 (Minuet)

GODFREY, Percy (1859–1945)
Symphony in G minor
    20.4.03 fp +

HARTY, Sir Hamilton (1879–1941)
Irish Symphony
    28.11.07 +   23.4.08 +   18.3.09 +   13.4.16 +   1.5.16 +

HOLLOWAY, H [Chorus-master of Bournemouth Municipal Choir] (1871–1948)
Symphony No 1 in E minor
    25.3.09 fp   3.5.09   22.11.09   24.10.10   ca. 5.12?
Symphony No 2 in D minor
    9.2.11 fp   13.3.11   22.1.12   14.12.16   12.5.20   15.12.21

HOLST, Gustav (1874–1934)
Symphony in F, Op 8 *The Cotswolds*
    24.4.02 fp (attended by Holst and RVW)

KEYSER, H A (1871–?)
Symphony in B flat
    7.3.10

LÖHR, Richard Harvey (1856–1927)
Symphony in D minor
    22.12.02 fp +
Symphony No 2
    10.5.09

PARRY, Sir C H H (1848–1918)
Symphony No 2 in F *Cambridge*
    19.12.01 +   30.4.08
Symphony No 3 *English*
    1.3.00 +   18.12.02 +   8.10.14   22.6.21
Symphony No 4
    29.12.04 +   13.4.11 + [rev. vers.]
Symphony No 5 in B minor
    17.4.13 +

PHILLIPS, Montague (1886–1969)
Symphony in C minor
    6.11.13 +

PROUT, Ebenezer (1835–1909)
Symphony in F
    30.12.97

SOMERVELL, Sir Arthur (1863–1937)
Symphony in D *Thalassa*
    4.5.14 [mvt. only]   7.5.14   4.3.15   30.3.16   ca.6.17

SPEER, W H (1863–1937)
Symphony in E flat
    5.3.06   7.11.07 +

STANFORD, Sir Charles Villiers (1852–1924)
Symphony No 3 in F minor *Irish*
    1.5.99 +   6.10.02   12.11.03   16.11.05   10.10.07   22.2.10   24.12.13
    26.4.15 ca 6.16   10.5.17 +   28.7.20
Symphony No 4 in F major
    15.4.09 +
Symphony No 5 in D minor *L'Allegro ed Il Pensieroso*
    12.1.05 +   8.12.10 +   (and 5 more times)
Symphony No 6 in E flat *In memoriam G F Watts*
    24.1.07 +
Symphony No 7 in D minor
    14.3.12 +   1.5.14 +

SWEPSTONE, Edith
Symphony in G minor
    3.2.02 fp

TAPP, F W [director of Bath Pump Room Concerts]
Symphony in E *The Tempest*
    17.12.14 +

TROWELL, Arnold [cellist and composer: 1887–1966 b. N Z]
Symphony in G minor
    16.10.11 (extracts)   19.10.11

VAUGHAN WILLIAMS, Ralph (1872–1958)
A London Symphony
    11.2.15 f. provincial performance [fp of reconstructed score; original being lost in Germany]
    11.11.20   21.4.21   21.9.21

WALLACE, William (1860–1940)
Symphony *The Creation*
    23.10.02 +

WINGHAM, Thomas (1846–1893)
Symphony No 2 in B flat
    18.11.01   24.2.08

Bournemouth is a good index to the prevailing tastes and activity and, as we can see, the most performed symphonies in the period up to and including 1921 were: Sterndale Bennett's [late] G minor Symphony (12 times), Stanford's *Irish* (11), Frederick Cliffe's First (8), Harty's *Irish* (5), and the local composer Henry Holloway's First (5) and Second (6). We perhaps need to look again at Cliffe, a professor at the Royal College of Music – and John Ireland's piano teacher – who flourished briefly in the 1890s and whose First Symphony, after its first hearing at the Crystal Palace on 20 April 1889, achieved an amazing reception: 'It may be doubted whether musical history can show on any of its pages the record of such an Opus I. The Symphony is a masterpiece, and ... Mr Cliffe has by one effort passed from obscurity to fame'.[20] It was repeated at Crystal Palace by popular vote at a plebiscite concert on 25 March 1899. Although not closely programmatic, its first movement was influenced, like Cowen's Third, by a visit to Norway. At the time it was most noted for its slow movement, with which Cliffe broke new ground by calling it 'Ballade'. It is one of the still unknown works of the period that would be worth an early revival. This could take place without too much difficulty as it was published in full score and has printed orchestral parts.

COLERIDGE-TAYLOR

Samuel Coleridge-Taylor (1875–1912) has tended to be remembered for his vivid *Hiawatha's Wedding Feast*, now recorded for the third time. (All three parts of *The Song of Hiawatha* are recorded on Argo set 430 3562). He tended to be overwhelmed by its success, and the necessity to produce sequels must have become an onerous chore as the subsequent parts of the *Hiawatha* trilogy become increasingly laboured, until by the end of the third part any enjoyment of the music has evaporated in our sympathy with the poor composer's predicament in having to set such awful lines as 'Or the heron, the shuh-shuh-gah? Or the white god, Waw-de-waw?' for which he falls back mechanically on his own 'Hiawatha' rhythms allied with over-used Wagnerian formulae. Two of Coleridge-Taylor's other substantial choral works have also been heard again: *Meg Blane*, given by Robert Tucker at Slough in 1975 (the performing materials literally pulled from the junk-heap at the eleventh hour), and *A Tale of Old Japan*, given by Stephen Banfield at Keele University in 1983. Both these enterprises revealed a very worthwhile composer, with rewarding chorus work, striking solos and – in *Meg Blane* – evocative sea music and a colourful command of the orchestra.

The once popular orchestral Ballade in A minor, commissioned at Elgar's instigation and dedicated to their mutual friend Jaeger, which was first heard at the 1899 Three Choirs Festival, has also been an unknown quantity for modern audiences. However, although mentioned in many books on the period, until it was broadcast in 1983 it had remained unheard in living memory[21] save for an unsatisfactory piano reduction. On hearing it for the first time we run up against a familiar problem in reassessing works of the Victorian period in that its contemporary appeal was clearly to a less sophisticated audience than that of today, and was undoubtedly due to its composer's very successful assimilation of the elements of the then popular salon music, a recurring feature which now militates against the successful revival of many works of this period, and one really only well handled for us today by Elgar, and perhaps to a lesser extent by Bantock.

In the instrumental field, Coleridge-Taylor's Violin Concerto in G minor, when revived by the violinist Sergiu Schwartz at the Guildhall School of Music and Drama in November 1980 (a performance subsequently broadcast), also revealed itself as an engaging score, though stylistically showing similar traits to the Mackenzie concertos and thus very much a product of late nineteenth century romanticism, but

[20] *Daily Telegraph*, 21 April 1889.
[21] Now sympathetically recorded by Royal Liverpool Philharmonic Orchestra conducted by Grant Llewellyn, coupled with the later *Symphonic Variations on an African Air* which the *Gramophone* critic (June 1993, p 39) compared with Grieg's *Old Norwegian Romance*. Llewellyn projects the Ballade well, showing us a strong and enjoyable piece.

The orchestral full score of Cliffe's Symphony in C minor (No 1) (Novello & Co., 1904)
(The penultimate page of the Ballade: Sir Henry Wood's copy)

nevertheless full of character and certainly justifying the effort given to revive it. They both would find a wide audience if recorded.

We might briefly remember the talented but little-known figure of William Hurlstone, whose premature death in 1906 took a young composer of whom great things were expected. His single-handed championship by the Lyrita record company underlines the range and quality of the music of the period.[22] Hurlstone's orchestral music, particularly his attractive and brilliant Piano Concerto, three sets of orchestral variations and the delightful suite *The Magic Mirror*, is proof, if proof were ever needed, that excavating forgotten scores is a rewarding activity, and that we still do not have sufficient information to arrive at a final assessment of the British music of this period.

BANTOCK

In the case of Sir Granville Bantock (1868–1946) we come to a composer who, although he survived the Second World War, wrote most of his best music before the First. Bantock's output was vast, and from what one may justifiably regard as over-production it can be difficult to make a viable assessment of what is likely to be of lasting value. There can be little doubt that he has a place in the living music of this country, and out of the hundreds of works he wrote – the majority of them published – it is possible to sift quite a number that should receive attention. The Hyperion CD of the *Hebridean* and *Celtic Symphonies*, the tone poem *The Witch of Atlas* and the shorter 'sea poem' *The Sea Reivers* (CDA 66450), conducted by Vernon Handley, has had considerable success.

Among the most accessible of the composer's works are his cycles of songs with orchestral accompaniment, of which there are altogether nine sets. The poets set vary widely, from translations of Hafiz and Sappho to Blake, Browning and the composer's wife. The only fact that militates against some of the songs today, particularly the early ones, is the way in which the texts have dated. This applies especially to the Arnold translation of Hafiz, which is set in the *Five Ghazals of Hafiz* of 1903–5, and which spoils what – at least in the orchestral version of 1937 – is a fine cycle. There are many delightful things in the *Sappho Songs* of 1906, a cycle of nine songs with an extended orchestral prelude which together play for nearly an hour, but which is probably more viable when only selected numbers are given with the orchestral prelude.

Like the songs, the orchestral music too has become part of the inevitable vicious circle in which the neglected composer finds himself: he is not played because he is not known, and he is not known because he is not played. Much of Bantock's orchestral music still has to be properly explored. However, the *Helena Variations* (written in the year of Elgar's *Enigma* – 1899) was broadcast by the BBC Philharmonic Orchestra, conducted by Edward Downes, in 1984. While it is uneven music, including mock-oriental and neo-Elgarian episodes, it was well worth a hearing and has passages of real stature; had not Elgar's masterpiece appeared on the scene at that time it might well have lasted better than it has.

Bantock conducted a lot of Tchaikovsky at around the turn of the century, favourite scores including *Francesca da Rimini* and the *Pathétique* Symphony, and

---

[22] On LP: Piano Concerto (1896) and *Fantasie-Variations on a Swedish Air* (1904) on SRCS 100 and the Piano Trio in G and the Piano Quartet in E minor on SRCS 117. On CD: *Variations on an Original Theme* (1896), Suite *The Magic Mirror* (1900) and the *Variations on a Hungarian Air* (1899) which predated Elgar's *Enigma* by just three months (on SRCD 208).

their influence may be heard in *Fifine at the Fair* and other orchestral works that Bantock wrote at that time. Bantock's six numbered tone-poems were written between 1900 and 1912, and of these the splendidly colourful *Fifine at the Fair* (1901, revised 1911) is familiar from Beecham's recording (EMI CDM 7 63405 2). This has now been somewhat upstaged, unusually for Beecham, by Vernon Handley's recent CD recording, which restores Beecham's cuts and gives us the 35-minute score complete, in its luxurious orchestral sound (Hyperion CDA 66630). All of them are well worth a hearing, though excerpts from *Lalla Rookh* (1902) that were once played in a piano reduction at a Havergal Brian Society AGM clearly needed orchestral colour to make anything of them. When the Kensington Symphony Orchestra wanted to present a Bantock orchestral work in 1981, *Dante and Beatrice* of 1911 (a revision of *Dante* from 1902) was chosen, and although indebted equally to Tchaikovsky and to Strauss, it is engagingly vivid and deserves to be known. The delicate tone-poem *Pierrot of the Minute* (after Dowson) of 1909 contrasts with the orchestral opulence of its Straussian companions. It has some lovely moments (listen to Chandos CHAN 8373), but for some it relies too heavily on delicate tendrils of colour, too little on Bantock's usually forthright melodic invention. These two aspects of Bantock's style in the Edwardian period combine with great success in the short *Sapphic Poem* for cello and orchestra of 1906, recorded by the cellist Gillian Thoday and the pioneering Hull Youth Orchestra (Gough & Davy GD 2003).

Bantock's earlier choral works have not yet been revived, but *The Time Spirit* of 1903, to words by Bantock's wife, made an energetic finale to Robert Tucker's 1984 Broadheath Singers' concert at Eton. Bowing to Wagner and Tchaikovsky by turns, Bantock established his personality in it with idiosyncratic melody and impassioned orchestral writing. It was the Broadheath Singers, too, who in 1976 had revived its immediate successor, *Sea Wanderers* (also to a Helen Bantock text), later twice taken up by the BBC, and clearly the precursor to *Omar Khayyam*, which immediately followed it. *Sea Wanderers*, published in 1906, must have had a considerable impact at the time on an audience which was yet to experience Vaughan Williams' *A Sea Symphony*.

Bantock had the gift of being able to coalesce a lot of intricately detailed writing into an impressive sweeping large-scale canvas. This he does most notably in *Omar Khayyam* (1906–9), setting the whole of Fitzgerald's English text in three parts. However, a work on the scale of *Omar* presents the same sort of barrier to performance that had to be surmounted by those bringing Havergal Brian's *Gothic Symphony* to a hearing. The BBC revival of *Omar* in 1981 is perhaps the key Bantock performance so far and has revealed a work of far greater stature than even Bantock's most committed champions may have dared hope. It raises its composer to being worthy of consideration as a very substantial Edwardian composer indeed, and *Omar* certainly warrants assessment in the same breath as some of Elgar's big choral works. Also of importance is another BBC revival, that of Bantock's pioneering unaccompanied choral symphony *Atalanta in Calydon* (1911). Here we have been lucky to have had two different modern performances. They gave a very fair idea of the music, but were given with only 64 voices, which did not allow the intended effect to be fully made, particularly in quiet passages something was missing. In addition, Bantock asked for coloured light effects, but the brave attempt at the first of the BBC's two performances to project coloured lights on a screen was no substitute for massed choirs totally suffused in the colours Bantock requested. To emphasise the variety that can be found in Bantock's vast output, we should perhaps also remember his chamber opera *The Seal-Woman*, founded on tunes from Marjorie

Kennedy-Fraser's *Songs of the Hebrides*, last revived, by Hammersmith Municipal Opera, in 1975 and broadcast then by BBC Radio London. Bantock's much earlier opera *Caedmar* was one which found George Bernard Shaw in caustic mood when he wrote: 'within a stone's throw of the Strand we get the cream of all Bayreuth without the trouble and expense of journeying thither',[23] proved when revived not to bear out Shaw's criticisms. Indeed, one must say that the destruction of many reputations in this period has been a consequence of the constant quotation of Shaw's views, which at this distance do not always turn out to be fully justified when one actually listens to the music with his criticism in hand.

OPERA

Victorian operas by British composers have not featured to the same extent beside the revival of interest in the choral and orchestral music of the period. Nevertheless, there has been a continuing thread of interest, and Stanford has, in particular, from time to time been on the agenda of fringe opera companies, the John Lewis Partnership Music Society presenting *The Travelling Companion* and *Shamus O'Brien* in 1967 and 1971 respectively. *The Travelling Companion* (Reading University, 1981) and *Much Ado About Nothing* (Opera Viva, 1985) were both seen on the stage during the 1980s.

The most celebrated British opera of the late Victorian period was Sullivan's *Ivanhoe*. It ran for over 150 consecutive performances in 1891, yet the account in *Hazell*'s (see p 45) is curiously lacking in enthusiasm. In spite of massive adulatory press coverage, it was, as Shaw identified from the start, an artistic failure, and it is still difficult to say whether it could be a success on the stage. Subsequently revised, the opera appeared in Liverpool in February 1895 and was toured. A Berlin production, in German, in November 1896 was panned by the German critics. Revived only at long intervals, it never established itself in the repertoire and performances became more and more infrequent. The Beecham Opera Company at Covent Garden in 1910, a BBC broadcast in 1929 and Act II staged at the Royal Academy of Music in 1932 were all that preceded Joseph Vandernoot's gallant attempt to stage it with Beaufort Opera at the cramped venue of Hurlingham School Theatre, London SW6, in May/June 1973. One of these performances was issued on three LPs by Rare Recorded Edition (SRRE 143/4/5): it gives a feeling for the limitations of the enterprise, though it was important at the time as an opportunity to hear the music, in spite of a few cuts. However, a BBC concert performance on 21 August 1987 of a scene from Act III conducted by Barry Wordworth (broadcast in 1988) emphasised the personality of Sullivan's invention, and a shoestring performance on three CDs conducted by David Lyle (Pearl SHE CD 9615) confirms that the work has much to offer. A fully professional concert performance by the Boston Academy of Music conducted by David Daniels on 23 November 1991 was very well received, while the Gilbert and Sullivan Society of Victoria gave five well-received staged performances at the Union Theatre at the University of Melbourne the same month, respectively the American and Australian premieres. So we have to conclude that the jury is still out on this work, and that while it may never join the regular professional repertoire, a sympathetic staging may yet make a case for it. However, it has to be said that the centenary performance of Sullivan's cantata *The Golden*

[23] *The World*, 2 November 1892.

Legend which Sir Charles Mackerras conducted at Leeds Town Hall in March 1986 was a more immediate success, and caused one to wonder whether the dramatic cantata was what Sullivan was really aiming at in his opera.

In 1982 the City of Westminster Arts Council promoted a concert at St John's, Smith Square, London, in which Leslie Head presented a team of advanced student singers, with orchestra, in extracts from 13 British operas dating from the period 1876–1916. It underlined how many separate numbers – and indeed episodes – from British operas of the period are delightful, but that they do not necessarily add up to effective musical drama that can work on the stage.[24] Collectors of 78 rpm records have long had available to them arias from such operas, and many have been reissued on LP and CD collections of old recordings, usually to document the art of a particular singer. However, there is no reason why we should not enjoy the arias while selecting which might be worthy of consideration on the stage.

Over the last 25 years revivals of operas from our period have included works by Bantock (*Caedmar, The Seal-Woman*); Rutland Boughton (*The Immortal Hour, Bethlehem, Alkestis, The Queen of Cornwall* and *The Lily Maid*, the last three from the 1920s and 30s); all the operas of Delius; Lisa Lehmann (*Everyman*); Ethel Smyth (*The Wreckers, The Boatswain's Mate*, and from outside our period *Fête Galante*); Hamish MacCunn (*Jeanie Deans*); all the mature operas of Holst, including extracts from his unperformed opera *Sita*; and Sullivan's *Ivanhoe*.

During 1985, as an activity of European Music Year, the British Music Society promoted a competition for staged revivals of British operas by 'fringe' companies which, among others, prompted spirited stage productions of MacCunn's *Jeanie Deans* at Ayr, Stanford's *Much Ado* in London, and Ethel Smyth's *The Boatswain's Mate* at Cambridge. All triumphantly demonstrated their command of the stage.

We need to add Samuel Alman, well-known composer of Jewish liturgical music, whose opera *King Ahaz* was a short-lived success in London's East End in 1912, and from which extracts were revived in a concert in 1984 that have been made available on cassette.[25] Also, a little out of the mainstream, was Joseph Parry's *Blodwen*, widely regarded as the first Welsh grand opera, which was first performed in Aberdare in 1878. Although it was not published until 1917, nor documented by *Hazell's*, it swept the country after its early performances, and by 1896 it is said to have been seen more than 500 times. There have been recordings of extracts on 78s, highlights on LP and complete on two LPs.[26] Revivals of Loder's *Raymond and Agnes* (of 1855) at Cambridge in 1966, and Balfe's *Rose of Castile* which launched the Wexford Festival in 1951, all predate our period. Perhaps more relevant are the operas of 'the English Ring' (Balfe's *Bohemian Girl*, Wallace's *Maritana* and Benedict's *The Lily of Killarney*), which were extensively performed during this time, though they also date from earlier days. *The Bohemian Girl* was a celebrated Beecham revival in 1951 and all three operas have been extensively recorded.[27] Finally we need to mention the well-known operettas of Gilbert and Sullivan and the

---

[24] Issued on 2 LPs (OV 101/2), 11 of the extracts played at that concert demonstrate what a wide range of styles composers of the time were using.

[25] B'nair B'rith Records BB 001.

[26] Qualiton Daffodil Series DAF 213; Sain 1138R. This came from a BBC programme in 1978.

[27] 78rpm extracts of the main numbers from *Maritana*, recorded in 1929–31, were reissued on Opal 814. Highlights from all three 'English Ring' operas were once available on HMV CSD 3651, while a complete CD recording of *The Bohemian Girl* conducted by Richard Bonynge has now appeared on Argo 433 324-2.

light operas of Edward German, which have been consistently performed over the years and are too familiar to need documenting here.

★ ★ ★

To us, a century later, the music reported in the earlier part of the period covered by these annual reviews is much less familiar than that in the immediate post-First War issues, just before *Hazell's* ceased publication. The dominance of choral music and opera in 1885, the consolidation of Wagner-worship — Wagner initially sung in Italian — the seemingly endless flow of musical prodigies, and the appearance in the UK of a host of famous musicians from abroad (many of whom are illustrated here in contemporary photographs) are constant features. The visit of Liszt in 1886 to an overwhelming reception sets the tone, later followed, among others, by Saint-Saëns, Grieg, and the darling of late Victorian choral festivals, *Herr* Dvorak. The visit of Mahler in 1892 to conduct the first London *Ring* cycles for 10 years is perhaps of greater significance to us today than it was at the time.

The Victorians in many ways liked to be larger than life, and the business basis of their musical exploits is amazing. The attendance at the Handel Festival at the Crystal Palace in 1883 was 87,784, and even though this had declined to 76,406 by 1894 it is still remarkable, indicating that over 20,000 must have been present at some performances. This was truly a popular art-form only comparable in its support to the pop festival of today. The size of the choirs taking part, too, is also a clue to the strength of Victorian choralism, *Hazell's* for 1895 referring to a choir of 3,500 for *Israel in Egypt*. These unexpected insights into the nature of the then musical scene also extend to the accounts of still familiar events, for example, unexpectedly, the story we have here of Elgar's *Gerontius* after its disastrous first performance at Birmingham is of a masterpiece recognised. There are also glimpses of the less pleasant reality of Victorian England — with passing reference in 1886 and 1888 to the starving and destitute choruses of foreign operatic touring companies that had suffered financial failure.

This was the time during which British music as a recognisable entity grew in stature and depth of repertoire, and even at the beginning of our period appear works that we are now beginning to know again in performance. At this time we can see a self-consciously national art slowly emerging — largely in the work of a small number of composers — and with it the capability of a later generation to mature into the many highly individual musical voices of a growing tradition.

Sir Frederic H Cowen

C H Lloyd   *Sir Frederick Bridge*

Sir Edward German

Sir Charles Hallé

Hans Richter

Sir August Manns

Samuel Coleridge-Taylor

Some famous vocalists (from top line, left to right) Patti, Melba, Tetrazzini, Albani, Caruso, Lloyd, Davies, Rumford (Clara Butt), Thornton, Crossley, Lunn, Black, Santley, Mills, Radford, Rumford, Coates, McCormack

Lady Hallé ('Norman Neruda')

Fritz Kreisler

Clara Butt

Pablo de Sarasate

Paderewski

Joachim Quartet

Edouard Colonne

Charles Lamoureux

Felix Mottl

Max Fiedler

Mischa Elman

Florizel von Reuter

Franz von Vecsey

Jan Kubelik

Music in 1885. A year that introduced to the notice of the public such important new works by British composers as Mr. Goring Thomas's opera "Nadeshda," Mr. F. H. Cowen's cantata "The Sleeping Beauty," Mr. E. Prout's third Symphony, Mr. A. C. Mackenzie's violin concerto, and Mr. C. V. Stanford's oratorio "The Three Holy Children," and that comprised in its operations four great festivals, cannot be regarded as uneventful in musical annals. Such a record speaks well for the activity of the present race of native composers; but, of course, such good results would not be obtainable were the bulk of English-speaking music patrons indifferent than usual, to the productions of their own country. In this, as in other branches of art, Great Britain has at length given such proof of her right to be placed in the front rank of contributors, that now to speak disrespectfully or sneeringly of British music manifests but little knowledge of modern progress, and still less of public opinion unhesitatingly expressed. The year 1885 being the **bicentenary of Handel's birth**, it very early became apparent that the occasion was to be seized for the performance, to a much larger extent than usual, of the more celebrated of his works. The only notable attempt at a revival of his less known, and in several instances undeservedly neglected compositions, was made by the Sacred Harmonic Society. This Association reproduced "Belshazzar," which had not been heard in London for some years previously; and the same oratorio was chosen (with the "Messiah") as representative of Handel's genius at the **Bristol Triennial Festival** in the autumn. The **Crystal Palace** directors, who by means of the triennial Handel Festival have done so much to make the name of Handel a household word, could not allow the bicentenary to pass without some special demonstration. If, in view of the recurrence of the festival in 1886, a single grand performance had been settled upon, it must, to fulfil its purpose, have consisted of the "Messiah," or "Israel in Egypt," in part if not wholly; and such a performance might reasonably be expected to seriously affect the festival proper of the succeeding year. Eventually it was wisely decided to fix the Handel Festival for 1885 instead of 1886, and all who felt any interest in the matter warmly approved of the resolve. Thus the great Handel orchestra was in June again filled with its 4,000 choralists, instrumentalists, and principals, Mr. August Manns being the conductor, as in 1883. The programme, as before, consisted of the "Messiah," a selection, and "Israel in Egypt," and the meeting was in every way a success.—At Easter **Mr. Carl Rosa's Opera Company** took possession of Drury Lane Theatre for a longer season than usual. Two new operas were promised in Mr. Goring Thomas's "Nadeshda"—having a Russian subject—and M. Jules Massenet's "Manon," the latter of which had been popular in Paris and elsewhere. Immediately on production both operas were received here with the highest favour. Virtually

a separate cast of principals was engaged for each: Madame Valleria, Mr. Barton M'Guckin, and Mr. Leslie Crotty appearing in Mr. Goring Thomas's opera; whilst Madame Marie Roze, Mr. Maas, and Mr. Ludwig, in the French work, neatly turned into English by Mr. Joseph Bennett. There was little chance for the older operas in the *répertoire* after these novelties appeared on the bill; nevertheless Mr. Carl Rosa continued to play a few more standard works, and an interesting and prosperous season terminated with a capital representation of "La Nozze di Figaro," with a strong cast. There seemed no probability of Covent Garden Theatre being opened for the annual Italian opera season until Mr. Mapleson gladdened the hearts of operatic *habitués* by announcing that he had engaged Madame Adelina Patti for a brief series of performances, under the conductorship of Signor Arditi. The unrivalled *prima donna*, who thus fulfilled her twenty-fifth consecutive season here, played several of her more familiar characters, and appeared for the first time as Carmen. The only other principal soprano was Mdlle. Alma Fohstrom, a vocalist who was said to have made a hit in Vienna, and who at Covent Garden created a favourable impression (but nothing more) as Lucia, Amina, and Gilda. Meantime the International Inventions Exhibition at South Kensington, with "Music" as its second department, was daily claiming its thousands of visitors. Here concerts were held very frequently in the Albert Hall, besides the band performances in the grounds; and there was a priceless loan collection of ancient musical instruments, manuscripts, portraits, etc. —The first of the provincial music meetings of the year was the triennial gathering at Birmingham, for which extraordinary preparations, including commissions for seven elaborate new works, had been made. Each of the four days of the festival brought forward some novelty concerning which singular curiosity was aroused, though the lion's share was naturally carried off by M. Gounod's second trilogy "Mors et Vita," which it was anticipated would be conducted by the composer. Those, however, who at Birmingham had hoped to congratulate M. Gounod as they had congratulated him three years before, when he superintended the performance of his "Redemption," were doomed to disappointment. "Mors et Vita" was conducted by Herr Richter, the successor to the late Sir Michael Costa as the musical chief of the Birmingham Festival. Mr. Cowen's cantata "The Sleeping Beauty," Dvorak's cantata "The Spectre's Bride" (a very remarkable work), Mr. Stanford's oratorio "The Three Holy Children," Mr. Prout's new symphony in F, Mr. Mackenzie's violin concerto, and Dr. Bridge's setting of the "Rock of Ages," were, like M. Gounod's trilogy, warmly approved. It should be added that the Birmingham verdict has been fully endorsed by the Metropolis respecting all of these compositions that have found their way to London platforms. The **Hereford Musical**

Festival (the **Meeting of the Three Choirs**) offered a cantata "St. Kevin," by Dr. J. Smith of Dublin, and a soprano solo with chorus, "**The Song of Baldir**," by Mr. C. H. Lloyd, as its only novelties; and Bristol fell back upon established successes, with Mr. Charles Hallé as conductor. The **Philharmonic Society** had a good season, with Sir Arthur Sullivan as conductor; and the **Monday Popular Concerts**, the **Crystal Palace Concerts**, the **Sacred Harmonic Society**, the **Royal Albert Hall Choral Society** and the **London Ballad Concerts** executed the same valuable functions in Metropolitan musical existence as for some years past. **Novello's Oratorio Concerts**, conducted by Mr. A. C. Mackenzie, and the **Brinsmead Symphony Concerts**, are new musical enterprises that promise exceedingly well.—The list of comic operas of the year is headed by "The Mikado" (one of Messrs. Gilbert and Sullivan's brightest efforts) at the Savoy; and merit in varying degree has been evinced in Messrs. H. Paulton and E. Jakabowski's "Erminie"(the Comedy Theatre), Messrs. H. Herman and Edward Jones's "The Fay o' Fire" (at the Opera Comique), and Messrs. Hamilton and Fullerton's "The Lady of the Locket" (at the Empire).

1886

Music in 1886. It would be easy to mention a year in which, taking the twelve months through, more musical activity prevailed in the British Isles, though it might be difficult to enumerate one presenting higher quality in the native productions. Three of our leading composers, whose nationality, together with their individuality of style, is not to be disputed, contributed important works, and in each case the result was extremely satisfactory. Certainly British art is the gainer by the musical proceedings of 1886. Strangely enough, the **compositions** to which we specially allude—Sir Arthur Sullivan's cantata "**The Golden Legend**," Mr. Mackenzie's "**The Story of Sayid**," and Mr. Villiers Stanford's "**The Revenge**"—were, like Antonin Dvorak's oratorio "**St. Ludmila**," written for the **Leeds** triennial festival held in October. The success of the three productions named were unquestioned, and public opinion in the Metropolis has since fully ratified the verdict of the Yorkshire musical centre. Sir Arthur Sullivan's cantata may take rank among his most original, elegant, and finished works, and in every sense warrants the warm encomiums it has received. "**The Story of Sayid**" was not Mr. Mackenzie's sole effort of the year. In June his opera "**The Troubadour**" was brought forward by Mr. Carl Rosa at Drury Lane Theatre, in the most elaborate manner and with a strong cast, but failed to take a firm grasp of public attention. In dramatic feeling Mr. Mackenzie's second opera is superior to his first—"**Colomba**," produced under the same auspices—though, unless some alterations be made in the construction of "the book," it is scarcely likely to be heard so frequently in the future. "**Colomba**" for a time undoubtedly attracted considerable notice. Through his connection with "Novello's Oratorio Concerts" this composer has become prominent as a conductor. To him was confided the superintendence of the performance of the "**St. Elizabeth**" of **Liszt**, when the distinguished composer and pianist was invited to this country to hear his oratorio rendered by British choralists and by the very first soloists of the day. Liszt had not visited England for more than forty years, and the announcement of his coming created such a stir in musical circles as was without parallel in modern times. For more than a fortnight our concert programmes teemed with his compositions. Besides the "St. Elizabeth" performance, concerts were organised in his honour, and his movements partook of the character of a triumphal progress. Wherever he appeared—whether at St. James's Hall, at the Crystal Palace, or at the concert-room of the Royal Academy of Music in Tenterden Street (where the intimation was officially made to him of the **scholarship** instituted in honour of his visit)—Liszt was everywhere received with the utmost enthusiasm. The extraordinarily effusive greeting thus tendered him by a nation that had hitherto regarded his more extended works with coldness—not to say indifference—was the last notable tribute to his great talents Liszt was destined to receive. He was here in April; less than four months afterwards he died at Bayreuth, beneath the shadow of the dramatic temple emblematic of the life-work of his friend and relative Richard Wagner. The **Wagnerian performances** for the year were not suspended, though their lustre was naturally dimmed by the great loss that particular school of art had just sustained. Besides Leeds, two other **provincial festivals** were held, at each of which new works of merit by British composers were introduced. At the time-honoured annual gathering of the **Three Choirs of the West**—held on this occasion at Gloucester—a decided success was achieved by Mr. Charles Harford Lloyd (formerly organist of the cathedral there) with his cantata "Andromeda," whilst at the **Wolverhampton triennial meeting**—which promises well—a very good impression was made with Dr. Swinnerton Heap's cantata "**The Maid of Astolat**" and Mr. F. Corder's "**The Bridal of Triermain**." The **Handel Festival** having taken place in 1885, a year earlier than usual, in consequence of the celebration of the bicentenary of the great composer's birth, the only public meeting of the choir bearing his name was for the performance at the Crystal Palace on a gigantic scale of "**The Redemption**." Among **miscellaneous works** of the loftiest class brought forward during the year may be mentioned a new symphony (in E minor) by **Brahms**, a new symphony by the industrious and painstaking **Mr. Ebenezer Prout**, and new orchestral pieces by Messrs. **Hubert Parry** and **Henry Gadsby**. A new instrumental organisation has been started in "The London **Symphony Concerts**," directed by Mr. George Henschel; and the older of our musical institutions—the **Philharmonic Society**, the **Crystal Palace Concerts** (with their indefatigable conductor Mr. Manns), the **Monday** and **Saturday Popular Concerts**, the **Sacred Harmonic Society**, the **Royal Albert Hall Choral Society** (patronised by the Queen, who in February attended a command performance of Gounod's "Mors et Vita"), the **Henry Leslie Choir**, and the **Bach Choir** (now conducted by Mr. Villiers Stanford), to wit—have well maintained their hard-earned reputation. The **operatic undertakings** of the year have been of a varied nature. The entire collapse of a weak scheme of Italian opera in the earlier months at Her Majesty's Theatre, when the painful spectacle was presented of a number of chorus-singers and supernumeraries appealing from the stage to the audience, assembled on the last night of the very brief season, for pence with which to purchase food, did not augur favourably for the prospects in London of this branch of enterprise. However in May Signor Lago opened Covent Garden Theatre for Italian opera, and by playing favourite operas with a strong cast—besides introducing three very capable **débutantes** in Mdlle. Ella Russell, Mdlle. Valda, and Signor D'Andrade—carried through his season prosperously. **Madame Adelina Patti**, who had previously sung at several concerts, delighted

Liszt

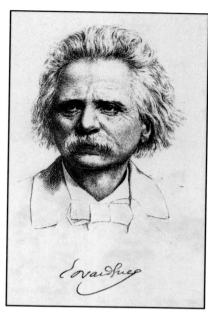

Grieg

Siegfried Wagner

Felix Weingartner

her multitude of admirers by appearing in "**Il Barbiere di Siviglia**" at a performance at Drury Lane for the benefit of Mr. J. H. Mapleson. Towards the end of the year **French opera** was played for several weeks at Her Majesty's Theatre, taken for the purpose by Mr. Mayer. In the field of **comic opera** the chief honours were gained by Mr. Alfred Cellier's tastefully written "**Dorothy**," the other works of a somewhat similar class being Mr. Ivan Caryll's "**The Lily of Léoville**" and M. Hervé's "**Frivoli.**" Of a more extravagant type were the "**Indiana**" of Audran, "**La Béarnaise**" by Messager, and "**La Diva**" (a version of the French "Joséphine vendue par ses Sœurs") by Victor Roger. The operas produced abroad having a chance (if a remote one) of being heard in this country, either in their native or some other tongue, are the "**Merlin**" of Goldmark (composer of "Königin von Saba"), the "**Otto der Schutz**" of Victor Nessler (whose "Piper of Hamelin" was given at Covent Garden in English a few years ago), the "**Cid**" of Massenet, "**Les Templiers**" of Litolff, and the "**Patrie**" (a musical setting of Sardou's well-known play) of Paladilhe.

1887

Music, '87. That the year of Jubilee would be marked by considerable productivity on the part of our native composers was to be expected. In consideration of the circumstance that neither of the recognised arts has made such rapid and continuous progress during the reign of Her Majesty, it was only fitting that some special display of English proficiency should be made on such an interesting and altogether exceptional occasion. Not so much, however, in the compositions born of the Jubilee as in miscellaneous productions was the musical year remarkable. Not many examples can be cited of music penned for some noteworthy Royal celebration being altogether worthy of the reputation of the favourite composers undertaking the task, and to their number but two of the new works dealing with the Jubilee can be added. These are **Dr. Bridge's anthem**, written expressly for the service attended by the Queen and Royal Family in Westminster Abbey, and the **Ode** composed by **Dr. Mackenzie**, produced the following day as the leading feature of a *fête* at the Crystal Palace. The last-named has since been heard at the Norwich Musical Festival, and at the Novello Oratorio Concerts in St. James's Hall. In nearly every other department of the art British composers have been active. True, no such success has been achieved as Sir Arthur Sullivan's "**Golden Legend**," the popularity of which seems almost as great as ever, notwithstanding that it has been before the public since the late autumn of 1886; but several meritorious works swell the list of productions of which the nation has every reason to be proud. Among these are **Mr. Cowen's** oratorio, "**Ruth**," written for the Three Choirs Festival at Worcester, and subsequently repeated with indications of increasing favour at the Novello Concerts and at the Crystal Palace; **Professor Stanford's** "**Irish Symphony**," extremely well received wherever heard; and **Mr. Prout's** cantata, "**The Red Cross Knight**," composed for the Huddersfield Festival. Of course slighter works were brought forward that deserve a word of praise, but to particularise a few productions out of many of the same calibre would be invidious. Of our **younger composers**, or—as perhaps it would be more correct to say—those who are beginning to be known by the general public, **Mr. George**

J. Bennett distinguished himself by some orchestral pieces, **Mr. Hamish M'Cunn** by an **overture** played late in the year at the Crystal Palace, and **Mr. Oliver King** by a violin **concerto.** Sir **Arthur Sullivan's** sole contribution was the comic opera "**Ruddigore**," another of the series having Mr. W. S. Gilbert as author of the "book," with which from its opening. The opera contained some of the prettiest solos the famous composer has ever incorporated into like works, but *Ruddigore* did not seize the public fancy to anything like the extent of preceding productions from the same pens. When it was withdrawn the management resorted to an elaborate revival of "**H.M.S. Pinafore**," with the delightfully buoyant music of which everybody was delighted to renew acquaintance under such excellent conditions. The **Carl Rosa Opera Company** paid its annual visit to the Metropolis, and was again located at Drury Lane. The novelty of the season was an **opera** by **Mr. Corder**, entitled "**Nordisa**," the subject of which was Norwegian. It secured such hearty acceptance from musical audiences of several of the more important provincial cities, that anticipations of a prosperous career in London were freely indulged in. The result was somewhat disappointing. Apparently Mr. Corder had endeavoured to conciliate the two extremes of opposite taste, and the issue was much the same as that recorded in a familiar fable. Far more successful was the **revival** of "**Lohengrin**," with Mr. Barton M'Guckin as the Knight of the Swan, and Madame Marie Roze as Elsa; whilst once more "**Carmen**" (with the prima donna just mentioned) drew crowded houses whenever played. In the latter opera a most favourable impression was created by Miss Fanny Moody (the Michaela), who has since been gaining further experience in the provinces. The season of **Italian Opera** was the busiest ever known in the Metropolis. For a few nights three operatic companies, respectively occupying the three established London opera-houses, were pitted against each other. Early in the spring Mr. Mapleson commenced operations at **Covent Garden Theatre,** and at the first performance ("La Traviata") reintroduced **Madame Nordica**, who was found to have developed a pure and telling soprano voice, in combination with a good stage style, since she made a not particularly promising essay in this country some years ago. Among operatic soloists this lady was destined to make the hit of the season. With **Signor Ravelli** as his chief tenor, Mr. Mapleson produced a number of works in creditable fashion, and towards the close of his tenancy produced for the first time in England Bizet's "**Les Pecheurs de Perles.**" He also revived Gounod's "**Mireille**," which did not prove so attractive as might reasonably have been hoped. When **Signor Lago** entered upon possession of the theatre he had the advantage of the services of **Madame Albani**, who went through a round of her favourite characters, and also played in Glinka's Russian opera, "**Life for the Czar,**" which, although regarded as a representative work, had not before been heard in Great Britain. Meantime Mr. Augustus Harris was pursuing a season of **Italian Opera** memorable for the perfection with which even the most hackneyed works in the Italian *répertoire* were placed upon the stage. Mr. Harris gave "**Norma**," "**Rigoletto**," and "**Lucia di Lammermoor**" among the productions of this stamp, but he naturally favoured the more spectacular works, whilst his vocal ensembles were magnificent. He did not give any new work, having failed in his negotiations for Verdi's *Otello*, produced a few months previously in Milan, but revived the last act of "**Les Huguenots**," and played the ballet act (absolutely new to England) of Gounod's "**Faust**," written to make that celebrated work suitable for the boards of the Parisian Grand Opera. The cast of these two operas was incomparable, the **Brothers De Reszke** being respectively the tenor and bass (both these *artistes*, by the way, being invaluable throughout the season), and Madame Nordica the soprano. **Mdlle Sigrid Arnoldson**, of whom we are certain to hear more in the future, also made a successful *début* in "**Il Barbiere di Siviglia**." Whilst Covent Garden and Drury Lane were in active competition, Mr. Mapleson opened **Her Majesty's Theatre. Madame Adelina Patti** drew an immense audience for "**La Traviata**," **Madame Trebelli** appeared in "**Carmen**," **Madame Lehmann** played in "**Fidelio**," and Boito's impressive "**Mefistofele**" was revived. The Norwich Festival novelties were a devotional oratorio, "**The Garden of Olivet**," by Signor Bottesini, and a dramatic oratorio, "**Isaias**," by Signor Luigi Mancinelli, the latter of which was specially successful. The performances of the **Philharmonic Society**, of the **Sacred Harmonic Society**, of the **Royal Albert Hall Choral Society**, of **Novello's Oratorio Concerts**, and of the **Crystal Palace Concerts**, have again been highly commendable. Other **notable musical events** of the year were the **Thousandth Monday Popular Concert**; the celebration of the **centenary** of the production of "**Don Giovanni**"; the **Welsh Eisteddfod** at the Albert Hall; the appearance in England of the wondrously gifted **boy-pianist, Josef Hofmann**, who had not attained his tenth year when he made his bow to a London audience at the Prince's Hall, and who has since become the object of idolatry of the New York musical public; the performance, in the autumn in London, of a **symphony by Wagner**, composed before he was out of his teens, and showing none of the individuality that was first displayed (and never afterwards lost) in "The Flying Dutchman"; and the **Conference of Musicians** from all parts of the country, held Jan. '88, for the second time in the Metropolis, with two concerts respectively of unpublished and published works by members of the society.

1888

Music, '88. There would be no difficulty in recalling an English musical year in which more important novelties were produced than in '88, but no season can be considered uneventful that includes the celebration of a Handel Festival under such conditions as are afforded at the Crystal Palace. By drafting contingents from the leading musical centres of the country, the **triennial meeting** has assumed the character of a national gathering that is both significant and impressive. Greater honour could not be paid to any representative of Art, whether past or present, than that bestowed at these fixed intervals upon the genius of Handel. Though the programme is virtually the same—being of necessity indeed almost unalterable—the patronage of the general musical public remains as steady as it was ten or fifteen years back. With such an enterprise the fluctuation of three or four thousand persons in the attendance matters little. The numbers cannot be always the same, and a few less or more are not worth mention when the total is about 80,000 during the three days of the Festival and the preliminary rehearsal. In '88 as much interest as ever was evinced in proceedings long since familiar to the great majority of supporters, and the entire performance, under the direction of Mr. August Manns, was in every detail equal to the best in preceding years.

As usual, the Monday and Friday were respectively devoted to "**Messiah**" and to "**Israel in Egypt**," those imperishable monuments to the power of the master; but in the Selection on Wednesday a successful attempt was made to exhibit in chronological order various specimens of his workmanship, from early Italian operas to his latest productions in the domain of sacred music. This arrangement allowed of the performance of some excerpts from operas, cantatas, and oratorios not previously heard at Sydenham. The result of the Festival was again eminently satisfactory to all concerned. Having acquired **Covent Garden Theatre for Italian Opera**, Mr. **Augustus Harris** soon bestirred himself to fulfil the expectations created by his initial venture with this costly branch of entertainment at Drury Lane in '87. He now trusted to singers for whom his subscribers had already shown great partiality. The catalogue of his **company** included nearly a dozen ladies who had earned the right to be considered *prime donne* both here and elsewhere; and among the male principals were the Brothers De Reszke, M. Lassalle, Signor Del Puente, and Signor Ravelli. Signor Mancinelli and Mr. Randegger were once more the conductors. Mr. Harris, by personally directing the *mise-en-scène*, not only secured pictorial completeness, but evolved much that was new in the way of grouping, etc. The co-operation of Madame Albani and the De Reszkes in "**Lohengrin**," the further assistance in "**Faust**" of Madame Scalchi and M. Lassalle, and the appearance in "**Les Huguenots**" of Madame Nordica, Miss Ella Russell, Madame Scalchi, the two De Reszkes, Signor Del Puente, and Signor Navarrini, caused these three fine examples of varying styles of composition to be so frequently heard during the season (always to densely crowded audiences), that Mr. Harris was induced to prolong the performances a fortnight beyond the period announced at the outset of his campaign. During these extra representations the attendance did not decline, and on the final night (when *Les Huguenots* was played) the assemblage did not depart until they had summoned the manager and extorted a few words of grateful acknowledgment, in which better things, if possible, were promised for the succeeding year. Mr. Harris was not rash enough to say exactly what he hoped to do during his **second season** at **Covent Garden**, but as it was whispered that he intended to witness the performance of the *Meistersinger* at Bayreuth, the conclusion was arrived at that he would probably place the only comic opera of Wagner upon the stage in the Italian language. It has since transpired that **Mr. Goring Thomas's** English opera "**Esmeralda**" (originally produced by Mr. Carl Rosa) has been translated into Italian with a view to **Madame Albani**—for whom the composer has provided an additional air—playing the heroine. **Madame Minnie Hauk** appeared several times in "**Carmen**," and celebrated the tenth year of her performance in London of the gipsy girl; **Mdlle. Sigrid Arnoldson** played some lighter characters, and as Cherubino joined **Madame Albani** and **Miss Ella Russell** in **Le Nozze di Figaro**. A pronounced success was gained by **Miss MacIntyre**, a *débutante*, that Mr. Harris towards the close of the season permitted her to represent Margaret in Boïto's "**Mefistofele**," the character of Helen of Troy (hitherto in the Metropolis assigned to the same *prima donna*) being sustained by Miss Ella Russell; and a favourable impression was made by **Madame Rolla**, whose useful readiness was shown by the manner in which at short notice she sang the music of Donna Elvira in the Mozartian *chef d'œuvre*. Mr. Harris gave about twenty operas with perfection of *ensemble*, and on no occasion throughout the season was compelled to change the performance advertised. For the first time for many years **Mr. Carl Rosa** did not bring his company to London, so that enterprise in elaborate opera was restricted to Covent Garden. The **provincial musical festivals** of the year were held at **Birmingham, Chester, Hereford,** and **Bristol.** Of the three latter nothing need be said, inasmuch as the programmes were chiefly made up of pieces often heard elsewhere. True, the **Three Choirs meeting** on the banks of the Wye brought about the first performance in England of the **Ode** for chorus and band composed by **Mr. F. H. Cowen** for the inauguration of the **Melbourne Exhibition,** and also led to the **revival** of **Sir F. G. Ouseley's** oratorio "**St. Polycarp,**" written as his "degree exercise" more than three decades back ; but neither of these could be looked upon as musical items of supreme consequence. The committee of the **Birmingham Festival** was called upon to endure a series of provoking disappointments. It was not designed to have so many altogether fresh works as in '85, when novelty was rather overdone, but two or three composers who had been invited to contribute were for divers reasons unable to respond. At length the list of new compositions dwindled to two—**Dr. Hubert Parry's** oratorio "**Judith ; or the Regeneration of Manasseh,**" and **Dr. F. Bridge's** cantata "**Callirhoë.**" Both these works were received with hearty approval, and were generally held to manifest qualities with the possession of which their respective composers had not heretofore been credited. Dr. Parry's oratorio was found to be clear, melodious, and based on the methods of the distinguished producers of sacred music in the past ; while Dr. Bridge's cantata displayed dramatic strength in addition to the elegance and knowledge of instrumental resource patent in former essays. **Sir Arthur Sullivan's** "**Golden Legend**" (which here, as elsewhere, drew an overflowing audience), **Berlioz's** "**Messe des Morts**" and **Handel's** "**Saul**" were also given during the Festival week, with Herr Richter wielding the bâton. The question of the **conductorship** of the concerts of the **Philharmonic Society** was settled by the appointment of **Mr. F. H. Cowen,** notwithstanding that it was known he would soon have to leave for Melbourne, in order to direct the musical performances in connection with the Centennial Exhibition. To fill the void thus occasioned the directors hit upon the happy idea of persuading **M. Tschaikowsky, M. Widor,** and **Herr Grieg,** as **representatives** of the **Russian, French,** and **Scandinavian schools,** to bring to England (and conduct) some of their newest compositions. In each case the issue of the visit proved decidedly interesting. Certainly the Philharmonic directors had no reason to regret their liberal policy. Another foremost artist absent from England during some weeks of the busiest portion of the season was **Mr. Edward Lloyd,** the tenor singer, who accepted an engagement for the **Cincinnati Festival.** As was expected, he was received with enthusiasm, and was compelled to promise that he would again visit America professionally. In October, after a series of **revivals,** of which "**The Mikado**" seemed the most welcome, a new Gilbert-Sullivan opera called "**The Yeomen of the Guard**" was produced at the **Savoy,** and the composer's share in the work was unanimously and cordially approved. For the **second year** continuously, "**Dorothy**" was a fixture at the **Prince of Wales's ;** "**Carina**" at the **Opera Comique** contained some pretty music in the Balfe-Wallace vein by **Madame Julia Woolf** ; the mirthful opera "**Nadgy**" at length ousted "**The Old Guard**" from the Avenue ; and "**Pepita**" at **Toole's Theatre** justified the good opinion delivered for many months in the provinces. **Novello's Oratorio Concerts,** the Richter Concerts, the **London Symphony Concerts,** the **Crystal Palace Concerts,** the **London Ballad Concerts,** and the **Monday** and **Saturday Popular Concerts,** profitably pursued their respective paths. The **Royal Albert Hall Choral Society,** in May, gave a performance of "**The Golden Legend**" by command of the Queen, who was present, and Mr. Barnby's force is henceforward to be called the "**Royal Choral Society.**" As usual, there were **Promenade Concerts** at Covent Garden Theatre in the autumn.— Among **occurrences** that had some bearing upon the musical proceedings of the year was the **death** of **Sir George Macfarren,** and the consequent **vacancy** in the lofty position of **Principal of the Royal Academy of Music.** As the time approached for the election, the number of candidates was reduced to two, Dr. A. C. Mackenzie and Mr. Joseph Barnby, the former being ultimately chosen. The boy pianist, **Otto Hegner,** delighted the admirers of rare juvenile talent, just as did **Josef Hofmann** twelve months before ; and other noteworthy incidents of the year were the **farewell** (at the Royal Albert Hall) of **Madame Nilsson,** the revival in November by Mr. E. Prout and the **Hackney Choral Society** of Handel's long-neglected oratorio "**Joshua,**" the performance of the ill-fated **Georges Bizet's** beautiful music to **Daudet's** "**L'Artésienne**" during representations of the drama at the Prince of Wales's Theatre in January, and the arrival of a **Russian Opera Company.** The latter acquired a very sad experience. After playing in the provinces, they gave some concerts at the **Royal Albert Hall** under circumstances that afforded little hope of their talents being effectively demonstrated. Subsequently they appeared in Rubenstein's opera "**The Demon**" at the Jodrell Theatre (the newly-named Novelty), but here again ill-luck attended their performances. The work they chose had been tried in London nine years before, with an exceptionally strong cast, and had failed. Operatic amateurs were disappointed that the company did not play Tschaikowsky's "**Mazeppa**" (one of the favourite operas in their *repertoire*), which would have been a novelty here. When the speculation suddenly, but not altogether unexpectedly, came to an end, a number of Russian choralists, ignorant of the English language, were found helpless, starving, and destitute at the East End, and for funds to send them back to their native country an appeal was made to the public. Towards the end of November **Mdme Patti** (q.v.) sang at Paris in Gounod's opera "**Romeo et Juliette**" (conducted by the composer) with great success. The **150th anniversary** of the Royal Society of Musicians was celebrated on Nov. 29th by an unusually imposing performance of "**The Messiah**" in Westminster Abbey.

1889

Music, '89. During the year most of our native composers gave proof of their activity, and in the majority of instances the result was highly satisfactory. Among the earliest novelties claiming attention in the Metropolis was **The Dream of Jubal,** a cantata composed by Dr. A. C. Mackenzie to an original poem by Mr. Joseph Bennett, given at Novello's Oratorio Concerts, after it had been heard at the jubilee celebration of the Liverpool Philharmonic Society, for which it was written. Employing for much of the narrative portion a reader whose utterances were accompanied by picturesque instrumentation, the work was somewhat akin to Mendelssohn's **Athalie** and

Antigone music. For the present day it was a bold experiment, but the favour accorded was quite commensurate with reasonable expectations, and subsequent performances had the effect of completely endorsing the original verdict. Both in its choral and instrumental features (the latter being particularly conspicuous) the work may be pronounced worthy to stand beside the most finished labours of its accomplished composer. It was among the productions chosen for the Festival of the Three Choirs—held this year at Gloucester—and attracted considerable attention.—In the autumn Dr. Mackenzie composed an elaborate violin piece for Señor Sarasate, called **Pibroch**, which was first heard at the **Leeds Festival** in October. To this festival it was hoped that Sir Arthur Sullivan would be able to contribute some new work that would further have associated his name with a triennial gathering that already contained on its roll of exceptional successes the English composer's **Martyr of Antioch** ('80) and **The Golden Legend** ('86), but it was understood that he had been too busy with the new opera to follow **The Yeomen of the Guard** at the Savoy Theatre. Sir Arthur, however, arranged for concert purposes his incidental music to **Macbeth**, composed for Mr. Henry Irving's magnificent revival at the Lyceum ; and this, with the ever popular **Golden Legend**, was played to a crowded assemblage at the "extra" concert which is customary at the great musical meeting of Yorkshire. To the Leeds Festival Dr. Hubert Parry, Dr. Villiers Stanford, and Mr. F. Corder furnished novelties that awakened much curiosity. Encouraged by the commendation accompanying his "new departure" in his oratorio **Judith** (Birmingham, '88, and one of the principal items of the Gloucester Festival this year) Dr. Parry pursued the same path in his setting of Pope's ode on **St. Cecilia's Day**, and the issue again commanded universal praise. As his choral ballad **The Revenge** (Leeds, '86) did so much to extend his popularity throughout the United Kingdom, Dr. Stanford acted wisely in taking up another of the Poet Laureate's works for treatment in Yorkshire. **The Voyage of Maeldune**, is, however, a much more important work than its predecessor. Solo voices are utilised as well as band and chorus, and the fancifulness of Lord Tennyson's theme is reflected by the musician in the most touching manner. Abounding with grace and melodic charm, and at the same time scholarly, a good reception for **The Voyage of Maeldune** may be guaranteed whenever it is adequately interpreted. Gauged by his pleasing opera **Nordisa**, Mr. Frederick Corder's cantata **The Sword of Argantyr** was somewhat disappointing. The remaining novelty of the Leeds Festival—a busy gathering for all engaged—was a brief cantata called **The Sacrifice of Freia**, composed by Dr. William Creser, the organist of the parish church, a work that suffered by being only a portion of the original design, the sudden death of the author of the book (the learned Dr. Francis Hueffer) preventing the completion of later sections that had been determined upon.—The one absolute novelty of the Gloucester Musical Festival was a church cantata, **The Last Night at Bethany**, modelled by Messrs. Joseph Bennett and C. Lee-Williams (the cathedral organist), upon those texts of Bach, composed with a view to the congregation participating at certain points of the sacred story. In all quarters the venture was approved, and the expressively devotional character of Mr. Lee-Williams's music created so deep an impression as to warrant further essays in a like direction. In every respect the **Three Choirs Festival** of '89 was eminently successful. That very promising young Scottish composer, Mr. Hamish MacCunn (*q.v.*), in **The Lay of the Last Minstrel** added another agreeable composition to his characteristic settings of well-known poems. This was given by Mr. Manns at the Crystal Palace Concerts, where in April, at the benefit concert of the esteemed conductor, Mr. Frederic Cliffe obtained his opportunity by the introduction of a symphony from his pen. Fresh in style, full of glow, and spirited in execution, this work (originally intended, it was rumoured, for the Leeds Festival) at once made its mark, and before the summer musical season ended was adopted by the **Philharmonic Society**, the subscribers to which appended their congratulations to those so liberally bestowed upon the composer at Sydenham. In connection with the oldest musical institution of which London can boast, it may be mentioned that during its annual series of concerts the Russian pianist M. Sapellnikoff, another pianist Mdme. Bäcker-Grondahl, and the Belgian violinist M. Ysaye, respectively made their first appearance here and were cordially received. Fraulein Geisler-Schubert (a grand-niece of the ill-fated composer) visited the Metropolis as a pianist, and Otto Hegner (*q.v.*), the boy pianist, both in the spring and the late autumn, fully maintained the reputation he had previously gained without affording the slightest indication that he was being overtaxed either physically or mentally. Edward Grieg (*q.v.*), the Scandinavian composer, who was one of the musical "lions" of '88, accompanied by his wife, again came to England for a few weeks, and they drew crowds wherever they appeared. **Madame Adelina Patti** (*q.v.*) in January gave some concerts at the Royal Albert Hall prior to leaving Europe for a South American tour, and again sang in the autumn on her return—each occasion of her appearance, whether in London or in the provinces, seeming to demonstrate that her popularity is as great as of old. Two interesting features in the season of the **Royal Choral Society** at the **Royal Albert Hall** were the production in London in February of Mancinelli's oratorio **Isaias** (given at the Norwich Festival of '87), and in April of the Flemish composer Peter Benoit's sacred cantata **Lucifer**, a strikingly original work. Late in the year came the announcement that the operations of **Novello's Oratorio Concerts** would henceforth be **amalgamated** with those of **Mr. Barnby's** choir. Before the Novello season ended a hearing was afforded of Dudley Buck's thoughtful work **The Light of Asia**, and of Handel's **Saul** as given at the Birmingham Festival the preceding autumn. The departure of **Mr. Santley** (*q.v.*), the celebrated English baritone, for Australia was severely felt, particularly at the provincial musical festivals. To compensate in some measure for this temporary loss to the United Kingdom, Mr. F. H. Cowen returned from his highly prosperous visit to the Antipodes, and resumed his post as conductor of the Philharmonic Society. Great was the satisfaction when it became known that he had ready for production a new dramatic cantata called **St. John's Eve**, the libretto by Mr. Joseph Bennett. During April, May and June the concerts of lesser known vocalists and instrumentalists—many of them as yet scarcely free of their tutors—were more numerous than ever, but as a rule the proceedings were only of interest to the executants and their friends. Mr. Henschel, as conductor of the London Symphony Concerts, invited Mr. Broughton's Leeds choir to the Metropolis to sing in **The First Walpurgis Night** and Beethoven's "Choral Symphony," and the reception of the Yorkshire choralists was in harmony with their widely acknowledged deserts. The Monday and Saturday Popular Concerts continued their steady course. In terminating the record of concerts it may be said that from time to time creditable displays were made by the pupils of the Royal Academy of Music (q.v.), the Royal College, the Guildhall School, and like institutions.—A good deal was done in the department of Opera from the middle of May until the end of July. The Royal Italian Opera at Covent Garden was recommenced on the 18th of May by Mr. Augustus Harris, with a very strong company, that included Mmes. Albani, Nordica, Ella Russell, Melba, Valda, MacIntyre, Van Zandt, and Scalchi, and MM. Lassalle, the brothers D'Andrade, Barton M'Guckin, Winsgradow, and last, but very far from least, the brothers De Reszke. The conductorship was shared by Signors Luigi Mancinelli, Randegger, and Arditi. Mr. Harris made arrangements for the addition to his répertoire of Gounod's Roméo et Juliette (in French), Les Pecheurs de Perles, Die Meistersinger (in Italian), and Le Prophète ; but the last-named had to be relinquished in consequence of the hindrance to preparations through the special visit to the opera of the Shah of Persia and the English royal family, when a brilliant spectacle was presented that will not soon be forgotten by those who witnessed it. During the ten weeks Mr. Harris played sixteen operas, the honours being carried off by Gounod with Faust (with grand combination casts), and Roméo et Juliette (with Madame Melba and the two De Reszkes) each of which was given seven times. The Italian version of Die Meistersinger, with Madame Albani and MM. Jean De Reszke, Lassalle, Montariol, and Isnardon (a Belgian singer engaged for the part of the spiteful Beckmesser), as principals, was played four times—a number that would certainly have been exceeded had Wagner's work been produced earlier in the season. The whole of the operas were finely mounted, and both from the artistic and financial aspects the issue of Mr. Harris's third Italian Opera campaign was very gratifying. A memorable event was the bringing to London in July by Mr. Mayer of Verdi's last opera, Otello, first produced at La Scala in Feb., '87. Instead of playing it at the Lyceum, with a scratch company and makeshift accessories—conditions that might not have checked the eagerness of English amateurs to make acquaintance with the work, however much the effect of the music may have been spoiled—the enterprising director secured Signor Tamagno and M. Maurel, the respective representatives of Othello and Iago chosen by Verdi, and transferred here the La Scala band, chorus, and scenery, together with the famous conductor, Signor Faccio. Thus the performance was the nearest approach to the original that seemed possible after the lapse of two years. That the stupendous cost of the venture, independently of the dramatic qualities of the music and the fine acting and singing of the two male principals, should be extensively discussed, was inevitable, and on all sides it was admitted that patrons of opera owed a debt of gratitude to Mr. Mayer. The veteran impresario, Mr. Mapleson, opened Her Majesty's Theatre for Italian Opera, and brought forward several singers new to this country. He gave a few familiar works, and revived Donizetti's charming L'Elisire d'Amore ; but before he could produce the promised Italian version of Bizet's La Jolie Fille de Perth the season came to an abrupt conclusion. The most fortunate essays in light opera were made at the Prince of Wales's Theatre and the Lyric. At the former, Planquette's Paul Jones had the exceedingly valuable co-operation of that pleasing vocalist Miss Agnes Huntington ; and at Mr. Leslie's new house, Dorothy, after 931 representations, yielded its place to the same com-

poser's Doris, while the Red Hussar (Nov. 23rd) seemed attractive. Other operas produced during the year were Signor Tito Mattei's La Prima Donna (at the Avenue in October), Major George Cockle's The Castle of Como (Opera Comique, October), Mr. Henry Parker's Mignonette (Royalty Theatre, May), Mr. Walter Slaughter's Marjorie (Prince of Wales's, July), and Mr. Edward Solomon's tuneful trifles Pickwick and Penelope (both at the Comedy). During August, September, and October, Covent Garden and Her Majesty's Theatres were in opposition with promenade concerts. The Ballad Concerts commenced Nov. 19th, at St. James's Hall.

1890

Music, '90. Close observers of musical activity in England, who fancied that pianoforte recitals were declining in favour, must have been undeceived when, during May, June and the greater portion of July, St. James's Hall, Prince's Hall, and other rooms suitable for the purpose, were in extraordinary demand for this species of entertainment. Never, in the Metropolis, was there so much professional pianoforte playing in public within such a limited period. Apparently still confident that England is a veritable Tom Tiddler's ground for performers whose gifts are rather above the average, foreign executants of all degrees came to this country in the spring with the view of trying their fortune,—in several cases, it is to be feared, with unsatisfactory results. Of course some of our visitors—Madame Sophie Menter, M. Sapellnikoff, and the Belgian violinist, M. Ysaye, among others—were old friends, whom all appreciating true art were glad to see again, and these probably had no reason to repent their journey. The most brilliant of the absolutely new-comers was M. Paderewski, a pianist whose power and facility were calculated to surprise even those whose experience of the modern school had created the belief that they were never likely to be again really astonished. Undoubted gratification was evoked by the appearance of Mr. Leonard Borwick (q.v.), a young Englishman who demonstrated at a Philharmonic Concert that he was able to hold his own both in classical works and in lighter pieces against Continental rivals. In fact, he fully realised the expectations that were the outcome of rumours concerning his ability. Our more famous composers have not been very prolific during the year. Sir Arthur Sullivan (q.v.) was known to be engaged on his serious opera Ivanhoe, for the completion of which his mind was freed by the pronounced success of his comic opera The Gondoliers (book by Mr. W. S. Gilbert) at the Savoy Theatre towards the close of last year. No work of its series was more highly praised. Mr. F. H. Cowen (q.v.), whose cantata St. John's Eve belongs to last year, added a grand opera to the Carl Rosa répertoire in Thorgrim ; Professor Stanford has been preparing a new oratorio of large dimensions, called Eden, for the Birmingham Festival next autumn ; Dr. A. C. Mackenzie (q.v.), in March, at the Royal Albert Hall, submitted his setting of Burns' "The Cotter's Saturday Night," received with marked approval, and subsequently provided some delightful incidental music to Mr. Robert Buchanan's poetic play The Bride of Love, and to Mr. Herman Merivale's Lyceum play Ravenswood ; Dr. Hubert Parry (q.v.) supplied "Allegro ed il Penseroso" for the Norwich Triennial Musical Festival ; and Professor Bridge (q.v.) was represented at the Three Choirs Festival at Worcester by a vigorously dramatic oratorio

Eugene Ysaye

(text by Mr. Joseph Bennett) called **The Repent-ance of Nineveh.** This is far from an extensive catalogue of important native productions; but, as indicated, there is reason to hope for a better result of the next twelve months' operations. Foreign musicians were very much in evidence during the season of the **Philharmonic Society.** No less than six works new to England were conducted by their respective composers. **M. Peter Benoit,** whose oratorio **Lucifer** was intro-duced to this country the preceding year, ap-peared at the desk to direct the performance of a selection of his music to the drama "Charlotte Corday," a work not calculated to increase his reputation here ; **Herr Dvorak** (*q.v.*) took the bâton for his Symphony in G, which made a good impression ; Signor Mancinelli did the same for his picturesque orchestral suite, "Scène Veneziane"; M. Moszkowski for an orchestral suite in G minor; M. Widor, for a fantasia in A flat for piano and orchestra (the solo part played by M. Philipp); and M. Huberti for some vocal pieces. There was thus some special feature of interest for nearly every concert, and the issue was such as to afford the conviction that our oldest musical institution still possesses abundant vitality. **Mr. Cowen** was conductor-in-chief throughout, and con-tributed to the programme an orchestral suite arranged from Grétry's ballet, "Cephale et Procris," whilst Mr. Frederic Cliffe, who bounded into notoriety in '89 with a well-written sym-phony, to which Mr. August Manns stood sponsor, was congratulated upon the pleasing quality of his new orchestral picture "Cloud and Sunshine," composed expressly for the Society. The performances by the band, almost entirely English, were, taken as a whole, un-surpassable. In the domain of serious opera Mr. Augustus Harris had matters entirely his own way. He superintended a brief season of the Carl Rosa Opera performances at Drury Lane, commencing at Easter ; and in the middle of May began ten weeks of opera in a foreign tongue at Covent Garden Theatre. The Carl Rosa representations included Gounod's **Romeo and Juliet** (first time in English), **L'Etoile du Nord, Mignon, Lohengrin, Faust,** and of course **Carmen,** the young *prima donna,* **Mlle. Zelie de Lussan,** making such a hit as the fickle heroine of Bizet's opera that she was secured for the same *rôle* at the Royal Italian Opera a few weeks afterwards. The chief event of the English season, however, was the production of Mr. Cowen's **Thorgrim,** the story founded by Mr. Joseph Bennett upon a Norse legend not unlike those of which Wagner was so fond. Concerning this work considerable curiosity was aroused, as Mr. Cowen's single preceding opera, **Pauline,** was penned early in his career, and is now only faintly remembered. **Thorgrim** betrays a stronger tendency towards the "ad-vanced school" than either of the composer's works yet presented; but, in the endeavour to be thoroughly dramatic, he did not lose sight of the fact that a fund of melody is happily indispensable to English opera, whatever form it may assume. It is a work that vastly im-proves with acquaintance. The original inter-preters were Mlle. Zelie de Lussan, Madame Tremelli, Messrs. Barton M'Guckin, Crotty, and Celli. As for months Mr. Augustus Harris had made no secret of his intentions, it was un-necessary for him to go through the formality of publishing a prospectus for his "Italian Opera" season. It was known that the **Brothers De Reszke, M. Lassalle, Madame Melba,** and **Miss Ella Russell,** had been re-engaged ; that a gor-geous revival of **Le Prophète** in the original French might be relied upon ; and that there would be an effort to give the English **Esmeralda** of Goring Thomas in the Gallic language. In neither of these particulars did disappointment

ensue. Mr. Harris also revived **La Favorita** and **Hamlet,** both in French. **Romeo et Juliette** (in French), **Die Meistersinger, Lohengrin,** and **Faust,** again drew immense audiences, in some measure perhaps due to the fact that in each of these **M. Jean de Reszke** was the hero. From the beginning of the season to the close the famous Polish tenor was, if possible, more popular than ever. As the theatre was open every night, Mr. Harris was enabled to give a total of **eighteen operas,** all carefully and the majority magnifi-cently mounted. In **Le Prophête,** indeed, he excelled himself. Two exceedingly valuable additions were made to the company in Madame Tavary, a dramatic soprano of Teutonic origin, and Madame Richard, a dramatic contralto for some time esteemed in France. The latter achieved a great success as Fides to the Prophet of M. Jean de Reszke, in Meyerbeer's imposing opera. The season was understood to be highly remunerative. The best seats fetched a fabulous price when, as an "extra night," Mr. Harris offered **Carmen** in French, with Mlle. de Lussan, M. Jean de Reszke and M. Lassalle in the three most prominent characters. The duties of con-ductor at this memorable performance were shared between Signor Mancinelli, Mr. Ran-degger and Signor Bevignani, who had been in turn responsible for the performances through-out the former ten weeks. For the annual operatic representation by the students of the **Royal College of Music,** Mozart's **Cosi fan Tutte** was selected. As the work had not been heard in the Metropolis for many years, a crowd of amateurs flocked to the Savoy Theatre, where **Professor Stanford** (*q.v.*) presided over a very creditable rendering of this delightfully tuneful, if otherwise weak work. Before quitting the field of **opera,** it must be mentioned that Mr. Walter Slaughter's **Marjorie** succeeded **Paul Jones** at the Prince of Wales' Theatre, and remained on the bills until the end of August, when it was superseded by Planquette's **Captain Thérèse,** written specially for the Carl Rosa light opera troupe. **The Red Hussar** quitted the Lyric Theatre in the summer and proceeded to America. The house then came under the management of Mr. Horace Sedger, who in October produced Audran's **La Cigale** with unequivocal success. For several weeks in the summer **Les Cloches de Corneville** were to be heard at the Opéra Comique ; and to the contiguous establish-ment, the Globe, Mr. Luscombe Searelle brought from Australia his melodramatic opera **The Black Rover.** The old farce **Domestic Economy** was turned into an operetta by Mr. Burnand, music by Mr. Edward Solomon, and was produced at the Comedy Theatre. The same gentlemen were associated in a slight musical piece, **The Tiger,** brought out at the St. James's. The comic opera, **Gretna Green** (book by Mr. J. Murray Ford, music by Dr. J. Storer), was played for a while at the Opéra Comique. There were two **oratorio performances** of a particularly noteworthy character in the Metropolis. Perceiving the growing appre-ciation for "St. Paul," the Crystal Palace directors decided upon Mendelssohn's noble work for the annual gathering of the Handel Festival Choir. Never before in England had it been given under such circumstances. The huge Handel Orchestra was of course filled. An extra force of five hundred boys was engaged for the treble part of "Sleepers, awake" and certain other choruses. **Mr. Manns** conducted, and the four soloists were **Madame Albani, Madame Patey** (who, by the way, soon after proceeded on a tour to Australia, thus depriv-ing us for a while of another member of "the representative English quartet"), **Mr. Edward Lloyd** (fresh from triumphs gained a second time in America), and **Mr. Watkin Mills.** The effect of the more massive choruses was superb, and financially the festival exceeded the most sanguine anticipations. The next month (July) a **Handel Festival** took place in Westminster Abbey, when, under the conductorship of Dr. Bridge (appointed Gresham Professor in place of the deceased Dr. Henry Wylde), a liberal selection from the great Saxon's masterpieces was gone through by eminent soloists and a numerous band and chorus.— Of the five provincial festivals of the year, **Worcester** demands the first place both in point of time and of musical importance. Here, as already stated, was given Professor Bridge's "Repentance of Nineveh." The lesser novelty was a spirited concert-overture entitled "Froissart," by Mr. E. Elgar, a local musician. Mr. Done, the organist of the cathedral for nearly half a century, resigned his claim to the bâton, which was given into the hands of the capable **Mr. C. Lee Williams**, the Gloucester organist. A further change in the arrangements was the substitution of another evening oratorio in the cathedral, at reduced prices, for one of the two miscellaneous concerts in the Public Hall. The wisdom of this policy was shown in the large increase of the collections at the cathedral doors, the whole amount of which is invariably devoted to the fund for the widows and orphans of the poorer clergy of the three dioceses, on behalf of which the Three Choirs Festivals were originated. The four other festivals were held in October. At **Norwich** the two proposed novelties were reduced to Dr. Parry's "L'Allegro ed il Penseroso"; the rest of the programme was made up of standard oratorios and attractive short pieces, among the latter being Dr. Mackenzie's "Ravenswood" music. Next came the **North Staffordshire Festival**—two days at Hanley, where a new cantata by Dr. Swinnerton Heap, on the subject of "Fair Rosamond," was heard for the first time. **Bristol**, held a year in advance of the usual course, in order to no longer clash with the Birmingham triennial meeting, trusted to familiar works with distinguished soloists; and so, too, in the main did **Cheltenham**, at the end of the month. The occasional appearances of **Madame Adelina Patti** (*q.v.*) have been the signal for the Royal Albert Hall to be besieged; and large audiences greeted **Mr. Sims Reeves** (*q.v.*) in his farewell performances in the autumn at Mr. Freeman Thomas' Covent Garden **Promenade Concerts**. The **Crystal Palace Concerts**, the Monday and Saturday "**Populars**," the **Richter Concerts**, and the **Royal Albert Hall Choral Society**, have respectively continued their good work with undiminished zeal and enterprise, and excellent support has also been awarded to the **London Ballad**, the **London Symphony**, and the **Sarasate** Concerts.

1891

Music in '91. With scarcely an exception, each of our leading native composers contributed some new work to the record of the year, and in a few instances the interest evinced by the musical public was altogether uncommon. Particularly was this the case with Sir Arthur Sullivan's romantic opera "Ivanhoe," written for the inauguration of Mr. D'Oyly Carte's new English Opera House in Cambridge Circus, and Professor Stanford's oratorio "Eden," specially composed for the Birmingham Triennial Festival in October; whilst as regards productions from foreign pens considerable attention was attracted to the Requiem introduced by Dvorak at the Birmingham meeting, and to Mascagni's powerful one-act opera "Cavalleria Rusticana," which, after an unchecked success of over eighteen months

throughout Italy and in various other parts of the Continent, was made the chief feature of an autumn opera season by Signor Lago at the Shaftesbury Theatre in the middle of October. The year was also marked by a **Handel Festival** at the Crystal Palace, and by the recurrence of the Chester and Hereford (Three Choirs) gatherings. The first of these in order was that at Sydenham in June, when honour to the mighty Saxon was again fitly paid by the performance of "Messiah" on the Monday, and "Israel in Egypt" on the Friday, with a lengthy selection from oratorios, cantatas, operas, and instrumental compositions on the intervening Wednesday. This was according to a custom that could scarcely be improved upon, since it represented the many-sidedness of Handel's genius. A special feature of the Selection programme was a "Gloria Patri" for double chorus and double orchestra, composed in Rome in 1707, when Handel was in his twenty-third year, and probably never previously performed. Some portions of the Chandos anthem "O come, let us sing," were also fresh to the Crystal Palace. The executive force was of the wonted strength and completeness, and Mr. August Manns again warranted his appointment as conductor of such a vast assemblage. The attendance at this (the tenth) triennial festival did not equal the highest figures yet attained, namely, 87,784 in '83, but it reached the very respectable total of 80,796 for the three days and preliminary public rehearsal. Considering that a Handel celebration is now very far from "a new thing," such an issue was eminently satisfactory. The next musical festival was at **Chester**, where distinct success accompanied the performance of a new cantata called "**Rudel**," by Dr. Joseph Bridge, the organist of the cathedral. In September came the **Hereford** meeting, under the conductorship, for the first time, of Mr. Robertson Sinclair, who was appointed the cathedral organist on the death, in '89, of Dr. Langdon Colborne. The absolute novelties here were a motet by Dr. H. J. Edwards for soprano solo, chorus and orchestra, entitled "Praise to the Holiest," the words from Cardinal Newman's "The Dream of "Gerontius"; "A Song of Judgment," a sacred cantata by Dr. C. Harford Lloyd, so closely associated with the Three Choirs annual gathering; and Dr. Hubert Parry's setting of "**De Profundis**." The latter, written for twelve part chorus, orchestra and soprano solo, proved one of the most notable compositions dated this year. The massiveness and sublimity of effect, no less than the singular skill exhibited in the simultaneous working of the three separate choirs, justified the designation of "the English Bach" being applied to a composer who during the past four years has made such rapid advance on the road to abiding fame. Noticeable revivals were Sir Arthur Sullivan's "Te Deum," Sir John Stainer's "St. Mary Magdalen," and Spohr's "Calvary." In more than one respect Mr. Sinclair showed a progressive spirit, and, favoured by splendid weather, the festival on the banks of the Wye was even more successful than had been hoped for. The diminution of late years in the receipts of the Birmingham Festival, whether there was an abundance or a paucity of novelties, demonstrated the desirability of a change in the arrangements. It being thought that the autumn holiday-making proclivities of the present generation had a great deal to do with the matter, it was decided to postpone the festival from the last week in August, when it has been generally held, until the beginning of October. This proved a step in the right direction. The Town Hall was well filled at each of the eight performances. Besides the novelties by Stanford and Dvorak respectively above referred to, there was a new and elegant setting by **Dr. A. C. Mackenzie**

43

The orchestral full score (Chappell, 1891, 3 volumes) of Sullivan's Ivanhoe;
Rebecca's aria, Act II sc. iii. This was one of the first British operas to be published
in full score.

of the "Veni, Creator Spiritus," as paraphrased by Dryden. "Eden" is in every way a remarkable work, original in design and execution. The poem by Mr. Robert Bridges, arranged in dramatic form, was issued separately some time before the performance. With its first act opening in "Heaven," and comprising the hymning of the new creation by the angels; with the second act devoted to the fierce maledictions and vain strivings of the fiends surrounding Satan in "Hell"; and with the illustration of the Fall in the "Garden of Eden," followed by Adam's vision of the various plagues afflicting earth as the penalty of his sin, and concluding with the promise of the advent of Christ, it afforded abundant scope for a composer resolved to cast aside the bonds of the conventional. A composition so unlike any other known oratorio—the nearest approach, perhaps, being M. Benoit's "Lucifer" heard at the Royal Albert Hall a few years back—could not but evoke considerable discussion. The difference of opinion concerning Professor Stanford's work did not extend to the **Requiem Mass of Dvorak**. Of this, high commendation was unanimous. The breadth, dignity and pathetic force contained in each section were as warmly recognised as the technical ingenuity and general structural merit, entitling it to a place beside the "Stabat Mater," by which the composer acquired his reputation. There can be no doubt that this "Requiem" is a noble addition to sacred musical art. Dvorak came to this country expressly to conduct the work he had specially written for Birmingham. The only other distinguished composer who honoured England with his company professionally was **Signor Sgambati**, who by invitation brought to the Philharmonic Society his "Sinfonia Epitalamia." At the close of January musical attention was absorbed by Mr. D'Oyly Carte's production of Sir Arthur Sullivan's opera **Ivanhoe**. This was a rather curious experiment. It had been often said that the comparative apathy evinced by British lovers of opera towards works of the more elaborate and thoroughly modern school penned by their own countrymen was in part due to the inability or objection of most operatic organisations to present an important novelty a sufficient number of times to make the public conversant with its merits. In reply it was pleaded that as one party of vocalists could not be expected to endure the strain of singing the same arduous characters night after night, frequent changes of programme were compulsory. Determined to give Sir Arthur Sullivan's first serious opera (the book by Mr. Julian Sturgis) every chance, Mr. D'Oyly Carte hit upon the plan of doubling and in a few instances trebling the cast of principals, so that all the more hardworked singers could obtain the prescribed rest. By this means the opera, magnificently mounted, could be played every evening, and the supporters of English lyric art be afforded time for accurately gauging the quality of the composition. The three companies were introduced at the first three representations, and the scheme of alternation was found to work extremely well. Although to many who had hitherto known Sullivan simply in connection with delightfully comic operas at the Savoy, and with platform ballads, it seemed strange that his pen should produce dramatic music of a vigorous and occasionally stern description, "**Ivanhoe**" was universally accepted as an able work warranting the hope that further efforts of a like order might diversify the composer's popular essays in another vein. Before the season terminated it had attained over a hundred and fifty consecutive performances—a circumstance unequalled in the history of English opera of the grand type.

"Ivanhoe," it may be added, brought into favour several vocalists hitherto but little known. Among these were Mr. Eugene Oudin (the Sir Brian), Mr. Norman Salmond (King Richard), and Mr. Avon Saxon (the burly Friar Tuck, whose song, "Ho! jolly Jenkin," and musical dialogue with the Black Knight in the forest, so vividly recalled the bright humour of the Savoy productions). Mr. D'Oyly Carte's announcement that he hoped this work would virtually prove the foundation of a national opera worthy of the name was widely endorsed, but as our supply of composers is hardly extensive enough just at present to meet the managerial demand for operas of the calibre of "**Ivanhoe**," resort to the Continent is still necessary. This was the explanation of Mr. D'Oyly Carte securing an English version of M. André Messager's "**La Basoche**" successfully produced at the re-opening of the house in Nov. Of foreign **opera** Sir Augustus Harris enjoyed a monopoly until the autumn. Having an exceedingly numerous force of distinguished vocalists at his command, he entered in April at Covent Garden upon a season of no less than sixteen weeks. There were ninety-four representations in all of twenty operas, most of which required great scenic preparation. The "bright particular stars" among the better known **artistes** were Mesdames Albani, Melba and De Lussan, the Brothers De Reszke, and MM. Lassalle, Maurel and Ravelli. The Sisters Ravogli, who in Signor Lago's autumn season in '90 had given new life to Gluck's **Orfeo**, joined Sir Augustus Harris, and opened the season with this work. A notable success was achieved by **M. Van Dyck**, a Dutch tenor who had acquitted himself most satisfactorily at the Wagnerian performances at Bayreuth. Here he made a host of friends in Massenet's **Manon** and in **Faust**, the only operas in which it was practicable for him to sing during his short stay here. **Miss Eames**, an American soprano, who had high credentials from Paris, was also well received here, and particularly distinguished herself as Margherita and as the heroine of Gounod's unjustly neglected **Mireille**. Another addition to Sir Augustus Harris' *repertoire* was **Tannhäuser**, with Madame Albani, Signor Perotti and M. Maurel as the three principals. The famous French baritone, by the way, had several opportunities during the season of illustrating his theory of voice-colour, previously expounded in a lecture at the Lyceum Theatre, by playing such contrasted parts as Rigoletto, Wolfram, Federico di Telramondo, Germont père, Di Nevers and Iago. Besides repeating such approved assumptions as Juliet and Lucia, **Madame Melba** redeemed a promise made the preceding year by appearing in the secondary part of Michaela in "**Carmen**" to the wicked gipsy of Mlle. Zélie de Lussan, the Don José of M. Jean de Reszke, and the Escamillo of M. Lassalle—altogether a cast unexampled for attractiveness, and in which the services of the Australian *prima donna* were thoroughly appreciated. The special event of the season, however, was the production of Verdi's "**Otello**" with M. Jean de Reszke as the Moor, Madame Albani as Desdemona, and M. Maurel (as already stated) in his original character of the treacherous Ancient. Interest was augmented by some postponements in consequence of the indisposition of the celebrated Polish tenor, who in undertaking a character hitherto identified in this country (at the Lyceum in '89) with Tamagno, was of course anxious to appear at his best. The performance, whether lyrically or dramatically, was not a whit disappointing. Towards the close of the season "**La Luce dell Asia**," a new cantata transformed into an opera, by Mr. Isidore de Lara, was announced, but circumstances arose to compel postponement. The presence of the German Emperor in London was made the occasion for a State performance at the Opera, when a splendid spectacle was presented before the curtain by the brilliant uniforms, the numerous gathering of Imperial and Royal personages in the huge central box, and the extraordinary decorative display of flowers. The programme consisted of the first act of "Lohengrin," scenes from "Romeo et Juliette" and "Orfeo," and the third act of "Les Huguenots." For political reasons, none of the eminent French artistes in the company took part in this gala representation. The Emperor also attended a concert at the Royal Albert Hall, at which a miscellaneous selection had as pendant the principal scenes from Sir Arthur Sullivan's "The Golden Legend." For the operatic performances in Oct. and Nov., Sir A. Harris had for mainstay several of the famed artistes of the Parisian Opera Comique, with M. Leon Jéhin as conductor. With this assistance he was enabled to present for the first time in this country Gounod's Philémon et Baucis and M. Bruneau's Le Rêve, both of course in French. The votaries of light comic opera were furnished during the year at the Prince of Wales's with Mr. De Koven's "Maid Marian," destined to give way to the musical dumb-show play "L'Enfant Prodigue"; at the Criterion with "Miss Decima," a version of the notorious "Miss Helyett" with M. Audran's pretty music; and at the Savoy with Mr. Edward Solomon's "The Nautch Girl." The latter, which was the first important work produced at Mr. D'Oyly Carte's Strand establishment without the signature "Gilbert and Sullivan," was eventually preceded by an amusing little piece called "Captain Billy," music by Mr. Francois Cellier. At the Lyric in October the deserving "La Cigale" celebrated its birthday. The students of the Royal Academy of Music gave an excellent performance of Gounod's "The Mock Doctor," which was also taken in hand by a company headed by Mr. Richard Temple. The Saturday afternoon concerts at the Crystal Palace were again noticeable for the unsurpassed efficiency of the performances under the baton of Mr. Manns, and for the abundant evidences of the resolve to keep abreast of the time. Besides Signor Sgambati's work before mentioned, the veteran Philharmonic Society included in the performances of the season Mr. Charles E. Stephens' Symphony in G minor, and Dr. Mackenzie conducted his effective music composed for the play "Ravenswood" at the Lyceum. The Royal Choral Society with old and modern oratorios; the Symphony Concerts conducted by Mr. Henschel; the Monday and Saturday Popular Concerts with the choicest of chamber compositions; the Handel Society; Sir Charles Hallé's Concerts, the Sarasate and Albeniz Concerts; the Wind Instrument Chamber Music Society, and the leading amateur associations also sustained their prestige. The custom of offering oratorios during the Lenten season was revived by Sir Augustus Harris, who in this way several nights turned Covent Garden Theatre to good account. Promenade concerts were held here in the early autumn for a few weeks. The Richter Concerts at St. James's Hall as usual relied mainly upon Wagner and Beethoven, but room was found for a few novelties, conspicuous among which was a stirring setting by Professor Stanford for choir and orchestra of Campbell's poem, "The Battle of the Baltic," the favourable verdict passed upon which was soon after endorsed at the Hereford Festival. The Bach Choir produced a new Mass by Mr. A. Somervell without forfeiting its pretensions to judgment and earnestness. The more interesting miscellaneous

events of the year included farewell of the public platform by Mr. Sims Reeves (in May at the Royal Albert Hall) after a brilliant career extending over half a century, the event being productive of much sympathy and countless testimonies of respect; the reappearance of Mr. Santley and Madame Patey after their respective lengthy tours in far-distant climes; the Tonic Sol-fa Jubilee gatherings; a performance of Messiah in Westminster Abbey in Nov. in aid of the Royal Society of Musicians; the celebrations at home and abroad of the centenary of Mozart's death; the representations of "Tannhäuser" at Bayreuth; and the performances in Paris, after preliminary threatenings that came to naught, of Wagner's "Lohengrin."

1892

Music in '92. The almost universal depression prevailing early in the year could not but seriously affect music, in common with other branches of art. The established institutions pursued their useful course, but no new ventures of importance were entered upon, and in the late summer, owing to the absence of promenade concerts, there was positive stagnation musically for a couple of months in the metropolis. Few foreign executants hitherto unknown here thought it worth while to tempt fortune by a professional visit to England, and these probably returned poorer than when they arrived. With two exceptions pianoforte recitals were a complete drug in the market. The exceptions were the performances of M. Paderewski, after his remarkably prosperous tour in America, and of the youth until lately known as "Master" Otto Hegner. Towards these the concert-going public exhibited all the former warmth of feeling, and general regret was expressed when the illness in Paris of the Polish virtuoso compelled the forfeiture of several engagements in this country. Most of the other candidates for favour were received with indifference. The most sensational incident of the season of the Philharmonic Society was reserved for the closing concert, at which Mr. F. H. Cowen as conductor apologised to the audience for any shortcomings that might occur in the immediately succeeding performance of Beethoven's Pastoral Symphony, on the ground that the number of works the directors placed in the programme had rendered sufficient rehearsal impracticable. As it happened the interpretation of the symphony left nothing to be desired. The wisdom of such an announcement to the subscribers being called into question by the Philharmonic authorities, Mr. Cowen resigned, and Dr. A. C. Mackenzie was appointed conductor in his stead. At the Popular Concerts (Monday and Saturday) Mr. Chappell made some additions, both from home and foreign sources, to his list of reliable players of chamber music; and Mr. Manns at the Crystal Palace fully maintained the prestige of his Saturday concerts, a series in one or two respects still unrivalled. The Royal Choral Society at the Royal Albert Hall gave a good selection of oratorios ancient and modern under the conductorship of Sir Joseph Barnby (q.v.), whom the vacancy in the Principalship of the Guildhall School of Music, occasioned by the death of Mr. Weist Hill, brought into exceptional prominence. At one period there were over thirty candidates in the field, but these were gradually narrowed down to two—Barnby, the Precentor at Eton, and W. G. Cusins, "Master of the Queen's Musick," and a professor at the Guildhall School. Eventually the first-named was elected, and soon afterwards the Queen conferred the honour of knighthood upon the two candidates, as well as upon Mr. Walter Parratt, the organist at Windsor. To the **Eton Precentorship**, resigned by Sir Joseph Barnby, was appointed Dr. Charles Harford Lloyd, formerly organist at Gloucester, and then at Christ Church, Oxford. As Dr. Richter, owing to his duties at the Vienna Exhibition, had but little time to spare for England, the concerts bearing his name were fewer than of late years, and, as before, the Wagner selections drew immense audiences to St. James's Hall. The London Symphony Concerts (directed by Mr. Henschel), the London Ballad Concerts, the Bach Choir, the Handel Society (of which in the autumn Mr. Manns became conductor), the Sarasate Concerts, the Wind Instrument Society's labours, and performances by Sir Chas. Hallé of Schubert's pianoforte compositions, attracted attention in differing degrees. Nor must the steady progress of the leading suburban societies be ignored, inasmuch as these are now sufficiently competent to take up elaborate modern productions without waiting for the older associations to lead. The oratorio at **the Crystal Palace** in June under Handel Festival conditions was "**Judas Maccabæus**," only once before heard in entirety—thirty years ago—beneath the glass roof of the fairy building, though excerpts are customary on the "Selection" day of the triennial Handel gatherings. "**Samson**" was first decided upon, but there was justification for the directors reconsidering their determination. The issue was in every way satisfactory. There was a large attendance, and on all sides it was admitted that the performance was worthy the festival choir. Higher praise could hardly be bestowed. Mr. Manns of course conducted; and after a separation owing to American and Antipodean wanderings for several years, the "**representative British quartet**"—Madame Albani, Madame Patey, Mr. Edward Lloyd, and Mr. Santley—reassembled on one platform. In **musical accompaniment to Shakespeare** two special successes were gained. For Mr. Beerbohm Tree's revival of "**Hamlet**" at the Haymarket Mr. Henschel composed some instrumental movements admirably expressive of the supernatural element of the plot and of the stage situations generally; the various numbers were brought into the shape of an orchestral suite, and as such were well received in the concert-room. For his "**Henry VIII.**" music at the Lyceum Mr. Henry Irving went to Mr. Edward German, who for Mr. Richard Mansfield's revival at the Globe a few years back of "**Richard III.**" had shown some aptitude for this description of work. The festal and more pompous strains of the later score were considered particularly happy, and the whole won approval for appropriateness and tuneful charm. By having a German as well as Franco-Italian opera season **at Covent Garden**, Sir Augustus Harris (*q.v.*) was exceedingly busy during May, June and July. The house was open every night, and overflow performances of certain works took place at Drury Lane, which the manager had kept in reserve for this purpose. He started by producing on a most complete scale Mascagni's (*q.v.*) "**Cavalleria Rusticana**," not previously seen on this stage, and by introducing to England as the heroine Madame Calvé, a genuine artist whose qualifications were at once recognised. A little later came the second opera from the same pen, "**L'Amico Fritz**" (new to this country), which was frequently played during the season; then, in the catalogue of novelties, Mr. Isidore de Lara's "**La Luce dell' Asia**" (postponed from the preceding year, and with M. Lassalle in the part originally intended for M. Maurel), and then M. Bemberg's "**Elaine**," an English version of

which Mr. D'Oyly Carte would have given at his handsomely appointed Royal English Opera House had enough support been tendered to warrant him continuing his zealous endeavours on behalf of opera in the native tongue. Thus in one branch of his enterprise alone Sir Augustus Harris added four works to the Covent Garden *répertoire*. In the two Mascagni operas Madame Calvé had for her chief companions Signor De Lucia and M. Dufriche; Madame Emma Eames joined M. Lassalle in Mr. de Lara's work; and Madame Melba and M. Jean de Reszke (*q.v.*) were secured for "**Elaine**." Unfortunately the famous tenor, betraying at the outset his just preceding American tour, was soon incapacitated. He played some half-dozen of his best-known parts, but could only appear once as Sir Lancelot in the new opera, and his frequent indisposition prevented the revival of "**Die Meistersinger**" and Verdi's "**Otello**," the latter of which Sir Augustus Harris had mounted in '91. "**Der Fliegende Hollander**" (in Italian) was restored to the Covent Garden stage for Miss Macintyre and M. Lassalle, and Gounod's dainty "**Philemon et Baucis**" (in French) was on nearly every occasion the prelude to "**Cavalleria Rusticana**." In number of performances the last-named surpassed any other presented in the course of the campaign. Mdlle. Giulia Ravogli, Madame Deschamps-Jehin, Mdlle. Sigrid Arnoldson, MM. Edouard de Reszke, Maurel, Plançon, and Montariol did good service, and M. Van Dyck appeared before he proceeded to Bayreuth. Signori Mancinelli, Bevignani, and Randegger, and M. Léon Jehin shared the responsibilities of the conductorship. **The German season** was distinct, though it ran contemporaneously. Band, chorus, and principals were brought from the Continent, in great part from Hamburg, with Herr Mahler—a musician thoroughly versed in Wagner's scores—as conductor. The feature of the scheme on which most stress was laid was the adequate representation in proper order of the colossal "**Ring des Nibelungen**," which no *impresario* had submitted to British operatic patrons since '82, when four cycles were gone through at Her Majesty's Theatre. Much, too, was expected from the revival of "**Tristan und Isolde**." When Sir Augustus Harris's plans were presented in full it was soon made clear that the financial prosperity of the undertaking was assured. In the result nothing was proved to be lacking in the artistic sense. The principal tenor of the *troupe* was Herr Alvary, a favourite with the Bayreuth pilgrims, and as he was particularly anxious to make his bow as Siegfried, the third section of the "**Ring**" began the German season. The success of this new-comer was unequivocal, and fresh friends were made in each character he played. For two or three performances the talented Frau Rosa Sucher came to England, and as Brunnhilde and Isolde demonstrated unimpaired powers both as singer and actress. The week after "**Siegfried**" came "**Tristan**," and then the four "**Ring des Nibelungen**" operas in regular sequence. During these representations at Covent Garden and Drury Lane another star arose in Frau Klafsky, who had played small parts in the tetralogy in '82, but was now found quite equal to the most arduous of Wagnerian *rôles*. The dramatic tenor and soprano so effectually carried all before them that the manager was induced before their departure to add "**Tannhauser**" to the German performances. Towards the close of her engagement Frau Klafsky also played in "**Fidelio**," but not so much interest was shown in Beethoven's only opera as in "**Rheingold**," "**Die Walkure**," "**Siegfried**," "**Gotterdämmerung**," and "**Tristan**." As a compliment to Herr Reichmann, the baritone, two performances were given at Drury Lane (Herr Feld conducting) of Victor Nesler's "**Trompeter von Sakkingen.**" By this time, however, the London public had been spoiled by the richness of Wagner's instrumentation, the complete grasp of the same by Herr Mahler, and the rare abilities of Herr Alvary and Frau Klafsky. The German season was an indisputable triumph for the manager as well as for the ardent advocates of Wagnerism. In October Sir A. Harris began a season of opera at cheap prices with Madame Melba and other members of his Italian company, together with several promising strangers, and again large audiences were drawn to "**Cavalleria Rusticana.**" Signor Lago opened a week later at the New Olympic with Tschaikowsky's "**Eugene Onegin,**"an opera hitherto unknown in this country. Notwithstanding frequent changes in the bill, the season only lasted a few days over a fortnight. A very fair supply of absolutely new works by native composers was reserved for the **autumn provincial festivals.** The hope that Sir Arthur Sullivan would contribute to the Leeds triennial gathering, of which he was conductor, was frustrated by a serious illness and the prior claim of the Savoy stage upon his pen; Dr. A. C. Mackenzie could not to his own satisfaction complete his oratorio "**Bethlehem**" in time for the Gloucester celebration (the Three Choirs); and a misunderstanding with the Leeds committee caused Mr. Cowen to withdraw his cantata, **The Water Lily.** Enough novelty remained, however, to attract musicians from distant districts. The Western cathedral city was able to put forth four entirely fresh compositions—a neat setting by Dr. J. F. Bridge of the Lord's Prayer from Dante's "Purgatorio," a tender and devotional Church cantata by Messrs. Joseph Bennett and Lee Williams, entitled "Gethsemane" (on the same lines as their successful "**Last Night at Bethany,**" dating from 1889), an elegant cantata by Miss Rosalind F. Ellicott, "**The Birth of Song**" (poem by Lewis Morris), and a short oratorio, "**Job,**" by Dr. Hubert Parry. The construction of the last-named is altogether unconventional; the subject as a whole is treated dramatically, albeit Job's lamentations form a bass solo occupying close upon twenty minutes, whilst the following chorus (the Divine reply) is of like duration. There is a peculiar power in the work that holds attention, whilst examination of the score reveals all the lofty attributes of musicianship of which Dr. Parry has previously shown possession. For its dimensions "**Job**" would be a credit to any composer. Handel's "**Joshua**" was among the miscellaneous works performed, and the attendance was good throughout. In September, also, **Cardiff** held a **festival** which the committee hope to make triennial. The conductor-in-chief was Sir Joseph Barnby, and Sir Arthur Sullivan and Dr. Mackenzie journeyed to South Wales to respectively direct their "**Golden Legend**" and "**Dream of Jubal.**" A decidedly good choice of works was made, and the exponent of local talent was Dr. Joseph Parry, who took the baton for his dramatic oratorio "**Saul of Tarsus,**" first given at the Eisteddfod at Rhyl a fortnight earlier. A magnificent body of choralists was brought together at **Leeds** in October, and as the novelties were reduced to two the four days' programme was framed to develop this specially strong element. Such a fine rendering of the choruses in "**Elijah**" and "**The Hymn of Praise,**" of several worthy examples of Handel's genius, of Mozart's "**Requiem,**" and of Bach's "**Mass in B minor,**" has seldom been heard even from a Yorkshire choir. A new symphony by Mr. Frederic Cliffe, written expressly for the festival, was pronounced to be an advance upon the striking work of the same description declined

by the committee of '89, and at once bringing the composer into fame[when it was performed under Mr. Manns at the Crystal Palace. Dr. Alan Gray's short cantata "**Arethusa,**" a setting of Shelley's poem, was also well received not only on its own merits, which were far from small, but on account of the promise of better things to come. The festival was well patronised.—**Comic opera** was to be met with in every quarter. The palm was again won by Mr. Gilbert and Sir Arthur Sullivan, though they worked independently of each other. The former was associated with the late Alfred Cellier (who died just before the work was produced) in the piquant "**Mountebanks**" at the Lyric, and the musical knight had Mr. Grundy for his companion in the melodic "**Haddon Hall,**" presented at the Savoy in September. Each work elicited deserved praise. Pending the restoration to health of Sir Arthur Sullivan and the completion of "**Haddon Hall,**" Mr. D'Oyly Carte revived at the Savoy the Grundy-Solomon whimsicality, "**The Vicar of Bray.**" "**Cigarette,**" a light opera by Mr. Haydn Parry (a son of the Welsh composer), was played first in the provinces, then at the Lyric, and then at the Shaftesbury. "**Incognita,**" an adaptation by Mr. Burnand of Lecocq's "**Le Cœur et la Main,**" was the autumn attraction at the Lyric; and Mr. Cotsford Dick's "**The Baroness**" was seen for a while at the Royalty. "**The Young Recruit**" (Sir A. Harris and Mr. Stephenson's version of "Les Dragons de la Reine") and "**Blue Eyed Susan**" (at the Prince of Wales's) also made a hit. Of a severer cast was "**Nydia, the Blind Girl of Pompeii,**" by Mr. George Fox, played at the Crystal Palace, and late in the season reproduced at Drury Lane. The opening of the Trafalgar Square Theatre was signalised by the production of "**The Wedding Eve,**" a three-act piece with music by Toulmouche. The Carl Rosa Opera Company, by offering engagements to Miss Ella Russell and Mr. Barton McGuckin, vastly strengthened its influence. On Nov. 15th the Company gave a "command" performance of "**The Daughter of the Regiment**" before the Queen at Balmoral. **In the provinces** Bizet's "**Djamileh**" and English editions of Mascagni's "**L'Amico Fritz**" and of Verdi's "**Otello**" were frequently performed; and Mr. Leslie Crotty and Miss Georgina Burns took a version of Rossini's "**Cinderella**" on tour. The most notable of **miscellaneous events** were the compact Musical Exhibition at the Aquarium; the distressing death of Goring Thomas, to whose memory it was resolved to found a scholarship at the Royal Academy of Music, on behalf of which a concert was given at the St. James's Hall with nearly all the singers of mark then in London; the closing of the Royal English Opera House as a purely musical resort; the performance at the Criterion of "**Haste to the Wedding,**" a farcical work by Mr. Gilbert, music by Mr. George Grossmith; and the successful introduction at Florence, on Nov. 17th, of Mascagni's latest opera, "**I Rantzau.**"

1893

Few new works of importance were submitted by British composers. Nearly all the productive musicians known to the public presented something, in order, perhaps, to escape the reproach of idleness; but, except in one instance, Art was not much the richer. The exception was Mr. F. H. Cowen's cantata "**The Water Lily,**" which had been withdrawn from the Leeds Festival programme in '92, and now found a home at Norwich. **Sir Arthur**

Sullivan was once more associated with Mr. W. S. Gilbert in Savoy opera, and the music he composed the year before for Tennyson's last play, " The Foresters," was heard when Mr. Daly mounted the work in October in his new London theatre. Dr. Mackenzie completed a pas'oral oratorio called " Bethlehem " for the Chicago Exhibition, and in the autumn was about to embark on his voyage across the Atlantic to conduct his latest production, when information was received that, owing to the indifference manifested by the public, it was compulsory to change the musical arrangements, and that there was no possibility of giving the new oratorio. English people were quite as disappointed as the Americans, because had it been known that there was some doubt respecting the performance of " Bethlehem " at the place originally intended, it might have been fitted into one of the autumn provincial gatherings. Dr. Hubert Parry did not produce another " Job," a work heartily received wherever heard ; but he wrote some charming incidental music to " Hypatia " at the Haymarket, and with a concert overture provided the sole absolute novelty for the Worcester meeting of the Three Choirs. Professor Villiers Stanford's chief works were a setting of an ode by Swinburne, " East to West," a theme suggested by the assembling of representatives of many nations at the World's Fair, and the music to Tennyson's " Becket," produced at the Lyceum by Mr. Henry Irving. Mr. Edward German, who gained so much commendation for his accompanying music to Mr. Richard Mansfield's revival of " King Richard III." at the Globe a few years ago, and to Mr. Irving's reproduction at the Lyceum of " King Henry VIII.," executed a similar task for Mr. H. A. Jones's poetical play " The Tempter " at the Haymarket, and had ready for the Norwich Festival in October a new symphony (his second), the success of which was immediate. Mr. Isidore de Lara was fortunate enough to get a second opera, " Amy Robsart," (the subject adapted from Scott's " Kenilworth "), produced in Italian at Covent Garden by Sir A. Harris. One of the earliest notable events was the representation at Liverpool by the Carl Rosa Company of the late Goring Thomas's comic opera " The Golden Web." Its reception was eminently favourable ; but though much of the music was voted extremely pretty, the opera failed to obtain a long run when brought to London about a month later by Mr. Horace Sedger, of the Lyric Theatre. Several distinguished foreign musicians visited England during the summer. To signalise the Jubilee of the Cambridge University Musical Society, the University decided to confer honorary degrees upon a few of the most famous composers of divers nationalities. Verdi and Brahms were invited to represent respectively Italy and Germany, but both were compelled to decline the proffered honour. Grieg (the Norwegian) accepted the invitation, but almost at the last moment was seized with illness, and could not undertake the journey. Four received the degree amid acclamations : Saint-Saens appeared for France, Max Bruch for Germany, Boito for Italy, and Tschaikowsky for Russia. The afternoon prior to the official ceremony the four musicians last named took part in a special concert at Cambridge, at which a composition of each was performed. The composers conducted, with the exception of Saint-Saens, who played with rare ability the taxing pianoforte solo of the fantasia he introduced. Two other celebrated visitors to London were Signori Leoncavallo and Mascagni. The arrival of both was in connection with new operas. Leoncavallo came for " Pagliacci," which proved a great success at Covent Garden ; Mascagni for " I Rantzau " (concerning which no enthusiasm was evoked) at the same house. He also occasionally wielded the *bâton* for his two earlier works—" Cavalleria Rusticana " and " L'Amico Fritz." Saint-Saens, Tschaikowsky, and Max Bruch accepted the invitation to the Philharmonic Concerts—conducted throughout the season by Dr. Mackenzie, as successor to Mr. Cowen—to direct a piece of their own composition. The visitors were everywhere well received. The Philharmonic, it may be added, gave a hearing during its satisfactory season to Mr. Somervell's ballad " Helen of Kirkconnel," and Erskine Allon's ballad " Annie of Lochroyan." Under the patronage of the ex-Empress Eugénie, Miss E. M. Smyth's " Mass in D " was performed in January by the Royal Choral Society at the Albert Hall, and made a favourable impression. The principal introduction by the indefatigable Mr. August Manns at the admirable Crystal Palace Saturday Concerts was a short " Mass in D " by Dvorák, written for a Bohemian village ceremonial in '87, the original organ accompaniment having since been scored for orchestra. The annual performance at the Crystal Palace under Handel Festival conditions was Sir Arthur Sullivan's " The Golden Legend," which once more brought together close upon 20,000 listeners. In May Mr. D'Oyly Carte gave at the Savoy a comic opera by Messrs. J. M. Barrie and Conan Doyle, music by Mr. Ernest Ford, entitled " Jane Annie ; or, The Good-Conduct Prize " ; but the leading feature in the history of the house for the year was the resumption of the partnership of Mr. Gilbert and Sir Arthur Sullivan, manifested by the new comic opera " Utopia (Limited) ; or, The Flowers of Progress," successfully produced in October. The gratification experienced by the public on the reunion was expressed in the heartiest fashion.

In the spring Sir Augustus Harris arranged a brief opera season at Drury Lane, giving a number of familiar works, and placing again upon the stage Halévy's " La Juive," which had not been seen in London for about forty years. The orthodox season at Covent Garden began as usual in the middle of May, and for two and a half months the utmost activity prevailed, a performance being held almost every night. No less than five works were added to the *répertoire* of the establishment—namely, Leoncavallo's " Pagliacci " (with Madame Melba, Signor de Lucia, and Signor Ancona in the three more responsible parts), Mascagni's " I Rantzau," Mr. de Lara's " Amy Robsart," Bizet's one-act " Djamileh," and Professor Stanford's " Veiled Prophet " (first given at Hanover in '81, and since revised). A stage version of Berlioz's " Faust " (for the two De Reszkes) was also prepared, but time did not permit of the performance. Twenty other operas were represented in French, German, or Italian ; but curiously enough not a single work by Mozart or Rossini figured in the catalogue of performances. Among the revivals were Bizet's " Les Pecheurs de Perles " (coldly greeted despite the popularity of Madame Calvé, who undertook the principal part) and the old-fashioned " La Favorita " (for the *début* of Madame Armand). The manager carried through a Wagner cycle, but owing to the difficulty in securing a German conductor more than half the music-dramas selected had to be rendered in Italian. These were " Lohengrin," " Tannhauser," " The Flying Dutchman," and " Die Meistersinger." At length Herr Steinbach, from Mayence, was engaged, and then the German troupe headed by Herr Max Alvary and Frau Moran Olden appeared in " Tristan und Isolde," " Die Walkure," and " Siegfried." Two or three repetition performances of these took place at Drury Lane, but at neither house was "**Rheingold**" or "**Götter-dämmerung**," the first and last of the **Ring des Nibelungen** series, given. Mesdames Albani, Melba, Calvé (who imparted new life to "**Carmen**"), Giulia Ravogli, the brothers De Reszke, MM. De Lucia and Lassalle fully retained the favour of the subscribers. So heavy was the instrumental work during the season that a second band was formed. Sir A. Harris, who in the preceding December had taken "**Carmen**" to Windsor Castle, was in July commanded by the Queen to pay another visit, this time with "**L'Amico Fritz**" (second act) and "**Cavalleria Rusticana**," the composer of both works conducting. On July 4th Gounod's "**Romeo et Juliette**" was performed at Covent Garden by command in honour of the royal guests for the wedding of the Duke of York and the Princess May, and the boxes from floor to ceiling were most lavishly festooned with real flowers.

The recurring **provincial festivals**, taking them in the order of their occurrence, were those of Worcester, Norwich, North Staffordshire (Hanley), Cheltenham, and Bristol. Of these it is only necessary to dwell upon the second. The **Norwich gathering** had not of late years been remarkable for novelty, but on this occasion five new works were presented. They were Mr. Cowen's cantata already referred to; Mr. Gaul's cantata "**Una**" (subject taken from Spenser's "Faerie Queene"); Mr. J. F. Barnett's cantata for female voices, "**The Wishing Bell**"; Mr. German's second symphony; and a Polish Fantaisie for piano and orchestra by M. Paderewski. The festival was in every way a great success, as also from the financial point of view was that of Worcester, where in contrast there was nothing to tempt the novelty lover but the overture by Dr. Hubert Parry. The Richter, the London Symphony, Bach Choir, Populars, Sarasate, and the London Ballad in their differing branches continued the same good work as for years past. Promenade concerts were offered by Mr. Farley Sinkins, with Mr. Cowen as conductor, at Covent Garden in the autumn. After a retirement of a little over two years, Mr. Sims Reeves reappeared for several nights to sing his favourite ballads, and the manager in concert form attempted to give some idea of Saint-Saens's Biblical opera "**Samson et Dalila**." Two juvenile prodigies, both pianists, came to London—namely, Raoul Koczalsky (extensively patronised) and Mlle. Frieda Simonson. Of the acknowledged virtuosi, M. Paderewski fully held his own. Other incidents of the year worth noting were the festival celebrating the 800th anniversary of the consecration of Winchester Cathedral; the performance in English by Royal Academy students of Lortzing's "**Czar und Zimmermann**," by the Royal College of "**Orfeo**" (a repetition), and by the Guildhall students of "**Faust**"; the reappearance in English at the Parkhurst Theatre of Adolphe Adam's "**Si J'étais Roi**"; the production at the Lyric Theatre of the opera "**The Magic Opal**," the music of which (by Señor Albeniz) was considerably above the average; the performance at St. James's Hall in May of the Rev. Mr. Moberley's Ladies' Orchestra; the jubilee of Dr. Hopkins as organist at the Temple Church; the reopening in October of the Princess's Theatre with a new opera called "**Miami**" (founded on the old drama "**The Green Bushes**"); the revival of Audran's "**La Mascotte**"; and the production at La Scola, Milan, in February, of Verdi's "**Falstaff**."

1894

The spread of orchestral societies indicates an increasing taste for loftier instrumental compositions that has not been ignored by concert managers. The past year witnessed the inauguration of several enterpises, both native and foreign, in this direction, and the patronage accorded was fairly commensurate with artistic aims. The same could hardly be said of pianoforte and violin recitals, which, speaking generally, seem to be declining in public favour. Some three or four players who are entitled to be considered *virtuosi* can still command crowded audiences in the Metropolis, but the majority are dependent on the support of friends. This was the lesson taught during the spring and summer to some of the Continental artistes who visited us. With many new claimants for a hearing; with the established institutions alive to the fact that rivalry was keener than ever; with an eleven weeks' Covent Garden opera season, in the course of which no less than seven works new to this country were presented; and with the recurrence of the Handel Festival at Sydenham; the first half of the musical year was remarkably busy. The customary six weeks' stagnation ensued, during which, there being no promenade concerts at Covent Garden, Metropolitan music-lovers had to proceed to the Crystal Palace if they wished to hear the compositions of the great masters. After the provincial festivals, unexampled activity for the period of the year, particularly in the instrumental department, set in.

The Philharmonic Society had a brilliant season at Queen's Hall. The "Pathetique" Symphony (No. 6) of Tschaikowsky, only submitted a short time before his death in November '93, was very early brought forward by Dr. A. C. Mackenzie, and created so much interest that it was repeated at a subsequent concert. Other works performed for the first time in England were Dvorak's symphony in E minor, "**From the New World**," in which the Bohemian composer deals to some extent with melodies of the negro and Indian pattern; and extracts from music to Bjornson's tragedy "**Sigurd Jorsalfar**," composed by Grieg, and conducted by himself. Advantage was also taken of the stay among us of Dr. Saint Saëns to invite him to conduct his symphony in C. The nautical overture "**Britannia**," by Dr. Mackenzie, a merry piece originally heard at a Royal Academy celebration, was added to the Philharmonic *répertoire*, and was extremely well received by the ordinarily severe listeners. Herr Felix Mottl, the well-known conductor, made his *début* in London in April, and came again towards the end of the year. Dr. Richter gave concerts in the Metropolis both in the summer and autumn, and, as before, relied chiefly upon the works of Beethoven and Wagner. Mr. August Manns continued his excellent service at the **Crystal Palace**, and whilst on the watch for novelties did not neglect the recognised masterpieces. Among the fresh works he placed in his catalogue was Mr. F. Dunkley's setting of "**The Wreck of the Hesperus**." The **London Symphony Concerts** did well under the bâton of Mr. Henschel, and a progressive spirit was maintained by the Stock Exchange Orchestral Society. The **Wolff Musical Union**, a new association, furnished some interesting performances, including a programme made up entirely of the compositions of Dr. Saint Saëns, and another consisting of pieces for M. Taffanel and his wind instrumentalists, who journeyed from Paris expressly for the purpose. The **Popular Concerts** exercised their olden influence. The summer did not pass without the advent of several prodigies, those attracting most notice being boys respectively named Argiewicz and Hubermann, both violinists, and both of Polish descent.

There were signs of a revived demand for choral music. An important feature of the **Bach Choir** season was the performance with the German text of the St. Matthew Passion. The **Royal Choral Society** at the Albert Hall varied its course of standard oratorios by producing Dr. Mackenzie's "**Bethlehem**," originally sent to America for performance at Chicago, but not given there owing to the collapse of the musical arrangements in connection with the Exhibition. The work was favourably received by the musical public, and gained further friends when the second part was given at the Hereford (the Three Choirs) Festival. The convenience afforded by the Queen's Hall resulted in the formation of two or three new choral societies in the late autumn. **Three Continential choirs** of repute came here in the summer. Male-voice parties from Berne and Upsala were welcomed, but a more ambitious venture was that of the Amsterdam *à cappella* Choir, a famous body of singers, whose rendering of compositions by the old Flemish musicians deserved more attention than it received. **The Handel Festival** at the end of June brought together during the four days (including the rehearsal) 76,406 persons as against 80,795 in '91. Considering all things, this falling off was not serious. It was certainly insufficient to demonstrate that London and provincial amateurs are becoming tired of the triennial gathering. Curiously enough, the greatest decline in attendance was on the " Israel in Egypt " day, hitherto regarded as one of the most popular because of the chances afforded the choir, numbering about 3,500. The bàton was again in the hands of the efficient Mr. Manns, and once more the Monday of the festival week was devoted to "**Messiah**," the Wednesday to a lengthy selection from Handel's sacred and secular works, and the Friday to "**Israel**." Since 1859, when the centenary of the great Saxon's death was commemorated, nearly all that has been pronounced worthy of the composer has been presented, so that with each succeeding festival the difficulty of imparting freshness to the selection programme is augmented. Among the principal singers were Mesdames Albani, Ella Russell, Anna Williams, Melba, and Marian Mackenzie, Messrs. Edward Lloyd, Ben Davies, and Santley ; and the choir maintained its reputation. To the band there was a very large accession of lady performers, there being a total of forty-nine, whilst in '91 there were but half a dozen ; and Mr. Walter W. Hedgcock succeeded Mr. A. J. Eyre (who had just previously resigned) at the organ.

In the course of sixty-seven nights Sir Augustus Harris at **Covent Garden Theatre** mounted twenty-one **operas**, whilst he produced eight German works during a short season carried on simultaneously at Drury Lane. He began boldly by presenting on the opening night at the first-named establishment Giacomo Puccini's " **Manon Lescaut**," a work approved on the Continent, and at the close of the same week gave the long-expected " **Falstaff** " of Verdi. The artistes for the two operas had been specially chosen, and with the exception of Mlle. Giulia Ravogli (the Mrs. Quickly of the Shakesperean comedy set to music), were not known in this country. Signor Pessina, who played " the fat knight," proved himself an actor and singer of great ability. The warm commendation passed upon " **Falstaff** " elsewhere was so thoroughly endorsed that the work was performed eight times during the season, and later was taken into the provinces by Sir A. Harris. Puccini's opera scarcely made the hit expected, neither did M. Massenet's " **Werther**," which came unexpectedly, awaken much enthusiasm, although M. Jean de Reszké selected it for his *rentrée*, and an admirable Charlotte was found in Madame Eames. The homeliness of the story was rather against the work on so large a stage, and since " **Cavalleria Rusticana**," the fancy of opera *habitués* has inclined to strongly dramatic themes, tersely set forth. Mr. Cowen's " **Signa**," after several adventures, at length reached London, for which capital it was originally intended ; but it was prepared in Italian, and in a very abbreviated form—four acts having been reduced to two. The title part was sustained by Mr. Ben Davies, and that excellent actor Signor Ancona was the avenging old farmer Bruno. It could not be given until late in the season, and a like fate befell Chevalier Bach's one-act work, " **The Lady of Longford**." But the novelties that, after " **Falstaff**," kindled most discussion were Massenet's " **La Navarraise**," and Bruneau's " **L'Attaque du Moulin**," both produced with a completeness of military spectacle agreeing with the respective subjects. The former was composed expressly for Madame Calvé, and the Judith-like heroine was found perfectly suited to the keen dramatic instincts of the prima donna, who on this stage had given new life to " **Carmen**." The music, too, was pronounced as spirited and forcible as it was melodiously expressive. The success of this novelty was incontestable. Owing to Madame Delna being detained in Paris, through the success of Verdi's " **Falstaff**," Bruneau's latest work was not introduced so early as was intended, therefore its performances only numbered three. The strength and vitality of the opera were universally recognised, whilst the finished acting and singing of Madame Delna as old Marcelline, and M. Bouvet as the stout-hearted miller, satisfied those whose expectations had been stimulated by the praise accorded these assumptions during the run of the opera in Paris. In his treatment of M. Zola's vigorous story, M. Bruneau exhibits some of the gifts of a really great dramatic composer. With seven novelties to be provided for, the older works in the *répertoire* naturally suffered. The requests for " **Roméo et Juliette** " (with Madame Melba, the two De Reszkés, and M. Plancon) resulted in seven performances, whilst " **Faust**," " **Cavalleria Rusticana**," and " **Pagliacci** " attained (with " **Falstaff** ") the maximum of eight performances. Most of the other operas were a long way behind. A revised version of M. Bemberg's " **Elaine** " was twice given, with Madame Melba and the brothers De Reszké in their original parts. Only two of Wagner's works were played, namely " **Lohengrin** " and " **Die Meistersinger**," the last-named as a special performance. There was no State representation in London called for, but Sir A. Harris took his company twice to Windsor to appear before the Queen, the operas being " **Faust**," and " **La Navarraise** " with " **Philemon et Baucis**." The conductors during the season were MM. Mancinelli, Bevignani, Seppilli, and Flon. Of the eight **German works** performed at Drury Lane in their original tongue, under the direction of Herr Lohse, five were by Wagner. The unsurpassable Frau Klafsky and the zealous Herr Max Alvary renewed former triumphs in " **Die Walküre**," " **Siegfried**," " **Tristan und Isolde**," " **Tannhauser**," and " **Lohengrin**." To the delight of her English friends, the German soprano repeated her exceptionally fine performance of " **Fidelio**," and also took part in an interesting revival of "**Der Freischutz.**" Although **The Carl Rosa Opera Company** did not come to London, their proceedings were eventful. At Liverpool in February they produced in English Berlioz's "**Faust,**" and in October at Manchester presented Tasca's "**At Santa Lucia.**" They also secured "**Jeannie Deans,**" a work by Messrs. Joseph Bennett and Hamish MacCunn, founded on "**The Heart of Midlothian.**"

The **Chester Triennial Festival** was held in July, before the London season had ended. There were two novelties during the three days—a short sacred cantata, "**The Soul's Forgiveness,**" by Dr. F. J. Sawyer (of Brighton), and a symphony by Dr. J. C. Bridge, the local organist, avowedly "suggested by incidents connected with the city of Chester." At Hereford in September a couple of absolute novelties were also provided in a setting by Dr. C. Harford Lloyd of a weird Danish poem to which the English adapter has given the title "**Sir Ogie and the Ladie Elsie**"; and in a canticle by Professor J. F. Bridge, "**The Cradle of Christ,**" the words being Neale's version of the old Latin hymn "**Stabat Mater Speciosa.**" The latter is a welcome addition to music specially suited to Christmas. Mr. G. R. Sinclair (the cathedral organist) was the conductor-in-chief of the festival. The most important native production of the year was reserved for the **Birmingham Festival** in October, and was obtained in **Dr. Hubert Parry's** oratorio "**King Saul.**" An impressive work, studded with dramatic points, had been anticipated, but few were prepared for the imaginative power and picturesque suggestiveness of the scenes between Samuel and Saul, the taunting tone of the Evil Spirit, prompting the king to his ruin, and the peculiar skill manifested in dealing with the interview at Endor between the troubled monarch and the witch. Whether in its vocal or instrumental elements every page of the score betrays the hand of a composer who knows how to infuse the modern spirit into all that is best in legitimate oratorio. The reception of the work was enthusiastic. Warm congratulations were also showered upon Mr. Henschel for his scholarly and devotional "**Stabat Mater.**" The remaining novelty was Goring Thomas's posthumous cantata "**The Swan and the Skylark,**" a tasteful composition scored for orchestra by Professor Stanford. Berlioz's "**Te Deum,**" Cherubini's Mass in D minor, and Schumann's "**Faust,**" Part III., were noteworthy revivals conducted by Dr. Richter.

With "**His Excellency,**" at the Lyric, at the end of October, Mr. W. S. Gilbert added another to his list of successes in comic opera; his musical partner on this occasion was Dr. Osmond Carr. M. Messager's bright and always elegant strains secured cordial approval of "**Mirette,**" produced at the Savoy. At the Lyceum "**The Queen of Brilliants,**" music by M. Jakobowski, was accompanied by Miss Lillian Russell, a singer who was no stranger to England. A cheery burlesque spirit pervaded "**Wapping Old Stairs,**" by Stuart Robertson and Howard Talbot, which, after preliminary trials at King's Lynn, found Metropolitan quarters at the Vaudeville. The new home of the Royal College of Music, the gift of Mr. Samson Fox, was formally opened by the Prince of Wales on May 2nd, with abundant state ceremonial. The Welsh National Eisteddfod was held at Carnarvon, and the musical contests were spiritedly conducted.

1895

Though in no sense, either at home or abroad, could they be regarded as epoch-making, many of the events of the year were of exceptional interest to British musicians. Orchestral compositions were again in great request—particularly Wagnerian selections—and indications of a revived taste for choral music were manifested in the late autumn. With its serial concerts, in addition to recitals and miscellaneous performances, November proved almost as busy a month for music as May or June, notwithstanding that during the accustomed holiday recess there was an eight weeks' season at Queen's Hall of promenade concerts under the conductorship of Mr. Henry J. Wood, and that the Sunday afternoon and evening concerts, commenced in October in various quarters of the metropolis, were more numerous (and in some cases more ambitious) in character than before. Of late years it has been proved that the increase of opportunities for listening to the highest-class music does not diminish the patronage accorded to associations boasting a satisfactory past. This is one of the results of the musical education so assiduously promoted at the Royal Academy, the Royal College, the Guildhall School, and elsewhere; whilst the means for performance are, of course, helped by the thousands of students yearly attending these prosperous institutions. Certainly the standard was never higher than at present. The nobler the aim of *entrepreneurs* the greater the chance of success. Indeed, there is no more gratifying sign of progress than the steady demand for acknowledged masterpieces adequately performed. The symphonies given in Queen's Hall in August and September received as much attention from the public as in the spring and winter.

Discussion respecting correct readings of Beethoven symphonies and Wagnerian excerpts was stimulated by visits from four of the most eminent of foreign conductors, as was Siegfried Wagner, the son of the Bayreuth master. Dr. Richter was here for a short time both in the summer and autumn, and his concerts retained their popularity despite rivalry. Herr Felix Mottl was again welcomed, and justified his claim to favour; and Herr Hermann Levi was most cordially greeted on making his *début* in this country. Another new-comer whose reception was of the heartiest, was Herr Arthur Nikisch, who, at a series of concerts at Queen's Hall in the height of the summer, won warm approval for his conscientious and exceedingly intelligent efforts. Herr Siegfried Wagner was not quite so successful. Speculation respecting his appearance and manner had been set at rest on a previous occasion, so that he was now judged solely by his labours. With some rashness he elected to figure in the double capacity of composer and conductor. His views of two or three works, especially the overture to "**Der Freischutz,**" were disappointing; whilst his own production—a symphonic piece having a poem by Schiller as its basis—was reminiscent of his grandfather Liszt rather than of the genius of his illustrious father. It is pleasant to state that from this competition a conductor who has virtually spent his artistic life in our midst, and has done more than any other musician of his time to familiarise the British public with the compositions of Schubert, Schumann, Berlioz, and others, did not suffer. To commemorate his seventieth birthday, and in recognition of indefatigable services to his art, a reception was given to Mr. August Manns at the Grafton Street Galleries, the attendance at which was of the most brilliant and representative description. The anniversary of the institution of the Saturday concerts at the Crystal Palace forty years ago was signalised by a programme consisting of works by British composers who owe much of the popularity they have acquired to the encouragement they obtained at Sydenham. In the honours freely bestowed at this concert Mr. Manns naturally to a great extent participated. During the **Philharmonic Society's** season an absolutely new symphony and a revised work of like nature were brought forward. Dr. Stanford presented his orchestral movements suggested by "**L'Allegro ed il Pensieroso**"; and Dr. Hubert Parry—now the director of the Royal College in place of Sir George Grove, resigned—offered his rewritten Symphony No. 3 in F, originally performed in 1883 by the Cambridge University Musical Society. Another incident of the season here was the appearance on the platform of Madame Adelina Patti. Sir A. C. Mackenzie was once more the conductor-in-chief. With undiminished energy Mr. Henschel carried on the **London Symphony Concerts,** and also found that Wagner was specially attractive.

It was not a Handel Festival year, but an excuse for the gathering of the choir was obtained by a performance at the Crystal Palace, in June, on an unwonted scale, of Mendelssohn's "**Hymn of Praise**," which passed off as well as could be wished. The **Bach Choir** is to be credited with a festival in April at Queen's Hall, at which the three performances consisted of the "**St. Matthew Passion**," a selection from the miscellaneous instrumental and choral works of the Leipzig cantor, and the massive B minor Mass, Dr. Stanford conducting. So much interest was evinced as to evoke the belief that the festival might with advantage be made a triennial event. The **Royal Choral Society,** at the Albert Hall, brought to London Dr. Hubert Parry's oratorio "**King Saul**" and Henschel's "**Stabat Mater,**" first heard the preceding autumn at the Birmingham Festival. Of the familiar sacred works of Handel and Mendelssohn Sir Joseph Barnby received convincing proof that the subscribers were not tired. The **Queen's Hall Choir** gave oratorios and cantatas in the building from which its name is derived; and two or three other societies had no reason to regret reliance upon "**Messiah**," "**Elijah**," "**St. Paul**," "**Creation**," and a few kindred productions that have successfully defied the freaks of fashion. The bi-centenary of Purcell's death was not allowed to pass unnoticed, attention being drawn to the matter early in the year by Professor J. F. Bridge issuing the original version of the "**Te Deum**," which, by a singularly lucky circumstance, had come into his possession.

The absolute novelties at the provincial festivals were much briefer than usual. The **Three Choirs Festival,** this time held at Gloucester, led the way with a Church cantata called "**The Transfiguration**," expressly composed by Mr. F. H. Cowen; another sacred cantata, simply styled "**A Dedication**," the music of which was by Mr. C. Lee Williams (the cathedral organist); an organ concerto in F minor by Dr. C. H. Lloyd, so well known at these festivals; and a fantasia for orchestra and pianoforte by Miss Rosalind Ellicott. Dr. Parry's "**King Saul**" and Purcell's "**Te Deum**" also attracted special attention. A week later came the **Cardiff Triennial Festival,** which was rendered noteworthy by the performance of the oratorio **St. Francis,** by the Belgian composer Edgar Tinel, who personally conducted the work. The imagination and grace exhibited in this musical illustration of

the life of the poet who obeyed the angelic command to devote himself to religion, more than compensated for sundry eccentricities of method. Dr. Stanford's setting for orchestra, chorus, and bass soloist of Gray's ode, "**The Bard**," not previously heard, was generally commended for its picturesqueness and vigour. Welsh musical art was represented by Mr. David Jenkins with a short cantata, "**The Psalm of Life**"; and important revivals were Verdi's "**Requiem Mass**" and Sullivan's unjustly neglected oratorio "**The Light of the World.**" The majority of the works were conducted by Sir Joseph Barnby. The financial issue of the festival, as in '92, was unsatisfactory. In October there was the **Leeds Triennial Meeting,** three of the concerts of which were attended by the Prince of Wales, who, before quitting the capital of the West Riding, had an interview with the choralists, and expressed the delight their admirable singing had given his sister (the Marchioness of Lorne) and himself. Four entirely new works were given during the eight concerts of the week presided over by Sir Arthur Sullivan. Dr. Hubert Parry composed for the festival a cantata entitled "**Invocation to Music**" (in honour of Purcell), which, though of limited dimensions, possesses most of the characteristics of a composer who is never more at ease than when dealing with such a lofty theme. The other novelties were a setting by Mr. Arthur Somervell of Matthew Arnold's poem "**The Forsaken Merman**," an orchestral suite in D minor, by Mr. Edward German, and an orchestral piece, "**Visions**," by Massenet. Wagner's "**The Flying Dutchman**," Parts I. and II. of Bach's "**Christmas Oratorio**," Dvořák's "**Stabat Mater,**" Parts I. and II. of Schumann's rarely heard "**Paradise and the Peri**," Samuel Wesley's "**Psalm cxiv.**," in eight parts, unaccompanied, Beethoven's "**Mass in D**," "**The Golden Legend,**" and "**Messiah**," were also among the performances. For the last-named, which had not been given at this festival for a long period, as it was thought that the patrons preferred less familiar works, the demand for tickets was so great that a fortnight beforehand they were sold at a premium. The festival was in every respect a very great success, and for volume, precision of attack, and respect for light and shade, the Yorkshire choralists were voted unsurpassed.

The operatic performances were extremely varied. Having induced Madame Patti to return during the summer season to the **Covent Garden** stage, from which she had been absent for ten years, Sir Augustus Harris made it no secret that for once he intended to rely upon star artists rather than upon new operas, of which in '94 he had produced no less than seven. Of the twenty-five operas given in the course of eleven weeks only two were novelties. These were Sir Edward Malet and Mr. F. H. Cowen's "**Harold**" and Mr. Maclean's "**Petruccio**," both of which were sung in English, believed to be an unparalleled circumstance at what used to be called the "Royal Italian Opera." Having introduced performances in the French and German tongues, Sir A. Harris felt justified in presenting the two works in question in the language in which they were written. Madame Albani associated herself with Mr. Cowen's composition, and the support she received was good, whilst the manager did all that was possible to effectively embellish the representation before the footlights of a moving chapter in English history. "**Petruccio**" was the outcome of a competition organised by Mr. Charles Manners, and the judges having given their award, the prize work (in one act) was brought before the public at a *matinée*. After the performance Madame Patti handed the composer the substantial

53

recognition of victory. The famous prima donna's reappearance for six nights in three of her most popular parts evoked great enthusiasm, the delight of the audience reaching the highest pitch when it was perceived that her histrionic skill still corresponded with the finish of her vocalisation. Madame Patti played in "La Traviata," in "Don Giovanni," and in "Il Barbiere di Siviglia," the lesson scene in the last-named provoking a demand for extra airs. The interest displayed by the general musical public in Madame Patti's *rentrée* ont he boards on which she made her London *début* in '61 thoroughly realised managerial expectations. Madame Sembrich also came back after being away eleven years, and Signor Tamagno appeared for the first time at Covent Garden, opening the season, and at once making himself at home, with his fine performance of Verdi's "Otello." Madame Melba sustained most of her favourite parts with unabated success, and towards the close of the season took part in "Carmen" with Madame Calvé (who was warmly welcomed). M. Alvarez, the tenor, with his fine voice and improved style, largely augmented his list of friends, and MM. Maurel and Plançon were always acceptable. For the first time during Sir Augustus Harris' management of opera he did not obtain the assistance of the brothers De Reszke. **Drury Lane Theatre** was set apart for the Grand Ducal Court Company of Saxe-Coburg and Gotha, whose *repertoire* included comedy and opera. They began with Zellner's "Der Vogelhandler," and later gave Smetana's long-expected "Die Verkaufte Braut" and Lortzing's "Der Wildschutz." neither of these having before been heard in London. "Hänsel und Gretel," "Fidelio," "Der Freischutz," and "Die Fledermaus" gave further scope for exhibiting efficiency in widely differing styles. Drury Lane opened at Easter for a few weeks with familiar operas sung in English by members of Sir A. Harris' company. A more important venture was made at Covent Garden in October by Mr. E. C. Hedmondt (formerly of the Carl Rosa troupe), who, trusting mainly to Wagner, produced "Die Walküre" in English in a telling manner, Mr. Henschel taking the *bâton*. "Tannhauser," "The Flying Dutchman," and "Lohengrin" were admirably conducted by Herr Feld.

The more eminent solo instrumentalists coming to England for the first time were Herr Moritz Rosenthal, the pianist, and Herr Willy Burmester, the violinist. Both are likely to become annual visitors, success in each case being immediate. Herr Sauer, M. Paderewski, and Señor Sarasate also drew large audiences. The Strauss Orchestra, under M. Eduard Strauss, were engaged at the **Imperial Institute** during the summer months. Mr. Edward German composed the incidental music to the latest "Romeo and Juliet" at the **Lyceum**. The **Monday** and **Saturday Popular Concerts** remained faithful to their original purpose, presenting a constant series of masterly chamber works, interpreted by such rare artists as Dr. Joachim, Lady Hallé, Miss Fanny Davies (who at her annual concert was able to offer two fresh works by Brahms for piano and clarionet), and others. Musically the tendency was decidedly progressive throughout the year.

1896

It would be easy to name years of greater musical productivity than '96 proved, particularly as regards native composers; but no decline was manifested in public support of the art. Orchestral concerts were more numerous, societies devoted to oratorio and cantata received a full share of patronage, recitals by well-known artists during the spring and autumn continued to draw large audiences, and the subscription to the **Covent Garden** summer opera season was declared to surpass preceding record. There was abundant opportunity for important novelties, but very few were forthcoming. This may be explained by professorial duties claiming so much of the time of British composers, whilst no work of Continental origin made sufficient mark to create a strong desire for performance in England. The unexpected death of Sir Joseph Barnby in January, and of Sir Augustus Harris in June, naturally exercised a depressing influence in the widely differing branches of musical enterprise of which each was virtually a leader. Sir A. C. Mackenzie conducted the Royal Choral Society until the end of the season, when Dr. J. F. Bridge (the organist of Westminster Abbey and the Gresham Professor) was appointed to fill the vacancy; whilst Mr. W. H. Cummings, after a brisk contest, was elected Principal of the Guildhall School of Music. At the Covent Garden Opera House an influential committee entrusted the future direction of affairs to Mr. Maurice Grau, who in America had acquired a vast experience in operatic matters. In this connection may be mentioned the sudden death in New York in October of Mr. Henry E. Abbey, the active manager who persuaded so many of the greatest European singers and solo instrumentalists to cross the Atlantic.

Though no novelties at **Covent Garden** were promised or provided, the season was eventful. Madame Adelina Patti did not reappear, but the two De Reszkés resumed their places in the company, and added to their *répertoire* in this country. After a revival of "Die Meistersinger" (in Italian), with M. Edouard de Reszké as Hans Sachs, came "Tristan und Isolde" (in the original tongue), with Jean de Reszké as the ill-fated hero, his brother as King Mark, and Madame Albani as the heroine. The performance of this complicated work was pronounced the best hitherto given here. The Polish tenor's impersonation of Tristan was instinct with the highest artistic qualities, his thorough grasp of the character and perfect delivery of the music surprising even staunch admirers who had long desired to see him in one of the most impassioned and arduous of Wagnerian *rôles*. Unfortunately Sir A. Harris, who had prided himself on the cast, did not live to hear the satisfaction expressed. "Tristan," which came late in the season, completely filled the house at each of the four representations it obtained. The experiment of giving "Die Walküre" in French was not so successful, despite the admirable embodiment of Siegmund by M. Alvarez. The language, not the interpreters, failed to bring out the peculiar spirit of the second section of the "Ring des Nibelungen" series. In "Tannhauser," also given in French, M. Alvarez, whose popularity has steadily increased, won much credit. The Wagnerian catalogue of the season was completed with "Lohengrin." Madame Melba, if possible a greater favourite than ever, sustained with undiminished effect several of the parts identified with her reputation; and Madame Emma Eames and M. Plançon again rendered specially valuable service. For certain singers two or three operas were brought from the shelf on which for several years they had rested without inquiry concerning them, but the result was not encouraging. Neither Madame Calvé nor Madame Sembrich appeared, although they were announced. In all, twenty-three operas were performed, and the total representations of Wagner's works far exceeded those of any other composer. It was the Bayreuth master, too, whom the Carl Rosa Company found most remunerative during a season of afternoon performances at **Daly's Theatre** early in the year. New to London was Mr. Hamish McCunn's "**Jeannie Deans**," libretto adapted from "The Heart of Midlothian," and originally produced at Edinburgh about fourteen months previously. It was also intended to give an English version of Godard's "**La Vivandière**," but this was postponed until March, when the troupe had returned to Liverpool, Miss Zélie de Lussan then playing the title part. At Daly's Theatre revivals of "**The Daughter of the Regiment**" and of "**Mignon**" took place. During his annual visit to the Metropolis Mr. Arthur Rousbey submitted "**Mercedes**," composed by Mr. Daniele Pellegrini, the subject being Longfellow's "**Spanish Student**." Prior to the regular season at Covent Garden Sir A. Harris gave performances of opera in English at **Drury Lane**, including "**Die Walküre**." Another operatic event deserving mention was the performance at a private house by the Sisters Ravogli of Mascagni's "**Zanetto**," a musical version of Coppée's "**Le Passant**," and virtually a duologue.

Musical farce almost ousted refined comic opera, but the **Savoy** remained true to its purpose. In March, after a long interval, an addition to the Gilbert-Sullivan series was made in "**The Grand Duke ; or, the Statutory Duel**," for a leading part in which the Hungarian actress Mlle von Palmay was expressly engaged. When it was withdrawn, after a few months' run, Mr. D'Oyly Carte fell back upon an old and well-tried friend in "**The Mikado**," and faith in this popular production was so completely justified, that on Oct. 31st the 1037th performance at the Savoy was commemorated amid great enthusiasm, the composer conducting, and the house being lavishly decorated with chrysanthemums, Japanese lanterns, and appropriate drapery. A bright little sketch, "**Weather or No**," written by Adrian Ross and W. Beach, music by Bertram Luard Selby, was acceptable as a first piece. At the **Opera Comique** a decided success was achieved by "**Shamus O'Brien**," a setting by Professor Stanford of an arrangement by Mr. G. H. Jessop of one of the best known of Sheridan Le Fanu's poems. Heart, life, and colour, together with a quick sense of humour, were recognised in music possessing all the charm of spontaneity. This opera made the talented composer known to many who were ignorant of his ambitious essays, and created the hope that he would soon submit another stage work on a genuinely Irish theme.

The autumn provincial festivals relied less upon new works than usual. **Norwich**, however, presented a notable novelty in Signor Luigi Mancinelli's "**Hero and Leander**," arranged for the theatre, though first heard in the concert-room. The old classical story was rewritten by Arrigo Boito, the composer of "**Mefistofele**" and friend of Verdi, and to the three solo parts justice was done by Madame Albani, Messrs. Edward Lloyd and Watkin Mills. Though his music for the most part reflects the modern Italian school, Signor Mancinelli has not disdained to revert to older methods of dramatic expression likely to serve his turn. But the mixture is skilfully compounded, for the work is both dramatic and poetic, extremely vigorous yet never deficient in dignity or persuasive power. Its reception was as hearty as could have been wished by all who are conversant with the abilities of the composer-conductor. Cordially welcomed also was Professor Stanford's new Irish ballad for orchestra and chorus, "**Phaudrig Crohoore**," another of Le Fanu's poems set to music with a breadth, freedom, and animation thoroughly suitable to a story of

the "Young Lochinvar" type. A third absolute novelty was a violin concerto in D minor, specially written by Mr. Frederic Cliffe, and played by Mr. Tivadar Nachez. The performances of these works were directed by their respective composers ; and Sir A. C. Mackenzie, Dr. Hubert Parry, and Mr. Edward German, with productions from their own pens, further assisted Mr. Randegger, the conductor-in-chief. The festival, honoured by the presence of royalty, was one of the most successful connected with East Anglia. The 173rd gathering of the **Three Choirs**, held at Worcester, was not quite so interesting, though it gave opportunity to a very able local musician. In his oratorio "**The Light of Life**" Mr. Edward Elgar realised the promise shown in former works. It was found to be rich in human feeling, besides being devotional, whilst structurally there was perfect mastery of effect legitimately produced. A still more creditable example of Mr. Elgar's sound workmanship and gifts of expression in a different direction was furnished in his dramatic cantata "**King Olaf**," a recital of scenes from the Saga, partly drawn from Longfellow, expressly composed for the triennial North Staffordshire festival held at the end of October at Hanley. For strength, ingenuity, and picturesque intensity, manifested alike in the vocal and instrumental portions, this cantata was the worthiest native composition offered during the year. Fresh to the festival lists was **Sheffield**, where, in October, two days' performances of high-class well-known works took place under the direction of Mr. August Manns. The festival at Bristol was more than ordinarily successful. As conductor Mr. George Riseley fully justified his election as successor to Sir Charles Hallé, and some half-dozen eminent native composers evinced their good feeling by conducting works of their own. For the first time in this country was performed Gounod's "**Requiem**," which, three years before, the composer was playing at the piano when he became unconscious and died. An absolute novelty was Mr. P. Napier Miles's setting of Coleridge's "Hymn before Sunrise." At one of the concerts Mr. Riseley returned to his old place at the organ, and played Professor Prout's second concerto, the composer wielding the baton. In the miscellaneous programmes scenes from Wagner's operas were assigned the foremost places.

For orchestral honours in England two new competitors appeared in **M. Lamoureux** (*q.v.*) and **M. Colonne**, (*q.v.*) each of whom brought his celebrated band from Paris. The first-named had the advantage of arriving earliest, and was so well received at three concerts at Queen's Hall in April that he was easily induced to come again in November. M. Colonne did not appear until October, when he gave four concerts. In the summer Herr Felix Mottl gave concerts, at which stress was laid on extracts from "**Der Ring des Nibelungen**" as a preparation for the Bayreuth festival, where the colossal work was reproduced for the first time since its original performance in '76. The **Crystal Palace Saturday Concerts**, to which amateurs owe so much, were resumed under Mr. August Manns. Rumours of contemplated abandonment were answered by increased spirit in the management, the season beginning a fortnight earlier than usual, whilst the performances were of undiminished excellence. Mr. Henschel, giving the **London Symphony Concerts** his own name, organised an interesting winter season. Herr Richter came both in the summer and autumn, and, when opportunity occurred, interspersed Beethoven and Wagner selections with pieces not hitherto heard in England, among these being excerpts from Goldmark's opera "**The Cricket on the Hearth**." Despite so much rivalry, the octogenarian **Philharmonic Society** held its own at Queen's Hall. Determination to avoid narrow grooves was evinced by the performance of Borodine's Symphony in B minor, whilst novelties were offered in a violoncello concerto in B minor by Dvorák (who conducted), and in a fanciful orchestral suite, "In Fairyland," by Mr. F. H. Cowen. For more than one reason a notable incident was the reappearance, after fourteen years' absence, of Mr. Eugen d'Albert, the pianist, who obtained such a friendly greeting that he subsequently gave a series of recitals at St. James's Hall. The **Westminster Orchestral Society** (at the local Town Hall) distinguished itself by introducing a clever Symphony in C minor by Mr. Barclay Jones.

It being the jubilee of the first performance of "Elijah," Mendelssohn's most favoured oratorio was given by every choral association of note throughout the country. Naturally it was selected in June for the annual gathering of the **Handel Festival Choir** at the Crystal Palace, Mr. Manns superintending a capital rendering. It was evident that in all directions this oratorio is as popular as ever. The **Royal Choral Society** at the Albert Hall repeated familiar works with undiminished success; whilst the **Queen's Hall Choral Society** (under Mr. Randegger) made a great advance in public favour as the result of able performances of recognised masterpieces. Attention was drawn to the **Bach Choir** by the introduction at Queen's Hall of Bruneau's new "Requiem," and by the rendering in German of the Leipzig cantor's "Passion Music according to St. John." At the People's Palace, Mile End, Handel's rarely heard "Hercules" was given by the **Handel Society.** The useful mission of the **Monday and Saturday Popular Concerts** was continued with unabated energy, and the **Sarasate Concerts** were well attended. Autumn brought another season of **Promenade Concerts** of a superior order at Queen's Hall, with Mr. Henry J. Wood as conductor. These were so successful that subsequently Mr. Robert Newman each Saturday night gave a concert on identical lines, and offered several works new to this country. In the same building the popularity of Sunday concerts—Mr. Newman's orchestral programmes in the afternoon and the National Sunday League oratorios at night—was fully maintained. A series of chamber concerts, with Señor Arbos as leader, was also started in the Queen's (small) Hall on Sunday evenings.

1897

Upon the creative as upon the executive branches of music the Jubilee naturally exerted considerable influence during at least eight months of the year. Commemorative programmes abounded in the summer, and later the tale was taken up at the provincial festivals. It cannot be said that art was made much richer, but the celebration of the record reign for a while undoubtedly promoted activity. Indeed, the rush of concerts and recitals during April, May, and the first week of June was unprecedented. Most of the distinguished foreign artists expected every year again came, but the majority arrived earlier than usual. Of these, among pianists, **M. Paderewski** to the full retained his exceptional popularity; and in the autumn a hearty welcome was accorded his famous teacher **Leschetizky**, whose visit, however, was not of a professional nature. Of native compositions only two were prominent as successfully representing alike in design and in performance the loftiest species of pro-

duction. These were a **Requiem** by Professor Villiers Stanford (penned for the Birmingham Festival), and a setting of the **Magnificat** by Dr. Hubert Parry (introduced at Hereford). These contained some of the very best workmanship of their respective composers, and by their freshness and energy were calculated to satisfy the comparatively uneducated lovers of superior music no less than the accomplished listener. The taste for orchestral concerts mainly devoted to modern works continued to increase; for although Mr. Henschel, after eleven seasons, suspended his instrumental series formerly known as the "London Symphony" at St. James's Hall, the Wagner concerts directed by Mr. Schulz-Curtius, the Saturday afternoon symphony concerts of Mr. Robert Newman, and the Sunday afternoon concerts at Queen's Hall became still more firmly established in public favour. On the other hand, evidence was afforded of less interest in choral concerts and in recitals restricted to a single instrument.

The first season of the Opera Syndicate, formed on the death of Sir Augustus Harris, at Covent Garden, passed off very well both financially and artistically. With Mr. Maurice Grau as general director, and Mr. Neil Forsyth as secretary, nearly all the special favourites of recent years rallied under the new standard, and on all sides wishes were expressed for the prosperity of the venture. During sixty-seven nights, beginning on May 10th, eighteen operas were mounted, of which two were novelties. Eight of these operas were performed in French, seven in German, and three in Italian. As usual of late years, the most popular works were "Lohengrin," "Faust," "Tannhäuser," and "Romeo et Juliette." The more important revivals were Massenet's "Manon" and Bruneau's "L'Attaque du Moulin." The first of the additions (July 2nd) to the Covent Garden *répertoire* was Dr. Kienzl's "Der Evangelimann," which had been successful throughout Germany. With M. Van Dyck as the longsuffering hero, a part admirably adapted to display both his histrionic and vocal gifts, the opera attracted the attention of thoughtful musicians, though it was only possible to give two performances. The other new work (July 10th) was the "Inez Mendo" of "Fred Regnal" (F. D'Erlanger), a graceful example of the tuneful modern French school. Italian operas were so much out of fashion that they were only represented by "La Traviata" and "Aida." Wagner and his imitators stood in the way of the appearance of Bellini and Donizetti, who in the preceding generation were virtually the mainstays of foreign opera in this country. Of the Bayreuth master's later works there were "Die Walküre," "Tristan und Isolde," "Siegfried," and "Die Meistersinger," the brothers De Reszke appearing in the three last-named to invariably crowded audiences. It was the first time the two famous vocalists had played here in the third part of the "Ring des Nibelungen" series. The poetic spirit and general charm of M. Jean's Siegfried were universally admitted, and a fair measure of praise was bestowed upon M. Edouard for the strength and solidity of his Wotan. In each of the Wagnerian music-dramas he conducted Herr Anton Seidl more than justified his engagement. As both Madame Calvé and Madame Nordica were unable to appear, the services of Madame Emma Eames were in great demand, and this refined artist always proved herself equal to the occasion. Madame Melba sang three times towards the close of the season, and other leading members of the company besides those incidentally mentioned were Miss Marie Brema, Frau Sedlmair, M. Plançon, M. Alvarez, Mr. David Bispham, M. Renaud (the French baritone, who appeared here for the first time), M. Bonnard, M.

Fugère (who made a hit as Leporello in "**Don Giovanni**"), and Madame Frances Saville. Signor Mancinelli was the conductor-in-chief. An opera concert immediately preceding the season served to introduce several of the artists, and in the Jubilee week a brilliant "Command" performance, consisting of excerpts, was attended by a host of royal personages.

The Carl Rosa Opera Company paid a couple of visits to the Metropolis, on each occasion giving a liberal selection from their extensive *répertoire*, and finding Wagner specially profitable. To the Garrick, early in the year, they brought Godard's "**La Vivandière**," with Mlle. Zélie de Lussan as the heroine ; and in October they began a month at Covent Garden with Puccini's latest work, "**La Bohème**" (book founded on Murger's romance), popular for several months in Italy. An absolute novelty was "**Diarmid**" (Oct. 23rd), book founded by the Marquis of Lorne on heroic Celtic legends, music by Mr. Hamish McCunn, of which three performances took place. One of the autumn recruits, Mr. Barron Berthauld, showed marked capacity for embodying Wagnerian heroes. In September Mr. Hedmondt opened Her Majesty's Theatre for a short season of opera in English. His initial essay was a new version of "**Rip van Winkle**" (libretto by William Akerman, music by Franco Leoni), in which he sustained the title part. Subsequently he submitted a one-act tragic opera, "**The Prentice Pillar**" (by Guy Eden and Reginald Somerville), and revived "**Hansel and Gretel**." In connection with the last-named may be mentioned the production in English, by Mr. Chudleigh, at the Court Theatre (Oct. 13th), of the fairy tale "**Die Königskinder**" (here called "**The Children of the King**"), by Ernst Rosmer, with music by Humperdinck, whose ingenious and suggestive orchestration made a deep impression. There was a significant revival of kindly feeling for genuine comic opera, as distinct from musical farce. At the Savoy, on Feb. 20th, was seen the long-expected work by Sir A. C. Mackenzie (book by Messrs. F. C. Burnand and R. C. Lehmann), "**His Majesty ; or, the Court of Vignolia**," additional interest to which was imparted by the return of Mr. George Grossmith for a short time to his old theatrical home, where his new companions included Madame Ilka Palmay, Miss Florence Perry, Mr. Charles Kenningham, and Mr. Walter Passmore. In the summer Mr. D'Oyly Carte, to the gratification of his friends, revived the Gilbert-Sullivan "**Yeomen of the Guard**." To the lot of the Prince of Wales's Theatre (Feb. 24th) fell one of the theatrical prizes of the year, Ordonneau and Audran's "**La Poupée**," of which an English adaptation was provided by Mr. Arthur Sturgess. The piquancy and melodic smoothness of the music, combined with the whimsical elements of the story, gave the work a claim to public favour that was promptly recognised. The success of "**La Poupée**" and the sustained popularity of "**The Geisha**" at Daly's indicated a willingness to revert to the Offenbachian school. Accordingly, on Sept. 14th, "**La Perichole**" (with new text) was revived at the Garrick, with Miss Florence St. John as the heroine, and met with hearty approval. A very quaint reproduction for curtain-raising purposes was Ferdinand Paer's one-act Italian opera buffa "**Il Maestro di Cappella**," at the Prince of Wales's in February.

The regularly recurring provincial festivals were prefaced by the triennial **Handel** gathering at the **Crystal Palace**, held a week earlier than usual to escape the Jubilee, which, nevertheless, told injuriously upon this worthy enterprise. Under the conductorship of Mr. August Manns, whose energy and watchfulness were as noticeable as ever, the customary general rehearsal took place on June 11th ; "**Messiah**" was performed on the 14th ; there was a splendid programme for the Selection on the 16th, and "**Israel in Egypt**" on the 18th once more closed the festival. The performances by the 3500 singers and players did not exhibit the slightest deterioration. The total attendance during the four days was 67,378, a serious decline on most of the Handel celebrations—the highest figures being 87,796 in 1886—but happily not the lowest record in the annals of nearly forty years. At the **Chester Festival** in July, under Dr. J. C. Bridge, Mlle. Giulia Ravogli made her *début* in English sacred music. The conductor offered a new work by himself in a cantata "**Resurgam**" and a new symphonic overture, "**Saul**," by Mr. Granville Bantock, both of which satisfactorily passed the ordeal of critical examination. Unfamiliar works were Adolf Jensen's descriptive scene for orchestra, "**The Walk to Emmaus**," and Spohr's symphony for double orchestra "**The Earthly and the Divine in Human Life**." An attractive item in the Thanksgiving programme was Sir A. Sullivan's too seldom heard "**Te Deum**." The 174th of the annual festivals of the **Three Choirs** was held in September at Hereford, Mr. Robertson Sinclair musically presiding. Here the absolute novelties were a "**Te Deum and Benedictus**," specially composed by Mr. Edward Elgar, and performed at a preliminary service on Sunday in the cathedral ; a "**Hymn of Thanksgiving for the Queen's Long Reign**," by Dr. C. Harford Lloyd, and Dr. Hubert Parry's firmly knit, stately, and thoroughly devotional "**Magnificat**," for choir, orchestra and soprano vocalist. As at Chester, scenes from Wagner's "**Parsifal**" were given in the cathedral. At the **Birmingham Festival** in October, again with Dr. Richter in command, expectations of a good financial issue were realised. By its loftiness, earnest expression, and clearness, Dr. Villiers Stanford's new "**Requiem**" at once gained unanimous favour. If for nothing beyond the introduction of this noble composition the great festival of the Midlands would have maintained its *prestige*. Mr. Edward German was complimented upon the cleverness of his symphonic poem "**Hamlet**" ; and the third new work was a cantata, "**An Ode to the Sea**," by Mr. Arthur Somervell. Considerable labour was bestowed upon a revival of Purcell's music to "**King Arthur**," specially edited by Mr. J. A. Fuller Maitland, and performed under Dr. Richter's direction. Of festivals in other lands it is only necessary to refer to that of Bayreuth, where in the early autumn English musicians mustered in force for three cycles of "**Der Ring des Nibelungen**," and eight performances of "**Parsifal**."

Excepting, perhaps, the C minor of Beethoven, no symphony was so frequently performed in the Metropolis during the year as the "**Pathètique**," the "Swan Song" of Tschaikowsky. It was conspicuous in the Richter *répertoire*, and it was many times played under the direction of Mr. Henry J. Wood at the Promenade and other concerts at Queen's Hall. The **Philharmonic Society** made a new departure by giving concerts in the autumn. During the orthodox spring season the novelties were Sir A. C. Mackenzie's Scotch concerto for piano, the solo part played by Paderewski ; Dr. Hubert Parry's "**Theme and Variations in E minor**," for orchestra ; and, for the Long Reign Commemoration Concert, Edward German's jubilant "**English Fantasia**," for orchestra, and Cowen's scena for tenor, "**The Dream of Endymion**." During the summer Richter Concerts place was found for Richard Strauss's tone-poem "**Don Juan**," and M. Gabrilowitsch, an able young pianist, made his *début*. Cowen's latest symphony, "The Idyllic," was also introduced. More concerts were given by Dr. Richter in October. **M. Lamoureux** also paid two visits to London, on the first occasion with his own Parisian orchestra. Subsequently, for a series of concerts, he conducted the Queen's Hall instrumental force. The **Crystal Palace Saturday afternoon Concerts**, twenty years back the only entertainments of their kind during the winter, were reduced in number; and in October Mr. August Manns succeeded in partially reorganising his band without impairing the efficiency of the performances. The scheme of the **Wagner Concerts**, conducted by Herr Felix Mottl, was varied, though of course Wagner's music was kept well to the front. One concert was devoted to "The Development of the Overture," the examples extending from Handel to Wagner, thus practically covering 150 years. At another concert Beethoven's Choral Symphony was performed with a chorus brought expressly from Leeds. Herr Mottl likewise had an autumn campaign. The Stock Exchange Orchestral and Choral Society and the Westminster Orchestral Society were among the associations that did excellent instrumental work.

The **Royal Choral Society**, at the Albert Hall, held its own under Professor Bridge, who on the Jubilee received the honour of knighthood. A Commemoration concert was held, at which were given a setting by the conductor of Kipling's poem "The Flag of England," and Eaton Faning's "The Queen's Song" (poem by Sir Edwin Arnold). The **Queen's Hall Choral Society** distinguished itself by performances of Saint-Saens's Biblical opera "Samson and Dalila." Three **Bach Festival Concerts** were given in the spring at Queen's Hall, the programme consisting of the Passion Music according to St. Matthew, a selection of choral and instrumental pieces, and the Mass in B minor, Professor Stanford conducting. At the People's Palace the **Handel Society** revived the master's "Susanna"; and the **Highbury Philharmonic Society** made a feature of the performance of Mendelssohn's music to "Athalie," in its proper connection with Racine's play. The **Monday and Saturday Popular Concerts** continued with undiminished spirit their useful career at St. James's Hall. In the summer the **Bohemian String Quartet** drew large audiences by their characteristic interpretation of chamber music of the Slavonic school; and the *ensemble* playing of the **Gompertz String Quartet** and of the **Kneisel String Quartet** was also much admired. The farewell concert (October 13th, at the Albert Hall) of **Miss Anna Williams** the oratorio singer; the production at the Alhambra of the ballet "Victoria and Merrie England," the whole of the music by Sir Arthur Sullivan; and the *début* of Bruno Steindel, a prodigy pianist, aged seven, were among the notable miscellaneous events of a busy musical year.

1898

Throughout the year Metropolitan musical taste was in a transitional state, except with regard to Wagner. Both in the spring and in the autumn miscellaneous concerts were less numerous than usual. At chamber concerts the claims of the younger school of composers were unhesitatingly admitted (sometimes to the detriment of the old), and there were indications of a slight decline in the demand for purely orchestral programmes. Amid these changes the Bayreuth master remained unshaken, alike on the platform and on the stage. Directly the scheme of cycles of **Der Ring des Nibelungen** at Covent Garden Opera House was matured, appreciation of Wagner was manifested in the most pronounced manner. Only two series of performances were originally decided upon, but the prompt sale of all the seats led to the announcement of an intervening cycle. The eagerness to hear the tetralogy was ascribed to two causes. There being no festival at Bayreuth, the faithful English Wagnerian pilgrims proclaimed their willingness to patronise representations at home, and the arrangements for the performances comprised much that was novel here. In the most emphatic manner it was officially declared that no "cuts" in the score would on any account be permitted, and that the representations of the three later sections of the colossal music drama would commence at a very early hour in order to provide a long interval after the first act, during which the theatre would be cleared of the audience and ventilated. None but experienced Wagnerian artists were engaged, and it was announced that the two De Reszkés would appear both in "Siegfried" and in "Götterdämmerung." **Herr Anton Seidl**, who had been such a favourite at Covent Garden the year before, was named as conductor, but to the universal regret of the musical world this distinguished interpreter of Wagner died suddenly in New York in the spring. In his place, solely as regards the "Ring" cycles, **Herr Felix Mottl** was secured, and the appointment gave general satisfaction. Practically June was filled with the "Ring" and other operas from the same pen, and the unprecedented spectacle was presented of full houses for "Die Walküre" and "Siegfried" at five in the afternoon, and for "Götterdämmerung" at four. Excitement was increased by the arrival in London of **Frau Cosima Wagner**, for the purpose of attending one of the cycles. As regards the rendering of the music, apart from the attempt to copy Bayreuth conditions as far as the differing circumstances of locale would admit, the performances of the "Ring" considerably eclipsed all predecessors in this country. Mottl's control of the orchestra was superb, and none witnessing them will speedily forget the imposing embodiments of Brunnhilde by Fraulein Ternina (who was new to England), of Wotan by Herr van Rooy, and of Erda and Waltraute by Frau Schumann Heink. Excellent, too, were the efforts of some dozen other artists, though in most cases falling short of the absolute genius marking the impersonations named. Unfortunately, during the first cycle there was a serious hitch. Through a misunderstanding, M. Jean de Reszké and M. Edouard de Reszké in the third section of the tetralogy played Siegfried and the Wanderer respectively as they had been in the habit of doing—that is to say, with a few "cuts" in the score. Staunch Wagnerites were at once in arms, and accusations were made of breach of faith. The discussion was fierce, but it came to an end when M. Jean de Reszké eventually sang the music of Siegfried in entirety, and supplemented this concession to Wagnerian enthusiasm by appearing as the fearless hero in "Götterdämmerung." Altogether the "Ring" cycles, which drew tremendous audiences, formed the most eventful chapter in the musical history of the year.

Independently of Wagner, the opera season commencing on May 9th had several interesting features. During the eleven weeks there were in all 67 representations, no less than 32 of which were of works by the Bayreuth master. Madame Calvé returned to Covent Garden, and appeared for the first time there as Marguerite in Gounod's "Faust," as the same character in Boito's "Mefistofele," and as Ophelia in

Ambroise Thomas' "**Hamlet**" Madame Melba came late in the season for four performances, and to the delight of her multitudinous admirers added Rosina in "**Il Barbiere**" to her London répertoire. Two other memorable evenings were those on which the gifted Fraulein Ternina played Isolde and Fidelio respectively. Mesdames Eames and Nordica were also among the stars. There were two novelties in Mancinelli's "**Ero e Leandro**" (July 11th)—originally heard as a cantata at the Norwich Festival two years before—and Saint-Saëns' fifteen-years-old "**Henri VIII.**" (July 14th), the latter being specially well received. Signor Mancinelli was conductor-in-chief, and the season was exceedingly successful throughout. The old régime of the **Carl Rosa** opera organisation came to an end in the summer, but after a while the company was taken over by Dr. Osmond Carr, who continued the performances on tour of popular works. The Savoy again reverted to **Gilbert-Sullivan** opera. "**The Gondoliers**" did well in the spring, but had to give place to the Pinero-Carr-Sullivan novelty, "**The Beauty Stone**" (May 28th), a work more serious in tone than had hitherto been given on these boards. But "**The Gondoliers**" soon returned, and afterwards (Sept. 22nd) came a revival of "**The Sorcerer**," with "**Trial by Jury**" as a pendant.

There were two important regularly recurring provincial festivals—those of **Gloucester** (the Three Choirs) and of **Leeds**. At the former the inaugural service took place for the first time on the Sunday afternoon (Sept. 11th)—a new departure received with general approval. This service included four works composed for the occasion—a "**Festival Overture**" by Dr. C. H. Lloyd, a "**Magnificat**" and "**Nunc Dimittis**" by Mr. C. Lee Williams, and a setting of Psalm xcviii., "**O Sing unto the Lord a New Song**," by Mr. Herbert Brewer—three régimes of the Gloucester Cathedral organistship being thus represented. The "**Stabat Mater**," the "**Te Deum**," and a quartet for female voices—all by Verdi, given a few months before in Paris—were introduced to England, whilst the absolute novelties were an impressive cantata, "**A Song of Darkness and Light**," by Sir C. Hubert Parry, a setting by Dr. Basil Harwood of Psalm lxxxvi., "**Inclina, Domine**," and a vigorous orchestral work, "**Ballade in A Minor**" by Mr. S. Coleridge Taylor. Mr. Brewer was the conductor-in-chief, and in all respects the festival was the most satisfactory given for a long period. Exceptionally successful, too, was the festival in October in the West Riding. Here there were six positively new works. Of these the most imposing were a well-written dramatic cantata, "**Caractacus**," by Mr. Edward Elgar, a masterly setting of the "**Te Deum**" by Professor Stanford, and a very tasteful version by Mr. F. H. Cowen of Collins's "**Ode to the Passions.**" The other specially composed works were an ode by Dr. Alan Gray, "**A Song of Redemption**" (Mason Neale's hymn, "The foe behind, the sea before"), a short ode by Mr. Otto Goldschmidt, "**Music**" (words by Sir Lewis Morris), and a "**Moorish Rhapsody**" for orchestra, by Engelbert Humperdinck (composer of "Hänsel und Grete."). Sir Arthur Sullivan was again the conductor. It was at this festival that the intended retirement of Mr. Edward Lloyd, the tenor, became known.

Incidents of the 86th season of the **Philharmonic Society** were the appearances of **Moritz Moszkowski** as a pianist (May 12th) and of **Saint Saëns** as an organist (June 23rd), each playing a work of his own composition. On June 9th **Eugen d'Albert** conducted his Symphony in F, and played Beethoven's Pianoforte Concerto in E flat. Another autumn season

was proposed, but it was eventually abandoned. The **Crystal Palace Saturday Concerts**, under the veteran August Manns, were less in number than before, but their interest and excellence were unimpaired. The excuse for the annual assemblage of the **Handel Festival Choir** (1898 not being a festival year) was the celebration of the 60th anniversary of the Queen's coronation. The stupendous "**Dies Iræ**," from Berlioz's *Requiem*, was given as nearly as possible according to the peculiar conditions demanded by the composer, and Madame Adelina Patti took part in the programme. There was a short series of **Richter Concerts** both in the summer and autumn. At a Wagner concert on May 17th, **Felix Weingartner**, a shining light among modern German conductors, made his *début* here with the utmost success. As a composer he won favourable opinion with his symphonic poem, "**King Lear**." Mr. Newman's **Symphony Concerts** at Queen's Hall, with Mr. Henry J. Wood as conductor, retained their hold of the public, and with the same orchestra special concerts were conducted by **M. Lamoureux** early in the year. The **Promenade Concerts** in the autumn under the same roof were carried on with the accustomed spirit and liberality, several compositions not previously heard in England, by Tschaikowsky and other modern masters, being submitted. The Stock Exchange Orchestral Society, under Mr. Arthur W. Payne; the Royal Amateur, under Mr. Ernest Ford; the Imperial Institute Orchestra, under Mr. Randegger; and kindred associations, also did meritorious work. The **Royal Choral Society**, under Sir Frederick Bridge at the Albert Hall, adopted Beethoven's "**Ruins of Athens**" music (rearranged for concert purposes), and Franco Leoni's new oratorio, "**The Gate of Life**" (March 16th). The **Bach Choir** at Queen's Hall brought to London Professor Stanford's Birmingham Festival "**Requiem**," and gave a Brahms "**In Memoriam**" concert, the programme of the latter including the "**German Requiem**." A few oratorio performances were given by the **Queen's Hall Choral Society**, which was afterwards utilised by Mr. Newman for his Sunday evening concerts. The zealous labours of the **Handel Society** comprised the revival of the master's "**Athaliah**" and "**Nisi Dominus**" (Psalm cxxvii.).

For the first time since they became a recognised Metropolitan musical institution, no **Monday Popular Concerts** were given prior to Christmas, but the Saturday series was resumed. Concerts of **chamber music** were successfully given by Messrs. Walenn, G. A. Clinton, Simonetti, and others; whilst the foreign visitors representing this branch of art included the Fitzner Quartet and the Bohemian String Quartet. Pianists who had no reason to regret giving recitals were Moritz Rosenthal, Vladimir de Pachmann (reappearing after long absence), and Arthur Friedheim. The reconstructed Salle Erard was opened in April by Paderewski. Mozart's **Don Juan** was performed by the Royal College students at the Lyceum in January. Sullivan's "**The Martyr of Antioch**" was played as an opera by the Carl Rosa troupe in February. **Herr Karl Klindworth** reappeared in London as a conductor. Mr. David Jenkins, the Welsh composer, brought his "**Legend of St. David**" to Queen's Hall on April 4th. During the annual conference of the **Incorporated Society of Musicians** held in London in January, Tallis's Forty-Part Motet was performed by a choir of about 400 voices under Dr. Mann.

1899

Upon the attention of so many of our leading musicians professional duties in connection with the larger schools make such a heavy claim as to allow little time for composition. This was more patent than ever. Very few of the better-known British composers produced works of such importance as to greatly stimulate curiosity. For novelty the provincial festivals had to rely upon comparative fresh comers and upon musicians less occupied with teaching and training. Of the younger men Mr. S. Coleridge-Taylor (*q.v.*) was the most fortunate. His cantata "**Hiawatha's Wedding Feast**," the first of a trilogy dealing with scenes from Longfellow's "Song of Hiawatha," was so warmly approved that it was taken up in all directions. At the Norwich Triennial Festival in October it was preceded by a specially composed overture, and later in the month the second of the set of cantatas, "**The Death of Minnehaha**," was introduced at the North Staffordshire (Hanley) Festival. It was also announced that the third cantata, "**Hiawatha's Departure**," completing the series, would be ready for performance in the coming March by the Royal Choral Society at the Albert Hall. To the Three Choirs' gathering at Worcester in September Mr. Coleridge-Taylor contributed an expressive "**Solemn Prelude**" for full orchestra, and his orchestral "Ballad in A minor" (written for Gloucester the year before) found its way to the Philharmonic Society. Mr. Edward Elgar's name was also frequently met with. His Leeds cantata "Caractacus" was given by the Royal Choral Society, whilst his orchestral "Meditation" from "Lux Christi" became quite a popular piece. In June, at a Richter concert, a set of "**Variations on an Original Theme**" commanded praise, and at the Norwich Festival he submitted a series of five graceful songs, "**Sea Pictures**," for contralto. Respecting the already celebrated composers, Sir A. C. Mackenzie brought from his desk incidental music for a contemplated revival of "**Manfred**" at the Lyceum, and Sir Hubert Parry composed music for the short tragic play "**A Repentance**" at the St. James's Theatre. At the Philharmonic a set of clever and humorous "**Variations for Piano and Orchestra**," by Professor Villiers Stanford, on the air "Down among the Dead Men," was heard, and a new orchestral suite called "**The Seasons**," by Mr. Edward German, was given at the Norwich Festival. Mr. Frederick Corder composed an overture and incidental music for "The Black Tulip" at the Haymarket.

Modern foreign art was as well represented on the concert platform as usual. In October, at Queen's Hall, Dr. Richter afforded a hearing of **Dohnanyi's Pianoforte Concerto**, and two or three excerpts were given from Siegfried Wagner's comic opera, "**Der Bärenhauter**," first produced in January at Munich. At the Philharmonic appeared Richard Strauss with his symphonic poem, "Tod und Verklärung"; Rachmaninoff, as composer, conductor, and pianist; and Giuseppe Martucci (director of the Bologna Conservatoire) with his Symphony in D minor, op. 75. Moritz Moszkowski also visited England. It was inevitable that interest should attach to the sacred works of Don Lorenzo Perosi, the young priest-composer of whose talent such glowing reports had been received from Italy. The Norwich Festival committee early secured "**The Passion of Christ**," the first of the four short oratorios then completed of a series of twelve intended to illustrate passages in the life of the Saviour. This could not be given until October. But the second, third, and fourth oratorios, respectively entitled "**The Transfiguration of Christ**," "**The Resurrection of Lazarus**," and "**The Resurrection of Christ**," were performed in May, under the conductorship of Mr. George Riseley, at the London Musical Festival organised at Queen's Hall by Mr. Robert Newman. Perosi was invited to England, but did not come, and the curiosity concerning his works failed to acquire augmented intensity. Many other foreign compositions were given at this festival, which extended over a week and employed two orchestras—the Queen's Hall players under Mr. H. J. Wood, and the Lamoureux Paris force under its distinguished founder, each appearing alternately until the closing performances, when the bands were united. At Mr. Newman's Symphony Concerts, at the successful Promenade series in the autumn, and at the Sunday concerts—all under the same roof—Continental sources were freely drawn upon, and as a rule with excellent results. At Queen's Hall acquaintance with modern Russian composers was considerably increased. A few works received their first performance in England under the *bâton* of Mr. August Manns at the Crystal Palace Saturday afternoon concerts.

As two cycles of "Der Ring des Nibelungen," separated by performances of "Die Meistersinger" and "Parsifal," had been determined upon at the Bayreuth Festival, the colossal tetralogy was not given as a whole during the Covent Garden summer Opera Season. There were, however, two cycles of Wagner's works, comprising "Lohengrin," "Tristan und Isolde," "Die Walküre," "Der Fliegende Holländer," "Die Meistersinger," and "Tannhäuser" followed by occasional performances of three or four of these music-dramas. Of each of the two first-named, at the beginning of the series, Herr Felix Mottl directed a fine performance, with Frau Mottl, Frau Schumann-Heink, Madame Litvinne (a *débutante*), M. Jean de Reszké and Herr Van Rooy among the principals. The other Wagnerian representations were directed by Dr. Mück, of Berlin, and in these the genius of Frau Gadski and Frau Lilli Lehmann was immediately recognised. Herr Scheidemantel was engaged for two representations of "Die Meistersinger," and his Hans Sachs was greatly admired. During the sixty-seven nights twenty-one operas were given, and of these three were additions to the *répertoire*. First came Puccini's "La Bohème" (June 24th), with Madame Melba as Mimi. This melodious example of the modern Italian school had been performed in English on the same stage by the Carl Rosa Opera Company eighteen months before, but this was the first representation here in the original tongue. Following a performance before the Queen at Windsor Castle, Adolphe Adam's little opera, sixty-five years old "Le Châlet," was revived on July 8th. Some discussion was evoked by the production (July 13th) of Mr. Isidore de Lara's "**Messaline**," originally given at Monte Carlo during the preceding March. The leading parts were taken by Madame Heglon, M. Alvarez, and M. Renaud, and the spectacle was of the most liberal description. Signor Mancinelli was again the conductor-in-chief, and M. Philippe Flon presided over some of the French operas. Old-fashioned works restored to Covent Garden were "Norma" (for Frau Lehmann), "Lucia di Lammermoor" (for Madame Melba), and "Les Huguenots" (in which Mlle. Lucienne Bréval made her *début*). Well-earned reputation was maintained by

Mesdames Nordica, Zélie de Lussan, Suzanne Adams, and Marie Brema, and MM. Van Dyck, Saléza, De Lucia, Dippel, and Plançon. Although the non-arrival of Madame Calvé was a disappointment, the season was the most prosperous on record. The Carl Rosa Opera Company paid several visits to London. In January and February they were at the Lyceum, and elsewhere in the summer they produced Mr. Victor Holländer's "San Lin," founded on the Chinese drama "The Cat and the Cherub." The Moody-Manners Company revived Wallace's "The Amber Witch," and the operatic students of the Guildhall School in February gave Gounod's "The Mock Doctor." •

To most of the chief features of the festivals at Worcester (conductor, Mr. Ivor Atkins), Norwich (Mr. Randegger), and Hanley (Dr. Swinnerton Heap) incidental references have been made, but it remains to be said that at the first-named city were introduced an oratorio, "Hora Novissima," by Professor Horatio W. Parker, an American musician of high repute, and a revised version of Mr. C. Lee Williams' "A Harvest Song." The second triennial festival at Sheffield (in October), conducted by Mr. August Manns, proved a magnificent choral display. The volume of tone, the precision of attack, the evenness of execution, and the regard for light and shade, resulting from the training received from Dr. Henry Coward, made the gathering memorable, although the programme consisted of familiar works. Festivals on an imposing scale, but devoid of novelty, were also held at Lincoln in June (conductor, Dr. G. J. Bennett) and at Scarborough in October (conductor, Mr. F. H. Cowen). The Welsh National Eisteddfod took place at Cardiff.

Notable items of the season of the Royal Choral Society at the Albert Hall were performances, under Sir F. Bridge, of "The Messiah" without Mozart's "additional accompaniments," and of Wagner's little-known "Holy Supper of the Apostles" (March 9th). The Bach Choir was again in evidence under Professor Villiers Stanford, and at the Crystal Palace in June there was a performance of "Elijah" on Handel Festival scale under Mr. Manns in aid of the funds of the Royal Society of Musicians. The Bristol Choral Society, under Mr. Riseley, visited London to sing in Brahms' "Requiem" and Mendelssohn's "Hymn of Praise" at Queen's Hall, and a hundred Leeds choralists accepted an invitation from the Philharmonic Society to take part in Beethoven's "Choral Symphony" and in Sir Hubert Parry's "Blest Pair of Sirens." Mr. Charles Fry organised a recital in June at St. George's Hall of Byron's "Manfred," with Schumann's incidental music, the latter being conducted by Dr. Yorke Trotter. Decidedly an interesting concert was that at St. James's Hall in May, introducing compositions by Fritz Delius, whose force and originality were widely recognised. The Monday and Saturday Popular Concerts, the Elderhorst chamber series, and the Royal College of Music concerts pursued the even tenor of their way. There was a brief series of promenade concerts at Covent Garden in August under Messrs. Riseley and Jacobi.

Sir A. C. Mackenzie resigned the conductorship of the Philharmonic, and the directors appointed in his stead Mr. F. H. Cowen, who was Sir A. C. Mackenzie's predecessor at the desk. The Mendelssohn Scholarship was gained by Mr. Percy Hilder Miles, of the Royal Academy of Music. Another student of this institution who specially distinguished himself during the year was Mr. Harry Farjeon. His two-act opera "Floretta" (book by Miss Eleanor Farjeon, his sister) was performed in July at

St. George's Hall, and at the students' concert on Nov. 20th his Harmonic Variations in G, for two pianofortes, received a cordial welcome. Madame Adelina Patti (who in the summer became Baroness Cederström) appeared at several concerts at the Albert Hall, and interesting vocal recitals were given by Madame Blanche Marchesi and Herr Van Rooy. Nearly all the famous pianists and violinists visited the Metropolis during the year, but there were indications that "one-instrument recitals," were somewhat declining in popularity.

1900

Though the gloom of war for several months overhung the musical world, the result of the year's proceedings was eminently creditable to British art. Nearly all the best-known of our composers contributed some novelty either to the metropolitan concert-room or to the provincial festival, whilst the creative musicians whose talents were of comparatively recent discovery, in varying degree advanced their position. Notably was this the case with Mr. Coleridge Taylor and Mr. Edward Elgar, who, though essentially of the modern school, do not reject or despise the canons formulated by the greatest masters of past times. In the earlier months the prospect of commanding the interest of the musical public seemed so hopeless that many schemes were abandoned. A change came with the Covent Garden opera season, which proved exceptionally prosperous, but in June and July it was too late for concert-managers to avail themselves of the reaction. Except Johann Kubelik, the young Bohemian violinist, who made his *début* at St. James's Hall, at a Richter concert on June 18th, and by his perfection of technique created quite a sensation, no fresh instrumentalist of mark appeared. Paderewski, Moriz Rosenthal, Ernst von Dohnanyi, and Ysaye paid flying visits, but, contrary to custom, Joachim did not come to London in the spring. Unless given by a star of the first magnitude, recitals were so much out of fashion as to be virtually disregarded.

There were four great festivals employing both chorus and orchestra. The first was the triennial Handel gathering at the Crystal Palace, under the veteran August Manns. To keep pace with the altered condition of affairs—social no less than musical—since the first great Handel Festival at Sydenham in 1859, the days of celebration were changed from Monday, Wednesday, and Friday, to Tuesday, Thursday and Saturday (June 19th, 21st and 23rd), with a public rehearsal on the preceding Saturday. In other respects precedent was observed— Messiah being offered on the first day, a lengthy Selection (including two parts of Judas Maccabæus, "in celebration of the victories of the British armies in South Africa") on the second, and Israel in Egypt on the third. In the latter the army of efficient choralists again produced a series of most imposing effects, and the general performances were throughout entitled to high praise. The soloists included Mesdames Albani, Ella Russell, Marie Brema, and Clara Butt, Messrs. Edward Lloyd, Ben Davies, Andrew Black and Santley. The attendance during the four days reached the satisfactory total of 80,204, as compared with 67,378 in 1897. On July 25th and two following days the triennial festival at Chester recurred under Dr. Joseph Bridge. An absolute novelty was a *Requiem* by the conductor, forming part of a commemorative service for those who had fallen in the war. Unfamiliar works for which places were found were the curious Funeral and

Triumphal Symphony of Berlioz, and Saint-Saens' cantata The Deluge, The Three Choirs' Festival, held at Hereford, occupied the week commencing Sept. 9th. For a "patriotic performance" Sir Hubert Parry specially composed a Thanksgiving "Te Deum," of the most spirited and masterly character. Its dignity, energy, and constructive skill demonstrated that the hand of the English composer had not lost its cunning. In the same programme was a vigorous choral and orchestral piece, Last Post, words by Mr. W. E. Henley, music by Professor Villiers Stanford. Professor Horatio Parker, of Yale, whose oratorio "Hora Novissima" was favourably received at Worcester the preceding year, brought a new work called A Wanderer's Psalm (a setting of Psalm cvii.), which both for taste and artistic finish realised expectations. The fourth novelty was a setting by Mr. Coleridge-Taylor of four sonnets by Mrs. Browning, under the general title of The Soul's Expression, the interpretation of which was entrusted to Miss Marie Brema. Besides the usual examples of Handel, Haydn, and Mendelssohn, there were works by Bach, Leonardo Leo, Beethoven, Verdi, Wagner, Brahms and Tschaikowsky. The cycles, drawn entirely from the three cities interested (Gloucester, Worcester, and Hereford), was far above the average. Just prior to the festival, Dr. Robertson Sinclair, the conductor, was appointed conductor of the Birmingham Festival Choral Society in succession to the late Dr. Swinnerton Heap. The fourth festival was that of Birmingham — October 2nd, 3rd, 4th, and 5th—conducted by Dr. Richter. For musicians eager to welcome native efforts of the loftiest type the special attraction was Mr. Edward Elgar's setting of Cardinal Newman's celebrated poem The Dream of Gerontius. A more exacting task was never undertaken by a reflective composer than that of illustrating the hopes and fears of the dying Gerontius, the strange emotions experienced by the soul of Gerontius, floating through space with the accompanying angel to the judgment throne, and the incidental contrasts between demoniacal and celestial spirits. The cantata made a very deep impression, and for its scholarly attributes, in union with beautiful treatment of a sublime theme, was deemed worthy to rank among the best modern productions of its kind. The expressive solos of Gerontius and the angel were sung by Mr. Edward Lloyd and Miss Maria Brema respectively. The only other novelty was a baritone song, "The Soldier's Tent," by Sir Hubert Parry, the poem by "Carmen Sylva." The same composer's noble "De Profundis," Bach's "Passion" (St. Matthew), Mendelssohn's "Elijah," Handel's "Messiah," Coleridge-Taylor's "Scenes from the Song of Hiawatha," a selection from Byrd's Mass for five voices, Dvorak's "The Spectre's Bride," Brahms' "Requiem," and symphonies by Mozart, Beethoven, Schubert, and Glazounow, were also performed.

The Covent Garden Opera season, beginning on May 14th, extended over eleven weeks, during which twenty-one operas, representative of divers schools, were performed with all the effect practicable on a stage not constructed for a different opera each night of the week. The season was inaugurated with "Faust," the part of the hapless heroine being sustained by Madame Calvé, who a few nights later repeated with undiminished force her dramatic impersonation of Carmen, and Santuzza in "Cavalleria Rusticana." The following week the gifted Madame Melba made her *rentrée* in Puccini's "La Bohème." She remained throughout the summer, playing Juliet, Marguerite, and Lucia, several times, and Rosina ("Il Barbiere")

once. Never was this popular prima donna in better voice.

Another extremely valuable artist was Fräulein Ternina, who greatly enhanced her reputation in a wide range of parts. She was seen in "Fidelio," "Tannhäuser," "Lohengrin," "Die Walküre," "Siegfried," "Götterdämmerung," and Puccini's "La Tosca." To the success of the latter, her fine singing and impassioned acting materially contributed. Indisposition interfered with M. Jean de Reszke's plans, but he took part in "Romeo et Juliette," "Lohengrin," and "Die Meistersinger." Two cycles of "Der Ring des Nibelungen" were given in proper order, and in these appeared, besides Fräulein Ternina, such distinguished artists as Frau Gadski, Frau Gulbranson, Herren Van Rooy, Krauss, and Dippel. These cycles, like the other Wagnerian operas by which they had been preceded, were conducted by Herr Mottl, who could not, however, remain until the end of the season. For the German operas, the services of Herr Emil Paur, who had won golden opinions with the company in America, were secured, and his ability was so manifest as to impart fresh interest to familiar works. The miscellaneous operas, comprising, in addition to those already mentioned, "Don Giovanni," "Aida," "Les Huguenots," "Pagliacci," and "Rigoletto," were conducted by Signor Mancinelli and M. Ph. Flon. Among favourites who maintained their popularity were MM. Saléza, Gilibert, Plançon, and E. de Reszke, Signori Scotti and De Lucia. New comers who had no reason to regret the journey to England were Fräulein Scheff, the tenor Signor Bonci, and the baritone Herr Bertram. Owing to the stage exigencies of the "Ring" Mr. Maurice Grau could not mount more than one novelty, "La Tosca," to which melodious and genuinely dramatic work he gave most picturesque embellishment. At the conclusion of the opera season preparations were commenced for an entirely new stage fitted with all the most modern mechanical appliances.

The principal concerts took place at Queen's Hall and St. James's Hall. At the former, constant appeals were made by Mr. Robert Newman to the lovers of symphonic works, and in every instance the Queen's Hall orchestra and its conductor, Mr. Henry J. Wood, proved equal to the occasion. It is impossible to say how many times during the year they performed Tschaikowsky's esteemed "Pathétique" symphony. Mr. Newman's second London Musical Festival filled the week beginning April 30th, the Queen's Hall orchestra being united with the Lamoureux orchestra from Paris. Mr. Wood and M. Camille Chevillard (son-in-law and successor as conductor to the lamented Lamoureux) directed the performances at alternate concerts. The bands combined in the great classic works, but French novelties were performed by the Lamoureux force and English novelties by the English orchestra. For nearly three months in the autumn Mr. Newman carried on a highly successful series of Promenade concerts; there were also Saturday afternoon symphony concerts at Queen's Hall and at the Crystal Palace by Mr. Newman's band. Dr. Richter had brief summer and autumn seasons at St. James's Hall, where, on March 19th, the fifteen hundredth of Mr. Arthur Chappell's Popular Concerts was held, with M. Ysaye as leader of the quartet party. The Royal Choral Society at the Albert Hall, on March 22nd, gave in complete form Mr. Coleridge-Taylor's "Hiawatha" trilogy, the concluding section of which, "Hiawatha's Departure," had not previously been heard.

A new chapter in the eventful history of the Philharmonic Society, now in its eighty-eighth year, was commenced on March 8th, when Mr. F. H. Cowen resumed the baton he had laid down eight years before. The compliments accorded him at Queen's Hall were as hearty as could be desired, and throughout the season the wisdom of the directors in reappointing him was justified. The chief novelty was a brilliant "Concertstück," composed by Mr. Cowen, and played on June 28th by M. Paderewski. Mention must also be made of a graceful new orchestral suite, called "Scenes from an Every-day Romance," by Mr. Coleridge-Taylor (May 24th), and of an "Ouverture Dramatique" in D minor, by Mr. Otto Manns (March 8th). Attention was drawn on July 13th to a new trio in G minor, for pianoforte, violin, and violoncello, by Professor **Villiers Stanford**, performed by "The London Trio" in the rooms of the Royal Society of British Artists, in Suffolk Street. This was the most striking essay in modern chamber music introduced to the metropolitan public during the year. A healthy sign was the renewed interest in the works of the unjustly neglected **Purcell**. An operatic society bearing his name was organised in the summer, and at the Hampstead Conservatoire some spirited performances were given of **Dido and Æneas**. A private representation of **The Fairy Queen** took place elsewhere.

A brass band competition on a gigantic scale was held at the Crystal Palace on June 21st, when the forty-eight entries represented about twelve hundred instrumentalists from all parts of the country. The prizes being worth winning, the contests were in several instances keen. The chief honour, that of holding a National Challenge Trophy for a year, was awarded the Denton Original (Manchester) band.

1901

A taste for **short compositions**, not exceeding half-programme length, has been manifested by the English musical public for two or three years past. A catalogue containing many names, both of creative and executive musicians, is now in favour, instead of the substantial works with few interpreters formerly approved. For the full play of imagination and of constructive skill the limit virtually imposed has in most instances proved too small as regards the production of works calculated to augment the reputation of composers already distinguished. Consequently, nearly all of those to whom well-wishers to the art looked for contributions of the highest importance have bestowed pains upon comparative trifles. To this, in a great measure, may be ascribed the decline of oratorio, which, except at the Albert Hall, is only to be heard in the suburbs and in the provinces. Doubtless "the whirligig of time" will in due course bring back massive sacred productions, but of this there is no indication at present. With the majority of concert patrons the orchestra remains far more popular than the chorus, and any composer who neglected to avail himself of the most modern instrumental resources would be voted old-fashioned. However short the work, the most imposing orchestral means must be employed, the result occasionally illustrating the danger of edged tools in inexperienced hands.

Thanks to the efforts of Mr. Henry J. Wood at Queen's Hall, acquaintance with **Russian composers** was greatly increased, but few new German, French, or Italian works were brought forward. The **death of Verdi** led to several performances, in memoriam, of his "Manzoni" Requiem. With respect to native productions, one of the greatest successes of the year was Madame Liza Lehmann's song-cycle, "**The Daisy Chain**," which, after introduction at a National Sunday League concert, speedily became known throughout the country, and for pleasant fancy was generally pronounced worthy the pen from which came "In a Persian Garden." Notwithstanding the deterrent influences of Court mourning, the **summer opera season** at Covent Garden was both busy and interesting. During a little over eleven weeks, sixty-seven representations were given, the repertory consisting of twenty operas, besides the Mad Scene from "Lucia." As general manager, M. André Messager succeeded Mr. Maurice Grau, retired. For a double reason it was decided not to include in the performances "**Der Ring des Nibelungen**" in entirety. Though the new stage, with all the latest mechanical and other improvements, was completed, it was advisable for a time not to attack the scenic and other difficulties of "Die Walküre" and "Götterdämmerung," and, secondly, there was the opposition of the pending Bayreuth Festival (with the "Ring," "Parsifal," and "Der Fliegende Holländer"), besides the opening of the magnificent Prince Regent Theatre in Munich. "**Siegfried**," however, was given, and the usual number of representations of "Lohengrin," "Tannhäuser," "Tristan und Isolde," and "Die Meistersinger" took place. Owing to Herr Van Rooy and several other Wagnerian artists being engaged at Bayreuth, these works were offered early in the season, and under the bâton of Herr Lohse, who, in every opera for the smooth rendering of which he was responsible, increased the favourable impression he had made at Drury Lane some years back. The artists included Fraulein Ternina, Frau Gadski, Fraulein Frankel Claus, Miss Marie Brema, M. Van Dyck, Herr Forchhammer, and Herr Knote. Madame Eames returned to the company, and, with M. Saleza, opened the season on May 13th with "Roméo et Juliette." Madame Melba, if possible a greater favourite than ever, appeared in Puccini's "La Bohème," supplemented by the "Lucia" excerpt, and in "Faust." Madame Calvé's impersonations were Carmen, Marguerite ("Faust"), and, for the first time in England, Messaline. For Signor Tamagno, who was engaged for a series of performances, Verdi's "Otello" was revived, the famous tenor's principal associates being Madame Eames and Signor Scotti. Later, he played in "Aida," and undertook his original part of the Gladiator in "Messaline." One absolute novelty, and a work new to this country, interspersed the familiar operas. More than ordinary curiosity was naturally aroused concerning Dr. Villiers Stanford's "**Much Ado about Nothing**" (May 30th), entrusted to English-speaking vocalists. Among these were Misses Suzanne Adams and Marie Brema, Messrs. John Coates and David Bispham. The only foreign singer in the cast was M. Plançon, who represented the Friar. The brightness and cleverness of the music were widely acknowledged, but it was only possible to give two performances during the season. From France was received Lalo's thirteen-years-old "**Le Roi d'Ys**" (July 17th), which served to make known the exceptional vocal and histrionic ability of Mlle. Paquot, a young artist who at once achieved success as the vindictive sister of the gentle heroine, embodied by Miss Suzanne Adams. Had the season lasted longer, a great deal more would have been seen of Mlle. Paquot. Mlle. Bréval appeared in her well-known assumption of Valentina in "Les Huguenots," and the readiness of Mlle. Strakosch was frequently demonstrated. The efforts of Signor de Marchi, Signor Anselmi, and M. Seveilhac (new-comers) won appreciation. The conductors of the Italian and French operas were Signor Mancinelli and M. Flon. The stage arrangements showed great improvement upon preceding seasons.

The **provincial festivals** receiving more than local attention were those of **Gloucester** (178th meeting of the Three Choirs) and **Leeds**. Both were highly successful. At the cathedral city, Sept. 8th to 13th, both days inclusive, eight brief works by British composers were heard for the first time—namely, a sacred cantata, entitled "**Emmaus**," by Mr. A. Herbert Brewer, the conductor-in-chief; a motet in memory of Queen Victoria, "The Righteous Live for Evermore," by Dr. Charles H. Lloyd; an orchestral "Idyll," by Mr. S. Coleridge-Taylor; a vigorous cantata, "**The Forging of the Anchor**," by Sir F. Bridge; an orchestral poem, "A Phantasy of Life and Love," by Dr. F. Cowen; a symphonic prelude, "A Song in the Morning," by Mr. W. H. Bell; an anthem, "Lord, I have loved the Habitation," by Mr. John E. West; and a setting by Mr. B. Luard Selby of the "Magnificat" and "Nunc Dimittis." The interesting revivals included Cherubini's Mass in D minor and Sir Hubert Parry's "Job," and again "Messiah," "Elijah," and "The Hymn of Praise" exercised a potent influence upon the attendance. The chorus, admirable throughout, consisted entirely of members of the Gloucester, Worcester, and Hereford Festival Societies. The Leeds triennial gathering (Oct. 9th to 12th) in two respects differed from former West Riding celebrations of a similar description. **Dr. Villiers Stanford** was appointed to the post filled from '80 to '98 by the lamented Sir Arthur Sullivan, and for a progressive musical city a curious policy was adopted with regard to the programme. The committee, without turning their backs upon Bach, Handel, Mozart, and two or three of the other classic masters, elected to make the festival, as far as was practicable, a "commemoration of nineteenth century music." An undertaking so large could not be carried through in eight concerts to the satisfaction of everybody. Although thirty-three composers in some degree belonging to the past hundred years were represented, a few curious omissions were noted. The list consisted of twelve British, ten German, five French, three Italian, and three Slavonic musicians. Tribute was paid to Sullivan, who for Leeds composed "The Martyr of Antioch" and "The Golden Legend," by the performance, at the outset of the festival, of his noble "In Memoriam" overture, throughout which the entire assemblage stood. The other British composers selected were Sir Hubert Parry, Sir A. C. Mackenzie, Sir W. Sterndale-Bennett, Drs. Stanford, Cowen, C. Wood, and Elgar, Messrs. Edward German, Goring Thomas, Pearsall, and Coleridge-Taylor. With the last-named came the leading novelty, a setting for orchestra, chorus, and soprano and baritone soloists, of "**The Blind Girl of Castel-Cuille**," Longfellow's translation from the Gascon of Jasmin. The other entirely new work was Walt Whitman's "**Dirge for Two Veterans**," effectively set for bass solo, chorus, and augmented orchestra by Dr. Charles Wood. The remaining unfamiliar piece was Glazounoff's "**Memorial Cantata**," penned in 1899 to celebrate the centenary of the birth of the Russian poet Pushkin.

Only for a few weeks towards the close of summer did Mr. Robert Newman suspend orchestral concerts at Queen's Hall. Among his most ambitious ventures was the annual **London Musical Festival** (April 29th to May 4th) of six concerts, held evening and afternoon alternately. With his celebrated Queen's Hall orchestra of 110 performers he obtained five eminent conductors, representing four nationalities. M. Colonne was responsible for the inaugural concert, M. Ysaye for the second, MM. Saint-Saëns and Ysaye (who also played on their respective instruments, the pianoforte and violin, whilst the programme was mainly drawn from the works of the first-named musician) for the third, Herr Weingartner for the fourth, and Mr. Henry J. Wood for the fifth and sixth. The selections were altogether different, and instrumental solos were contributed by Dr. Joachim, Lady Hallé, Signor Busoni, Herr Hugo Becker, and Mr. Harold Bauer. The enterprise of the manager was well rewarded. Early and late in the year Saturday Afternoon Concerts, conducted by Mr. Wood, successfully appealed to the public, and notable events at these were the performance of Dr. Cowen's new overture, "The Butterfly's Ball," of Sir A. C. Mackenzie's suite comprising the incidental music he had written for Sir Henry Irving's revival of "Coriolanus" at the Lyceum, and of Beethoven's Ninth Symphony, with the Wolverhampton Festival Choral Society for the concluding section. The **Promenade Concert** season, yearly increasing in popularity owing to the high-class programme and the excellent performances, began on Aug. 24th and ran into November. The numerous foreign compositions submitted to English audiences for the first time included Tschaikowsky's "Swan Lake" Suite, Hugo Alfvén's Second Symphony in D, Liapounoff's "Ouverture Solennelle," Glazounoff's "The Seasons" ballet music, Balakireff's Symphony in C, Weingartner's Second Symphony in E flat, and excerpts from Siegfried Wagner's opera, "Herzog Wildfang." It must be added that throughout the season British composers were not ignored, and that several nights were devoted to Beethoven as well as to Richard Wagner.

Among the old-established institutions, **the Philharmonic** firmly held its own. Dr. Cowen conducted the seven concerts, and novelties were forthcoming from Dr. Elgar (a picturesque concert-overture, "Cockayne," several times afterwards heard elsewhere), Mr. Landon Ronald (a song-cycle, "Summertime,' 'for tenor), and Mr. William Wallace (a symphonic poem). In its eighty-ninth year, the Society showed considerable vigour. The Saturday Concerts at the **Crystal Palace**—forty-fifth and forty-sixth annual series—were subjected to change. The veteran Mr. August Manns conducted the spring series with unflagging spirit, but of the autumn performances Mr. Newman, with Mr. H. J. Wood as conductor of the Queen's Hall band, took charge. The **Monday Popular Concerts**, established in '59 at St. James's Hall, were abandoned, but the Saturday afternoon series, of much later origin, were continued on the same plan as before. Professor H. W. Parker's "Hora Novissima" and Mr. Coleridge-Taylor's "Hiawatha" trilogy were in the list of works presented by Sir F. Bridge during the thirtieth season of the **Royal Choral Society** at the Albert Hall. **Dr. Richter** paid his usual visits to the Metropolis in the summer and autumn, and again his readings of the works of Beethoven and Wagner were enthusiastically received.

New to this country was the Quartet Party formed and led by Dr. Joachim, who successfully gave six concerts at St. James's Hall in April and May. Other Continental virtuosi, besides those incidentally mentioned, who gave recitals were M. Paderewski, Senor Sarasate, and Herr Kubelik. Devotees of **Purcell** rejoiced in a series of performances at the Coronet Theatre, in March, by the Operatic Society bearing the master's name, of "Dido and Æneas," followed by "The Masque of Love" from "Dioclesian." Specially interesting, too, was a platform performance on June 15th at St. George's Hall of "The Fairy Queen," under the direction of Mr. J. S. Shedlock, who had recently recovered the long-missing score under singular circumstances. Excellent work in an unobtrusive way was done by the Stock Exchange Orchestral and Choral Society, the Royal Amateur Orchestral Society, the Westminster Orchestral Society, the Victoria Madrigal Society, and several of the suburban associations.

Of **grand opera** in the English tongue the provinces had a virtual monopoly. In October, however, the Carl Rosa company came to town, and at the Coronet Theatre gave "Siegfried," and during a week spent at Kennington the Moody-Manners troupe revived Meyerbeer's "L'Etoile du Nord." Genuine **comic opera**, as distinct from modern "musical pieces," was better represented. At the Savoy, on April 27th, the place of the Gilbert-Sullivan "Patience" was taken by "**The Emerald Isle**," book by Captain Basil Hood, music by Sir Arthur Sullivan and Mr. Edward German, the latter proving himself thoroughly in sympathy with the esteemed musician whose labour he had consented to complete. Despite the additional shadow cast by the death of Mr. D'Oyly Carte, the manager of "Savoy opera" from the beginning, the charm of the new work secured for it an unbroken run of seven months. **Nov. 14th** brought a "double bill"—**The Willow Pattern**, an operetta by Messrs. Basil Hood and Cecil Cook, and a musical version of **Ib and Little Christina**, by Messrs. Hood and Franco Leoni. The Royal Academy of Music students played in March, at St. George's Hall, Herbert Scott and Edward German's operetta, "The Rival Poets," and in July at the Globe Theatre gave two performances of Ambroise Thomas's "Mignon." The Guildhall School of Music students in March revived upon their own stage Messager's "The Basoche."

Miscellaneous events were the opening of the new concert hall of the Royal College of Music, for which occasion Sir Hubert Parry composed an ode "To Music," poem by Mr. Arthur Benson; the performance at the Crystal Palace on June 22nd, under Handel Festival conditions, of "The Golden Legend," Mr. Manns conducting; choral and orchestral performances, under Mr. Allen Gill, at the reopened Alexandra Palace; the brass band contest at the Crystal Palace on Sept. 28th, when twenty-seven bands, almost wholly from the Midlands and the North, competed, and the championship trophy was gained by the Lee Mount (Halifax) contingent; and the visit in October of Mr. Sousa and his American band.

1902

As contributors to the **Coronation** of King Edward VII. and Queen Alexandra composers of the United Kingdom did their share. The earlier months of the year brought a large number of marches, songs, and festal pieces appropriate to the occasion. Besides **Mr. Percy Godfrey's march**, which gained the prize offered by the Worshipful Company of Musicians, specially composed Coronation marches by Sir A. C. Mackenzie, Dr. Cowen, Mr. Percy Pitt and Mr. Coleridge Taylor obtained frequent hearing. Of a more substantial character was **Dr. Elgar's** "Ode," for soloists, chorus, and orchestra, intended for the gala performance at Covent Garden Opera House, which did not take place owing to the serious illness of the King. When subsequently heard at the Sheffield festival and elsewhere the Ode (words by Mr. Arthur C. Benson) was pronounced not only

creditable to the composer's reputation, but in its breadth, fervour, and patriotic ring, a worthy production for a great national event. **Dr. Cowen** also penned a dignified **Ode** (poem by Sir Lewis Morris), which received its initial performance at the Norwich festival towards the end of October. At the **Coronation ceremony** in Westminster Abbey in August the pieces chosen represented five centuries of English church music. There were three new works. Sir Hubert Parry provided an introductory anthem, "I was glad," Sir Walter Parratt (Master of the King's Musick) an anthem, "Be strong and play the man," and Sir Frederick Bridge (who, by right of his position as organist of the Abbey, conducted) the Homage Anthem.

At the **Thanksgiving Service** for the cessation of the war in South Africa, held on June 8th in St. Paul's Cathedral, and attended by the King and Queen and many members of the Royal Family, was performed for the first time the lamented Sir Arthur Sullivan's "Te Deum." It was written by request, and was his last finished work. On Oct. 26th, at the Thanksgiving Service in the Cathedral for the King's recovery from illness, also attended by Royalty, the "Te Deum" was that composed by Sir George Martin for Queen Victoria's Diamond Jubilee in 1897.

With the gala performance in view the **Opera** season was more than ordinarily brilliant. It began on May 8th and ended on July 28th, seventy performances (three more than usual), and twenty-one complete operas, besides portions of two others, being given. There were two special cycles, in addition to occasional representations, of six of Wagner's works, whilst the real Italian school was more often drawn upon than for several preceding years. The revivals included Donizetti's sparkling **L'Elisir d'Amore**, long absent from Covent Garden, in which Signor **Caruso** (a tenor who speedily became one of the chief favourites of the season), and Mlle. **Regina Pacini** (a gifted light soprano), greatly distinguished themselves. Signor Mancinelli was again the conductor-in-chief. Madame **Melba** remained throughout the season, and with unabated success appeared in "La Bohême," "Roméo et Juliette," "Faust," "Rigoletto," and "La Traviata." She departed with the good wishes of the subscribers for a pleasant visit to Australia, her native land, where she was greeted with the utmost enthusiasm. At Covent Garden a cordial welcome also awaited Madame **Calvé**, who played in "Carmen" and "Cavalleria Rusticana." The principals in the Wagnerian performances were Mesdames Nordica, Lohse, and Fremstad, MM. Van Dyck, Pennarini, Kraus, Bispham, and Van Rooy, with Herr Lohse as conductor. In French opera Madame Suzanne Adams, Miss Mary Garden (a newcomer from Paris, for whom Massenet's "Manon" was restaged), MM. Saléza, Maréchale, and Plançon were of the utmost value. Other artists who returned, and invariably did good service, were Frl. Fritz Scheff, Madame Kirkby Lunn, MM. Scotti, Renaud, Seveilhac, Blass, Pini-Corsi, and Salignac. Well-known works with strong casts, and sometimes with entirely fresh *mise-en-scène*, proved so attractive that the **two novelties** were reserved until July. Both were by English composers speaking in a foreign tongue. First in order of production was "**La Princesse Osra**," a setting by Mr. Herbert Bunning of a French libretto by M. Maurice Berenger, founded on a story by Mr. Anthony Hope. The leading parts were sustained by Miss Garden, MM. Maréchale, Plançon, and Seveilhac. Then came Miss E. M. Smyth's "**Der Wald**," a picturesque work already heard in Germany. The effective combination of the idyllic and the realistic, both in the music and the book, secured much attention. In the cast were Frau Lohse, Frl. Fremstad, Herr Pennarini, and Mr. Bispham. Of each of these novelties two performances were given.

Very soon after the grand season had been brought to a successful termination Messrs. Frank Rendle and Neil Forsyth, with the assistance of the Moody-Manners company, started a five weeks' season of performances of **opera in English** at cheap prices, beneath the same roof and with the same decorative adjuncts. Both artistically and financially the result surpassed expectations. For such works as "Faust," "Carmen," "Lohengrin," "Tannhäuser," "Cavalleria Rusticana," "Pagliacci," and "Il Trovatore," there were crowded audiences. Mesdames Fanny Moody, Zélie de Lussan, Alice Esty, and Blanche Marchesi, Messrs. Philip Brozel, Joseph O'Mara, John Coates, and Charles Manners were among the best-known singers, and there was a capital chorus. Herr Richard Eckhold was principal conductor. On Sept. 26th a one-act tragic opera, called **Rosalba**, the composition of Signor Emilio Pizzi, was introduced to this country, the interpreters being Madame Fanny Moody, Messrs. O'Mara and George A. Fox.

Considerable activity prevailed at the more important **provincial festivals**. At Lincoln early in June Sir A. C. Mackenzie submitted the overture to his opera, "The Cricket on the Hearth," libretto based by Mr. Julian Sturgis on Dickens' Christmas story. Another novelty was a Suite in D minor by Dr. G. J. Bennett. The **Three Choirs' Festival** was held at Worcester in September, under the direction of Mr. Ivor Atkins. During the four days there was a full list of standard and classical works, together with three notable novelties. Dr. H. Walford Davies presented an elaborate oratorio, **The Temple**, Mr. Hugh Blair a cantata, **The Song of Deborah and Barak**, and Mr. Granville Bantock an orchestral poem, "The Witch of Atlas." An event of the festival was the success of the young contralto, Miss Muriel Foster, who was suddenly called upon to sing the music of the Angel in Dr. Edward Elgar's Birmingham festival oratorio "The Dream of Gerontius," a work that earlier in the year had won high praise at Düsseldorf. The **Sheffield** triennial gathering took place on Oct. 1st, 2nd, and 3rd, with Mr. Henry J. Wood as conductor. Again, the choralists, trained by Dr. Henry Coward, maintained their prestige for volume of tone and vigour, united with close observance of light and shade. Here the unfamiliar works, besides Dr. Elgar's "Coronation Ode," comprised a dramatic cantata, **Gareth and Linet**, by Dr. Coward, and a short cantata, **Meg Blanc**, by Mr. Coleridge Taylor, both specially composed for the occasion. It was unfortunate that the festivals at **Cardiff** and at **Bristol** were held on the same days in October, more particularly as each meeting was a revival of a triennial gathering for several years suspended. At Cardiff, where Dr. Cowen presided, a great impression was made (Oct. 9th) by the late César Franck's little-known oratorio, **The Beatitudes**, and the absolute novelties were a couple of dainty pieces for orchestra—respectively entitled "On the Heights" and "On the March"—by Mr. Arthur Hervey. Mr. George Riseley superintended the performances at Bristol, and among the most striking features were Dr. Horatio Parker's dramatic oratorio "St. Christopher" and Berlioz's "Grand Requiem." The orthodox festival season came to a brisk termination at **Norwich** with eight concerts, starting on Oct. 21st, under the bâton of Mr. Randegger. There were no less than nine compositions either absolutely new or not previously performed in England. The former

were Dr. Cowen's "Coronation Ode"; a very spirited topical suite for orchestra, "London Day by Day," by Sir A. C. Mackenzie; a stirring "Irish Rhapsody in D minor," for orchestra, by Sir C. Villiers Stanford; a fanciful cantata, "A Star Song," by Dr. Horatio Parker; the balcony scene from "Romeo and Juliet," set by Mr. Herbert Bedford as a duet for contralto and baritone; a concert overture, "Youth," by Mr. Arthur Hervey; and a scena for contralto, "The Triumph of Alcestis," by Mr. Frederic Cliffe. Mr Edward German brought forward a new version of his "Rhapsody on March Themes," and the dramatic cantata "Werther's Shadow," by Mr. Alberto Randegger, jun., equalled expectations of its power and effectiveness, kindled by reports of its performance on the Continent.

Orchestral concerts continued to be well supported, though they were not quite so numerous as in 1901. The ninetieth season of the **Philharmonic** Society was safe at Queen's Hall in the hands of Dr. Cowen, and among the additions to the répertoire were two orchestral pieces by Mr. William H. Bell and a new violin concerto in D minor by Mr. A. Randegger, jun. A few **Richter** concerts were given in the summer and late autumn. In the six concerts forming the **London Musical Festival** at Queen's Hall, commencing on April 28th, five eminent conductors took part—namely, Mr. Henry J. Wood, Herr Nikisch, Herr Weingartner, M. Ysaye, and Dr. Saint-Saëns. Herr Nikisch, being more of a stranger than the others, was engaged to conduct the Queen's Hall band at two extra concerts in June. The same band also supplied **Symphony Concerts**, which were directed by Mr. Wood until he became indisposed, when his place was taken by M. Colonne (Oct. 25th), Herr Emil Paur (Nov. 8th), and Dr. Elgar (Nov. 22nd). Mr. Wood's substitute during the final weeks of the busy **Promenade Concerts** season was Mr. Arthur W. Payne. In the summer the Queen's Hall Orchestra and Choral Society were several times conducted by Herr Richard Strauss, with whom came Herr Ernst von Possart, the celebrated Munich manager and reciter. On May 31st they gave "Manfred," with Schumann's music. The celebrated **Meiningen Orchestra**, conducted by Herr Fritz Steinbach, came to St. James's Hall on Nov. 17th to give five performances, and particularly distinguished themselves in the interpretation of works by Brahms. Apart from the stage, Mascagni's music composed for the drama "The Eternal City" received its first performance on Oct. 12th at a National Sunday League concert at Queen's Hall. The Stock Exchange Orchestral and Choral Society, the Westminster Orchestral Society, and the Highbury Philharmonic Society gave meritorious performances. A series of concerts was organised at the Empire in June for Johann Strauss's Imperial Band.

Chamber Music was rendered at Queen's Hall by M. Ysaye, Signor Busoni and others, and at Saturday Popular Concerts (Prof. Johann Kruse directing the winter series) at St. James's Hall, where also the Joachim Quartet appeared in April and May. **Renowned foreign soloists** who gave recitals during the year were MM. Paderewski, V. de Pachmann, Dohnányi, Sapellnikoff, and Godowsky among pianists; and MM. Kubelik, Kocian, Arthur Hartmann, and Fritz Kreisler among violinists.

The **Royal Choral Society**, conducted by Sir Frederick Bridge, varied the older oratorios by performing at the Albert Hall Mr. Coleridge Taylor's cantata "The Blind Girl of Castél Cuillé," revised since the Leeds festival, and Sir F. Bridge's Gloucester cantata, "The Forging of the Anchor," both being new to the

Fritz Steinbach

Metropolis. In the summer there was a miscellaneous concert at the Crystal Palace, employing the Handel Festival choir. The customary Ballad Concerts were held at Queen's and St. James's Halls.

Interesting **Handelian revivals** were " Alexander Balus," given by the Handel Society at St. James's Hall on Feb. 19th, " Messiah," as revised by Prof. Prout (Nov. 12th, Queen's Hall), and a series of performances in March on a draped stage at the Great Queen Street Theatre of " Acis and Galatea."

At the Savoy Theatre on April 2nd was produced **Merrie England**, a comic opera by Messrs. Basil Hood and Edward German, which perfectly complied with the traditions of the house. In the autumn the piece went on tour with the Savoy company. In June the operatic students of the **Guildhall School of Music** revived Goetz's " The Taming of the Shrew." At St. George's Hall on July 22nd the **Royal Academy students** performed an operetta by Mr. Harry Farjeon, "A Gentleman of the Road " (book by Miss Eleanor Farjeon); " The Moon Slave," a terpsichorean fantasy (music by Mr. Paul Corder); and incidental music by Mr. A. von Ahn Carse to Maeterlinck's tragedy, " The Death of Tiatagiles." In the preceding March the last-named composer had submitted at a students' concert a setting of Mrs. Browning's " The Lay of the Brown Rosary." For their annual operatic performance (Nov. 25th, His Majesty's Theatre), the pupils of the **Royal College of Music** gave " Fidelio," conducted by Sir C. V. Stanford.

Interesting events in the autumn were the return to the concert platform of the popular tenor **Mr. Edward Lloyd** (Albert Hall, Oct. 18th), and the commencement in November of **Broadwood Chamber Concerts** at St. James's Hall, and of Erard Popular Concerts at the Albert Hall. Herr Richard Strauss conducted his tone-poem " Heldenleben " at Queen's Hall on Dec. 6th.

The annual **brass band contest** at the Crystal Palace, open to all parts of the United Kingdom, took place in September. No fewer than eighty-eight bands competed for the various prizes. The champion band proved to be the Black Diké, and the second and third prizes were awarded to the Wyke and Luton Red Cross respectively.

1903

The **distinguishing features of the year** were the production at Birmingham of Dr. Elgar's oratorio " The Apostles," awaited with exceptional interest ; the *début* of **Miss Marie Hall**, the young English violinist ; three cycles of " Der Ring des Nibelungen " at Covent Garden under Dr. Richter ; the **Handel Festival** at the Crystal Palace ; the visit of **Herr Richard Strauss** to personally conduct several of his most elaborate orchestral works ; and the opportunities afforded to little-known **British composers** for the performance of their works under highly favourable conditions. The older creative musicians made few additions to the national store. Not for many years in this country had the younger generation received so much encouragement. This was in part due to the continuous **growth of the taste for orchestral** compositions. The Philharmonic and Queen's Hall bands, under Dr. Cowen and Mr. Henry J. Wood respectively, had several dangerous rivals. Dr. Richter brought the **Halle** (**Manchester**) orchestra to London ; Prof. Johann Kruse gave concerts with another fully equipped instrumental force, conducted by **Herr Felix Weingartner** ; and Herr Richard Strauss was

accompanied here by the **Concertgebouw orchestra** of Amsterdam and its conductor Herr Willelm Mengelberg. To the general musical public the result of this competition was eminently satisfactory.

The demand for **opera**, whether in English, German, French, or Italian, was adequately met. The summer season at **Covent Garden** was longer than usual, owing to the " Ring " cycles, and in the spring and autumn the Carl Rosa and Moody-Manners companies gave performances in various districts. The absolute **novelties** were " Maguelone," a short French tragic opera, and the English four-act opera " The Cross and the Crescent," both produced at Covent Garden. With the latter Mr. Colin McAlpin gained the prize of £250 offered by Mr. Charles Manners for the best native opera.

As regards **vocalists**, no new-comers from abroad made a very deep impression. There were indications of revived activity in the domain of **choral music**. Such favourite solo **instrumentalists** as Sarasate, Ysaye, Kubelik, Kreisler, Jean Gérardy, Pachmann, Busoni, Sauer, Mark Hambourg, and Homann gave recitals. For lovers of **chamber music** there were the Monday and Saturday Popular Concerts under Prof. Kruse, the Joachim Quartet, and the London Trio, each sustaining well-earned reputation.

Opera in London.

" **Der Ring des Nibelungen**," three cycles without cuts, beginning April 27th, under Richter, Covent Garden. In opening cycle the principals included Leffler-Burckard, Fremstad, and Kirkby Lunn ; Van Dyck, Kraus, Bertram, and Lieban. Later came Ternina, Anthes, Van Rooy, and Reiss. The tetralogy was newly staged.

" **Maguelone**," July 20th, Covent Garden (book by Michel Carré, music by Missa), in one act, first production on any stage. Calvé (in title part), Salignac, Seveilhac, and Journet.

Covent Garden summer season, April 27th to July 28th, with four conductors (Mancinelli, Richter, Löhse, and Flon). Twenty-three operas were given : " Faust," 8 times ; " Roméo et Juliette," 6 ; " Carmen," " Lohengrin," and " Rigoletto,' each 5 ; " Il Barbiere," " La Bohème," " Tannhäuser," " Tristan," and " Die Walküre," each 4 ; " Aïda," " Cavalleria Rusticana," " Götterdämmerung," " Die Meistersinger," " Rheingold," and " Siegfried," each 3 ; " Don Giovanni," " Lucia," " Manon," " Otello," " Pagliacci," " Maguelone," and " Der Wald," each 1. The " bright particular stars " were Melba, Calvé, Ternina, Suzanne Adams and Fritzi Scheff ; Alvarez, Van Dyck, Bonci, Van Rooy, Renaud, Scotti, and Plançon.

Gala Performance, July 7th, Covent Garden, by command of the King, in honour of the visit of President Loubet. Garden scene of " Rigoletto" (Melba, Bonci, and Renaud), second act of " Carmen " (Calvé, Alvarez, Plançon), and balcony scene of " Roméo et Juliette " (Melba and Alvarez).

Moody-Manners' five weeks' English season, Covent Garden, opened Aug. 24th. Thirteen operas were performed : " Faust," " Carmen," " Siegfried," " Cavalleria Rusticana," " Pagliacci," " Romeo and Juliet," " The Cross and the Crescent," " Tristan and Isolde," " Maritana," " Tannhäuser," " Il Trovatore," " The Bohemian Girl," and " Lohengrin." Among the principals were Fanny Moody, De Lussan, Alice Esty, Blanche Marchesi, and Toni Seiter, Arens, O'Mara, MacLennon, Magrath, and Manners. Herr Eckhold was chief conductor.

" **The Cross and the Crescent**," Sept. 22nd, Covent Garden (founded on J. Davidson's version of Coppée's " Pour la Couronne," music by Colin McAlpin). Fanny Moody and Toni

Seiter, O'Mara, W. Dever, Dillon Shallard, and Charles Magrath.
"A Princess of Kensington," Jan. 22nd, Savoy (book by Basil Hood, music by Edward German). Louie Pounds, Brandram, and Drever, W. Passmore, R. Evett, and H. A. Lytton.
J. W. Turner's annual season of popular operas in English began at the Standard Feb. 6th.
"My Lady Molly," March 14th, Terry's (book G. H. Jessop, music Sidney Jones). Sybil Arundale and Decima Moore, Richard Green, Walter Hyde, A. Winckworth and Bert Gilbert.
"Andre Chenier," April 16th, Camden, Carl Rosa Co. (music by Umberto Giordano). Lizzie Burgess, Arthur Deane, and Julius Walther.
"Véronique," May 5th, Coronet (book Vanloo and Duval, music André Messager). French company, including Mariette Sully and Angèle Vanloo.
"La Gioconda," May 6th, Kennington. Moody-Manners Co. (English version of Ponchielli's opera). Blanche Marchesi.
"The Marriage of Figaro," June 17th, Guildhall School. Students of operatic class.
"King Arthur," July 6th, Royalty (Colin McAlpin).
"Dolly Varden," Oct. 1st, Avenue (book Stanislaus Stange, music Julian Edwards). Mabelle Gilman and Sylvia Sablanc, George Ridgwell and Sidney Howard.
"Hansel and Gretel," Dec. 4th, Lyric, Royal College of Music pupils.

Principal Festivals.

Beethoven Festival, May 16th to 25th, Queen's Hall. Eight orchestral and chamber concerts, including the nine symphonies, organised by Kruse and conducted by Weingartner.
Richard Strauss Festival, June 3rd to 9th, St. James's Hall. Amsterdam orchestra, conducted by Strauss and Mengelberg. Programme included "Till Eulenspiegel," "Also sprach Zarathustra," "Don Juan," "Don Quixote," "Tod und Verklärung," "Macbeth," "Ein Heldenleben," excerpts from "Guntram," and songs. Some of the latter were given by Frau Pauline Strauss de Ahua.
Handel Festival, June 20th (rehearsal), 23rd, 25th, 27th, Crystal Palace. "Messiah," Selection (including "Acis and Galatea" and excerpts from "Solomon"), and "Israel in Egypt." Band and chorus, 4000; conductor, F. H. Cowen. Albani, Ella Russell, Macintyre, Clara Butt, and Clara Samuell; Ben Davies, John Coates, Charles Saunders, Santley, K. Rumford, Andrew Black, and Watkin Mills. Solo organist, Sir Walter Parratt. Total attendance during four days, 81,848.
Hereford Festival (Three Choirs), Sept. 6th-11th. Conductor, Dr. G. R. Sinclair. "The Wilderness," Sept. 8th, orchestral interlude (Granville Bantock). "The Atonement," Sept. 9th, sacred cantata (Coleridge Taylor). Albani, Muriel Foster, and Emily Squire; William Green and Andrew Black. "Indian Rhapsody," Sept. 9th, orchestral work (Cowen). "Voces Clamantium," Sept. 10th, motet for soli, chorus, and orchestra (Hubert Parry). E. Squire and Plunket Greene.
Birmingham Festival, Oct. 13th-16th. Conducted by Richter. "The Apostles," Oct. 14th, oratorio (Elgar). Albani and Muriel Foster; John Coates, Ffrangcon Davies, K. Rumford, and Black. Composer conducted. "Te Deum," Oct. 16th (Bruckner). Agnes Nicholls and Muriel Foster, W. Green and A. Black.

Orchestral and Choral.

Sousa and his band, Jan. 2nd, began short season at Queen's Hall, preparatory to tour.
Marie Hall's début, Feb. 16th, St. James's Hall. Played Paganini's Violin Concerto in D major, Tschaikowsky's Concerto, and Wieniawski's "Faust" Fantaisie.
"Once upon a Time," Feb. 22nd, Queen's Hall, cantata (book a new version by H. J. Jessop of "The Sleeping Beauty"), music by Liza Lehmann. National Sunday League Concert, conducted by Allen Gill
"The Light of the World," Feb. 25th, Albert Hall. Sullivan's oratorio, revived by Royal Choral Society under Sir F. Bridge.
"Pelleas and Melisande," Feb. 26th, Queen's Hall, new overture (Garnet Wolseley Cox). First concert of 91st year of Philharmonic Society. Cowen conductor.
Sauer's Second Pianoforte Concerto, in C minor, March 26th, Queen's Hall. Played by himself at Philharmonic concert.
"War and Peace," April 30th, Albert Hall, cantata (Hubert Parry), Royal Choral Society.
Edward MacDowell, the American composer, played his own Pianoforte Concerto in D minor, May 14th, Queen's Hall, Philharmonic Society.
"The Dream of Gerontius," June 6th, Westminster Cathedral (Elgar, who conducted). Muriel Foster, Ffrangcon Davies, and Ludwig Wüllner.
Stanford's Second Irish Rhapsody, in F minor, June 8th, St. James's Hall.
Glazounoff's Seventh Symphony, in F, and orchestral suite, "From the Middle Ages" (conducted by himself), June 11th, Queen's Hall, Philharmonic Society.
Band of Rome, June 13th, began concerts at Queen's Hall, Cav. Vessela conducting.
Ysaye, June 16th, St. James's Hall, played three violin concertos—Bach's E major, the Beethoven, and the Mendelssohn.
Promenade Concerts, Aug. 22nd, began at Queen's Hall, under Wood. Several interesting works by young composers were given during season, including Cyril Scott's symphony in A minor (Op. 22), Aug. 25th; Edwin York Bowen's symphonic poem, "The Lament of Tasso," Sept. 1st; Harry Farjeon's Pianoforte Concerto in D, Sept. 3rd; William Wallace's orchestral suite, "Pelleas and Melisande," Oct. 8th; Garnet Wolseley Cox's pastoral suite, "Ewelme," Oct. 10th; and Cyril Forsyth's Concerto for Viola and Orchestra, Oct. 12th.
London Choral Society, Oct. 26th, first concert ("Golden Legend"), Queen's Hall, Arthur Fagge conducting.
Dorothy Bridson, English violinist, Oct. 30th, début, St. James's Hall.
Queen's Hall Symphony Concerts, Oct. 31st, resumed under Wood.
Richter's Berlioz Concert, Nov. 3rd, Queen's Hall: "Harold in Italy."
Royal Choral Society, Nov. 5th, Albert Hall, began season with "Elijah."
Arensky's Violin Concerto in A minor (Op. 54), Nov. 11th, St James's Hall; introduced by Irene Penso, Queen's Hall band accompanying.
Kruse's Berlioz Concert, Nov. 12th, Queen's Hall, under Weingartner. "Cléopâtre," dramatic piece, first performance (sung by Mlle. Palasara); "Symphonie Fantastique" played.
Richter's Brahms Concert, Nov. 17th, Queen's Hall.
Richter's Wagner Concert, Dec. 1st, Queen's Hall.
London Welsh Musical Society, Dec. 3rd, first choral and orchestral concert, Queen's Hall.
Berlioz Birth Centenary Concert, Dec. 11th, Queen's Hall. Richard Strauss conducted Queen's Hall orchestra.
"Weihnachtsmysterium" (Philipp Wolfrum), Dec. 15th, Queen's Hall. Handel Society.

Miscellaneous.

Joachim Quartet Party, April 25th, St. James's Hall (reappeared).

Annual Brass Band Contest, Crystal Palace, Sept. 26th. 112 bands took part in the six sections. In the championship contest Besses o' the Barn was first, Rushden Temperance second, and Black Dike Mills third.
Saturday and Monday Popular Concerts, Oct. 24th and 26th respectively, St. James's Hall, resumed.
Chappell Ballad Concerts, Oct. 24th, Queen's Hall, resumed.
London Ballad Concerts, Oct. 28th, St. James's Hall, recommenced.
Broadwood Concerts, Nov. 5th, resumed, St. James's Hall.
Kubelik. Nov. 7th, played at Crystal Palace.
Robert Newman Testimonial Concert, Dec. 2nd, Queen's Hall.
Frau Strauss de Ahna's Strauss Song Recital, Dec. 9th, St. James's Hall. Richard Strauss at the piano.

1904

Virtually the musical year was made up of festivals, operatic performances, and the feats of child-violinists. No very ambitious work by a British composer kindled the curiosity manifested in 1903 in Elgar's "The Apostles," and few surprises were forthcoming. But whilst the younger generation failed to greatly advance upon preceding productions, there was evidence of the good likely to be accomplished by the generosity of Mr. S. Ernest Palmer in founding the **Royal College of Music Patron's Fund** for the performance in public of works by promising British students.

Public appreciation of the artistic gifts of **Sir Edward Elgar** was displayed in an unprecedented manner. A festival was organised in March at Covent Garden Opera-house, where as many works from his pen as could be brought into three evening performances were performed under the direction of Dr. Richter. For the occasion Elgar composed a concert overture, "**In the South (Alassio)**," which met with immediate favour.

The important **autumn provincial festivals** were, taking them in order of occurrence, those at Gloucester (Three Choirs), Cardiff (held a year earlier than usual in order to avoid clashing with Bristol), and Leeds. At each several novelties were submitted. In the Yorkshire centre Dr. Walford Davies distinguished himself with an impressive setting in cantata form of the old morality play "Everyman," whilst Sir A. C. Mackenzie was complimented upon "The Witch's Daughter," the text of which was a poem by J. G. Whittier. A successful novelty in quite a different line was Dr. Cowen's treatment at Cardiff of "John Gilpin."

Three distinct opera seasons on an extensive scale, besides visits from the Carl Rosa troupe, resulted in interesting revivals and the introduction of works new to this country. At **Covent Garden** in the summer Madame Melba was seen in Saint-Saëns' short poetic work "Hélène," and to Madame Calvé was due the production of Massenet's "Salomé," long known on the Continent as "Hérodiade." The revivals were Verdi's melodious "Un Ballo in Maschera" (for Signor Caruso, the celebrated tenor, whose return afforded great satisfaction) and "La Navarraise." To test the genuineness of the demand for "National English Opera," Mr. Charles Manners, whilst the Covent Garden season was in progress, opened **Drury Lane** for a three-months' series of representations in English. Amalgamating his companies, he gave many familiar works, and restored to the London stage Halevy's "The Jewess," and

Wagner's "The Flying Dutchman." In October Messrs. Rendle and Forsyth, through Mr. Henry Russell, induced the **San Carlo (Naples) Opera Company**, together with Signor Caruso, to enter upon a six weeks' season at Covent Garden, these performances being, of course, in Italian. Their novelty was Cilea's two-year-old "**Adriana Lecouvreur**," which was very favourably received.

Mr. Henry J. Wood's new regulations in connection with the Queen's Hall orchestra were followed by the formation of an independent body which, under the title of the **London Symphony orchestra**, gave concerts on its own account under various conductors, native and foreign. With his reconstituted force Mr. Wood presided over symphony concerts, over the Queen's Hall promenade concerts, and over the Sunday Concert Society's afternoon programmes.

The appearance in the provinces as composer and orchestral conductor of a little boy named **Max Darewski** paved the way for several talented children, the majority of whom were violinists. With credentials from Dr. Joachim and other eminent professors **Franz von Vecsey**, from Buda-Pesth, was so successful in his exposition of classic as well as modern masters that he drew crowded audiences until the end of the season. **Florizel von Reuter**, by adding composition and conducting to violin playing, was also well supported. The craze for "prodigies" extended, the supply being fully equal to the demand.

In May advantage was taken of the presence of **Dr. Joachim** with his quartet party to celebrate the diamond jubilee of the virtuoso's appearance in England, when at the age of thirteen he played Beethoven's violin concerto under Mendelssohn at a Philharmonic concert. At a reception at Queen's Hall (May 16th) his portrait painted by Sargent was presented to the veteran by the Prime Minister (Mr. Arthur J. Balfour). During the accompanying concert Dr. Joachim played the Beethoven concerto, with which his name will always be identified, and conducted his own "King Henry IV." overture.

As the **Monday and Saturday Popular Concerts** at St. James's Hall were not resumed in the autumn, chamber music during the greater part of the year was left to independent organisations such as the London Trio and the Joachim, Wessely, Kneisel, Bohemian, and Cathie quartet bodies. Among the **foreign virtuosi** who visited us were Sarasate (warmly greeted in November), Ysaye, Kubelik, Kreisler, Kocian, Busoni, D'Albert, and Pachmann.

Both in the quality of its performances and the judgment governing the selection of works, the **Royal Choral Society** under Sir F. Bridge at the Albert Hall maintained its prestige. The **London Choral Society**, conducted by Mr. Arthur Fagge, strengthened its position by careful rendering of modern compositions. The **Chappell Ballads**, the **London Ballads**, and the **Broadwood Concerts** were well patronised.

Opera in London.

At **Covent Garden**, as cycles of "**Der Ring des Nibelungen**" were announced at Munich as well as at Bayreuth, it was decided not to give any section of the tetralogy, but in lieu thereof to begin the season with a series of special performances of four works by Wagner ("Lohengrin," "Tristan," "Tannhäuser," and "Die Meistersinger"), and two works by Mozart ("Don Giovanni," and "Le Nozze di Figaro"), conducted by Dr. Richter. These inaugural representations, which evoked considerable interest, started on May 2nd, and

comprised in the solo department Mesdames Ternina, Knupfer-Egli, Kirkby Lunn, Destinn, Suzanne Adams, Alice Nielsen, Hertzer Deppe, and Plaichinger, MM. Van Dyck, Burrian, Van Rooy, Herold, Renaud and Journet. For operas of other schools MM. Mancinelli, Lohse, and Messager were the conductors. In all twenty works were performed, and the revived interest in purely Italian works was shown by a total of 37 representations, against 24½ and 20 of French and German respectively. Particularly in favour was **Verdi**, who a few years ago was under a cloud. From him came "Rigoletto," "Aida," "La Traviata," and "Un Ballo in Maschera." The **other operas performed** during the season were "Faust," "Carmen," "La Bohême," "Philémon et Baucis," "Pagliacci," "Roméo et Juliette," "La Navarraise," "Cavalleria Rusticana," "**Hélène**" (first performance June 20th, with Melba, Parkina, Lunn, and Dalmores as principals), and "**Salomé**" (first performance July 6th, with Calvé, Lunn, Dalmores, Renaud, and Plançon). Each of the two novelties was given twice. Artists not already mentioned who were conspicuous during the season were Frl. Russ, MM. Caruso, Dani, Scotti, Gilibert, and Reiss. The **San Carlo Opera Company's** season at Covent Garden, from Oct. 17th to Nov. 26th, comprised thirteen works. There were three operas by Puccini ("Manon Lescaut," "La Tosca," and "La Bohême"), who superintended their production, though Signor Campanini wielded the bâton. In "Adriana Lecouvreur" (Nov. 1st) Mme. Giachetti (an able dramatic soprano), Mme. de Cisneros, MM. Anselmi and Sammarco were the principals. "Aida," "Carmen," "Un Ballo in Maschera," "Rigoletto," "Cavalleria Rusticana," "Pagliacci," "Faust," "Lohengrin," and Verdi's "Otello," were also performed. In the last-named Maurel resumed his original impersonation of Iago, and M. Duc was the Moor. At a special representation, attended by the King and Queen of Portugal, on Nov. 25th, there were excerpts from "La Bohême," "La Tosca," and "Otello."
The **Moody-Manners season in English** at Drury Lane commenced on May 21st with "Faust" (Mr. and Mrs. Manners and Mr. Joseph O'Mara as principals). In rapid succession came "The Jewess" (May 25th, Misses De Vere and Ada Davies, Messrs. O'Mara, Manners, and F. Maclennan), "The Bohemian Girl," "The Daughter of the Regiment," "Il Trovatore," "Mignon," "Lohengrin," "Martha," "The Flying Dutchman," and "Tannhäuser," (with Madame Ella Russell as Elizabeth). Herr Richard Eckhold was conductor-in-chief, and prior to every performance a lecture on the work to be given was delivered.
"**Ib and Little Christina**" (Basil Hood and Franco Leoni), Jan. 11th, revived at Daly's; Ben Davies and Susan Strong.
"**Le Domino Noir**" (Auber), March 23rd, Guildhall School of Music pupils, G. Jacobi conducting.
"**The King's Prize**" (S. R. and Alick Maclean), April 29th. Royalty. London Music School.
"**The King's Diamond**" (Charles Harbury and Meredith Ball), May 30th, Kennington.
"**Alcestis**" (Gluck), Dec. 2nd, English version. Royal College students under Stanford. Title part, N. Tout. His Majesty's.

Principal Festivals.

Elgar Festival at Covent Garden, Richter conducting. "The Dream of Gerontius," March 14th (Kirkby Lunn, J. Coates, Ffrangcon-Davies), "The Apostles" (first time in London), March 15th (A Nicholls, Lunn, F. Davies, Coates, K. Rumford, A. Black). New concert overture

"In the South (Alassio)," etc., March 16th (Clara Butt, S. Adams, L. Chandos, C. Clark).
Prof. Kruse's Queen's Hall Festival of seven concerts, April 9th to 20th, Weingartner conducting. Symphonies by Beethoven, Mozart, Brahms, Schubert, Haydn, and Tchaikovsky; Wagner excerpts ; "The Dream of Gerontius," etc. Dr. Henry Coward's Sheffield chorus.
Gloucester (Three Choirs) Festival novelties were a Magnificat and Nunc Dimittis in G, by Ivor A. Atkins, and "A Song of Zion," by John E. West, both given on Sept 4th ; "A Festival Hymn," unaccompanied motet by C. Lee Williams, Sept. 6th ; a short oratorio, "The Love that Casteth out Fear," by Hubert Parry, for two choirs and two soloists (Muriel Foster and Plunket Greene), Sept. 7th ; "The Holy Innocents," oratorio by Herbert Brewer, Sept. 8th (Albani, M. Foster, Coates, F. Davies, and Dalton Baker). Brewer conductor-in-chief.
Cardiff Festival, presided over by Cowen, brought forward a "Welsh Rhapsody" for orchestra by Edward German, Sept. 21st ; "In the East," tone-poem by Arthur Hervey, Sept. 22nd ; "John Gilpin," choral ballad by Cowen, Sept. 23rd ; and "The Victory of St. Garmon," cantata by Harry Evans, Sept. 24th. Massenet's cantata "Eve," introduced to Great Britain, Sept. 22nd ; (Blanvelt, Ben Davies, F. Davies).
Leeds Festival, under Stanford, offered seven new works : "The Witch's Daughter," cantata by Mackenzie, was produced on Oct. 5th, (Sobrino and F. Davies) ; Walford Davies' "Every Man," (Gleeson-White, M. Foster, Coates, and Lane Wilson) ; and Joseph Holbrooke's poem for orchestra and chorus "Queen Mab," both Oct. 6th ; Charles Wood's cantata "A Ballad of Dundee" (soloist Plunket Greene), Stanford's new violin concerto in D major (Fritz Kreisler), and same composer's setting of "Five Songs of the Sea," by Newbolt (P. Greene), Oct. 7th. The programmes of the remaining day included Beethoven's Mass in D and Sullivan's "Golden Legend."

Orchestral and Choral.

"**War and Peace**" (Hubert Parry), Jan. 28th, given by Royal Choral Society at Albert Hall. Bridge's "Callirhoë" followed.
"**The Atonement**" (Coleridge Taylor), Feb. 17th, introduced to London by Royal Choral Society at Albert Hall.
"**Mazeppa**" (Liszt's symphonic poem), March 1st, Richter concert, Queen's Hall.
"**Manfred**" (A. von Ahn Carse's symphonic prelude to), March 2nd, first Philharmonic concert of 92nd year, Queen's Hall, Cowen conducting.
"**Dante**" (Liszt's symphonic poem), March 12th, Queen's Hall Orchestra, Queen's Hall, under Wood.
"**The Apostles**" (Elgar), April 21st, performed by Royal Choral Society, Albert Hall.
"**King Olaf**" (Elgar), April 25th, given by London Choral Society, Queen's Hall, under Fagge.
Franz von Vecsey's début. May 3rd, St. James's Hall. He played Wieniawski's violin concerto in D minor, Paganini's "Hexentanz," an air by Bach, and Hubay's Fantasia on "Carmen."
"**Jephtha**," May 10th, performed by Handel Society at St. James's Hall.
Miss May Harrison, youthful violinist, May 31st, appeared with Queen's Hall Orchestra at St. James's Hall.
Stanford's Concerto for Clarinet (C. Draper), and orchestra, June 2nd, Philharmonic Concert, Queen's Hall.
Crystal Palace Jubilee Concert, June 11th,

"Hymn of Praise" (Albani, Agnes Nicholls, Ben Davies, and Handel Festival Choir), and miscellaneous selection In the latter Santley and Muriel Foster joined. Manns conducted.

Florizel von Reuter's début, June 29th, Queen's Hall : played Vieuxtemps' violin concerto in E major, Bruch's "Scottish Fantaisie," and pieces by Sarasate and Bazzini ; also conducted orchestra in his own "Symphony Royale."

Promenade Concerts at Queen's Hall under Wood from Aug. 6th to Oct. 21st. Novelties included Stewart Macpherson's Concerto (alla Fantasia) in G minor for violin (Aug. 9th) ; Charles Macpherson's orchestral suite "Halloween" (Aug. 27th) ; Paul Juon's Symphony in A, (Sept. 6th) ; Norman O'Neill's ballade for contralto (Miss Grainger Kerr) and orchestra, "Death on the Hills" (Sept. 8th) ; and Cyril Scott's orchestral Rhapsody, Op. 32 (Sept. 10th).

The "**Kilties**," Scottish Canadian band, commenced English tour Sept. 24th, Albert Hall.

Evangeline Anthony, violinist, Nov. 5th, first appeared in London, St. James's Hall ; gave Bach's violin concerto in A minor, the Mendelssohn concerto, and the Paganini-Wilhelmj concerto in D.

Nikisch, Nov. 17th, conducted London Symphony Orchestra, Queen's Hall.

"**Ulalume**" (Joseph Holbrooke's symphonic poem), Nov. 26th, Queen's Hall Orchestra, Queen's Hall.

"**Everyman**" (W. Davies), Dec. 5th, performed Queen's Hall, London Choral Society.

Fritz Steinbach conducted London Symphony orchestra, Dec. 15th, Queen's Hall.

Miscellaneous.

Stanford's String Quintet in F major, Op. 85, Jan. 11th, St. James's Hall ; the Kruse quartet and E. Tomlinson.

Melba's Concert for Queen Charlotte's Hospital, May 5th, Queen's Hall.

Patron's Fund, Royal College of Music, first orchestral concert, May 20th, St. James's Hall.

Giulia Ravogli's performance in concert form of "Orfeo," for St. Bartholomew's Hospital, June 3rd, Queen's Hall. The Leeds Choral Union under A. Benton.

Annual Brass Band Contest, at Crystal Palace, Oct. 1st. 156 bands took part. National-Challenge Trophy ; Hebburn Colliery 1st, Wingates Temperance 2nd, Irwell Springs 3rd.

1905

The increasing interest of the general public in the **works of British composers** is a gratifying feature in the record of music during 1905, but apart from this recognition of native talent, the year was uneventful. There were the opera seasons and provincial festivals, and the usual recitals by more or less skilled instrumentalists and vocalists ; and a few new prodigies were brought forward, the best being **Mischa Elman**. It was anticipated that the **closing of St. James's Hall** on Feb. 11th, which had been connected with the musical history of the past 45 years, would have reduced the number of concerts, but the leading societies immediately transferred their performances to **Queen's Hall**, now the recognised centre of musical life, the miscellaneous recitals being held at Bechstein, Æolian, or Steinway Halls.

Provincial Festivals.

No important new works were introduced at the **Three Choirs Festival**, at Worcester, Sept. 10th, 12th, 13th, 14th, and 15th, the only novelties being "A Song of Eden," by A. H. Brewer, and Ivor Atkins' "Hymn of Faith," both attractive compositions ; and Bach's "Come, Redeemer of our Race" was given for the first time in England. The other works included "The Apostles" (conducted by Sir E. Elgar), "The Dream of Gerontius," Mozart's "Requiem," and Parry's "De Profundis."

The **festival at Sheffield**, Oct. 4th, 5th, and 6th, was conducted by Felix Weingartner, and was notable for the fine singing of the 300-voiced chorus. Nicholas Gatty's "Fly, envious time" and Fred Cliffe's "Ode to the North-east Wind" were specially composed cantatas ; and the familiar works that made up the programme were Berlioz's "Faust," Mozart's "Requiem," Bach's Mass in B minor, and Schumann's "Paradise and the Peri."

Three compositions new to England were performed at the **Bristol festival**, Oct. 11th, 12th, 13th, and 14th—namely, Mozart's Grand Mass in C minor, R. Strauss's choral ballad "Taillefer," and Berlioz's "Lelio," in which the reciter was Lawrence Irving, the vocal soloists Wm. Green and Chas. Knowles, and the pianists Adela and Mathilde Verne. An absolute novelty was Joseph Holbrooke's dramatic scena, "Marino Faliero." George Riseley, who conducted, also gave "Lohengrin" (without cuts), the whole of "Messiah," "The Dream of Gerontius," and "Engedi."

Fifteen British composers conducted their works at the **Norwich festival**, Oct. 25th, 26th, 27th, and 28th, the musical director of which was Alberto Randegger. These compositions were Stanford's "Te Deum," Sir F. Bridge's "Morte d'Arthur" overture, Mackenzie's ballad "La Belle Dame," Coleridge-Taylor's "Five Choral Ballads," Elgar's "The Apostles," A. Hervey's tone-poem "In the East," Hubert Parry's "Pied Piper of Hamelin" (the most successful novelty), H. W. Davies's overture to "Everyman," Edward German's "Welsh Rhapsody," F. H. Cowen's "John Gilpin," and miscellaneous songs by Granville Bantock, Joseph Holbrooke, Hamilton Harty, H. Bunning, and F. Corder. Mancinelli's cantata "St. Agnes" was the only foreign novelty at this interesting gathering.

Opera in London.

There were three seasons of opera in London, two of which were held at Covent Garden. **The spring season**, which was phenomenally successful, opened on May 1st with **two cycles of "Der Ring des Nibelungen,"** conducted by Dr. Richter. In "Rheingold" Clarence Whitehill was the Wotan, Zador the Alberich, Albert Reiss the Mime, Josefine Reinl the Fricka, Knupfer-Egli the Freia, Kirkby Lunn the Erda, and Hermine Bosetti the Woglinde. The Siegmund in "Walküre" was represented by Carl Burrian, Allan Hinckley being the Hunding, Marie Wittich the Brunnhilde, Agnes Nicholls the Helmweige, Edna Thornton the Siegrune, Luranah Aldridge the Grimgerde, Winifred Ludlam the Rossweise, and Fleischer-Edel the Sieglinde. In "Siegfried" Ernst Kraus impersonated the hero. On May 17th **Melba** made her reappearance as Violette in "Traviata," A. Scotti being the Germont. **A new work by Franco Leoni**, "L'Oracolo," the libretto of which was founded on the grim play "The Cat and the Cherub," was produced June 28th, and was well received, thanks to its dramatic interpretation by Pauline Donalda, the Canadian *débutante*, as Ah-joe, Charles Dalmores as Sanlui, and Scotti as Cim-fen. Puccini's "**Madama Butterfly**," after several performances in Italy, was introduced on July 10th, and at once won popularity owing to its charming melodies, picturesque orchestration, and interesting story; Emmy Destinn showed remarkable power and pathos as the married geisha, Enrico Caruso made the most of his opportunities as the faithless hero Pinkerton, and Scotti sympathetically impersonated the American consul Sharpless. "Orfeo" was revived with Kirkby Lunn in the title rôle, Jeanne Raunay as Erudice, and Elizabeth Parkina as Love; and "Les Huguenots" proved another attraction with Selma Kurz as Margaret, Whitehill as San Bris, Destinn as Valentine, Scotti as Nevers, Caruso as Raoul, and Marcel Journet as Marcello. The last-mentioned also distinguished himself as Mephistopheles in Gounod's "Faust," when Melba was the Marguerite, Dalmores the Faust, and Parkina the Siebel. Other features of the season, which closed July 25th, were the gala performance, June 8th, in honour of the King of Spain, and Mathilde Bauermester's farewell benefit, July 12th. The works given were "Faust" (7 times), "La Bohème" (6), "Rigoletto" (6), "Romeo et Juliette" (5), "Ballo in Maschera" (4), "Lohengrin" (4), "Madama Butterfly" (4), "Orfeo" (4), "Aida" (3), "Barbiere di Siviglia" (3), "L'Oracolo" (3), "Don Giovanni" (3), "Les Huguenots" (3), "Die Meistersinger" (3), "Tannhäiser" (3), "Carmen" (2), "Don Pasquale" (2), "Tristan und Isolde" (2), "Der Ring des Nibelungen" (2 cycles), and "Traviata" (1). The conductors were Luigi Mancinelli, André Messager, and Cleofonte Campanini.

On Oct. 15th the autumn season opened with "La Bohème," in which Melba appeared, supported mainly by the San Carlo company; and among the works presented were "Ballo in Maschera," which served for the *début* of Giovanni Zenatello, a young tenor of great ability; "Manon Lescaut," "Madama Butterfly," Boito's "Mefistofele," "La Tosca," "Aida," "Rigoletto," and Giordano's "André Chénier."

The Waldorf Theatre opened May 22nd with Paer's "Il Maestro di Cappella" and "Pagliacci." During the season of eight weeks the operas performed were "Cavalleria Rusticana," "Rigoletto," "Adrienne Lecouvreur," "Sonnambula," "L'Elisir d'Amore," "L'Amico Fritz," "Barbiere di Siviglia," and a new work by Amherst Webber, "Fiorella," produced June 7th. The principal vocalists were Alice Nielson, Emma Nevada, Pepita Sanz, Eleonora de Cisneros, Alessandro Bonci, Fernando de Lucia, Mario Ancona, Antonia Fini Corsi, and Vittorio Arimondi, and the conductor was Arnaldo Conti.

Prominent London Societies.

Seven concerts were given at Queen's Hall by the Philharmonic Society under the direction of Dr. F. H. Cowen. At the first, March 15th, Sir A. C. Mackenzie's "Canadian Rhapsody" was warmly welcomed, this work owing its origin to the composer's visit to the Dominion in 1902. Stanford's concerto in D was performed by Achille Rivard on May 25th; and at the last concert, June 22nd, a revised version of Cowen's fifth symphony was enthusiastically received.

The Bach Choir gave an interesting performance at Queen's Hall, April 12th, of Walford Davies's "Everyman," which the composer conducted, and the programme concluded with Bach's cantata "O Fire Eternal." On May 30th, in this hall, the Handel Society revived Max Bruch's "Odysseus."

Several excellent performances characterised the season of the Royal Choral Society at the Royal Albert Hall. On Jan. 26th Berlioz's "Childhood of Christ" and Mackenzie's "The Witch's Daughter" formed an interesting programme; and on Feb. 16th Sir Fredk. Bridge directed a fine rendering of Berlioz's "Faust." Handel's "Acis and Galatea" and his "Ode on St. Cecilia's Day" were noteworthy works performed on March 30th. Good progress was made at Queen's Hall by the London Choral Society, conducted by Arthur Fagge, and on Feb. 25th this body won special distinction for a superb rendering of "The Apostles."

Noteworthy Concerts.

Considerable activity was shown by the Queen's Hall Orchestra, conducted by Henry J. Wood, and the programmes of the Symphony Concerts at Queen's Hall included many unfamiliar items. On Jan. 2nd three early overtures by Wagner, "Polonia," "Christopher Columbus," and "Rule Britannia," were revived, but they failed to realise the expectations of those who desired to appreciate them for their artistic rather than for their sentimental value. R. Strauss's "Symphonie Domestica," Op. 53, first performed in New York, March 21st, 1904, when the composer stated that he wished it to be regarded as "absolute music," was introduced by Mr. Wood on Feb. 25th, after 17 rehearsals; it was repeated April 1st under the direction of the composer.

The Promenade Concerts at Queen's Hall started Aug. 19th and ran till Oct. 27th. A few interesting novelties were brought forward, including J. D. Davis's suite, "Miniatures" (Sept. 9th), Wm. Wallace's symphonic poem "Sir William Wallace" (Sept. 19th), Cecil Forsyth's "Four Studies from Victor Hugo's 'Les Miserables'" (Sept 23rd), and Hamilton Harty's "Irish" symphony (Oct. 14th). The concert on Sept. 13th was memorable for the performance of the "Symphonie Domestica."

Great success attended the symphony concerts at Queen's Hall arranged by the London Symphony Orchestra. That on March 8th was conducted by Sir E. Elgar, when the principal items in the programme were his third "Pomp and Circumstance" march and his new "Introduction and Allegro" for string orchestra and quartet.

Charles Williams directed several Orchestral Concerts at Queen's Hall, that on March 21st being specially notable for the *début* of Mischa Elman, a remarkably clever Russian violinist, 12 years of age, whose rendering of Beethoven's romance in G and Tschaikowsky's concerto in D aroused great enthusiasm. Elman reappeared on April 7th, and gave a beautiful interpretation of Mendelssohn's concerto; and on June 28th he played Max Bruch's concerto in G minor and Tschaikowsky's Serenade Mélancolique. On Oct. 17th he brought forward Glazounow's new concerto in A minor, a spirited work.

On June 1st the Ostend Kursaal Orchestra gave the first of six performances at Queen's Hall, conducted by Leon Rinskoff; and the following day Holbrooke's variations on "The Girl I Left Behind Me" were introduced.

The Royal College of Music Patrons' Fund organised two concerts, that at Queen's Hall on June 29th being interesting for the performance of Frank Tapp's clever variations on "Tom Bowling." Sir C. V. Stanford conducted, the composer being at the pianoforte.

Franz Beidler, of the Imperial Opera at Moscow, directed a Wagner-Beethoven concert with the London Symphony Orchestra at Queen's Hall on March 27th. Among other notable foreign musicians who appeared in London during the year were Fritz Kreisler, Hans Sauer, Arthur de Greef, Jean Gerardy, César Thomson, Jacques Thibaud, Ernst von Dohnanyi, Bronislaw Huberman, Leon Sametini, Florizel von Reuter, the Joachim quartet party, Ernst von Schuch (who conducted Kubelik's 25th concert in London, June 19th), Wilhelm Backhaus, Franz von Vecsey, Edouard Colonne, and Fritz Steinbach.

Maud MacCarthy, the Irish violinist, reappeared Feb. 2nd, after a seven years' absence from the concert platform. **Vivien Chartres**, a ten-year old pianist, made her *début* May 15th at Queen's Hall. **Mark Hambourg**, at his recital at Queen's Hall, May 20th, introduced a capriccio by Frank Bridge, which had won the prize offered by him for a short pianoforte piece ; there were 96 competitors.

The **Brass Band Championship Competition** at the Crystal Palace, Sept. 30th, aroused considerable interest, and the first prize was won by Irwell Springs (conductor, W. Rimmer).

1906

Nothing sensational occurred in the musical world during 1906. Numerous compositions by native musicians were performed, and won, in many instances, well-deserved praise, the most important being Edward Elgar's oratorio "The Kingdom." The growing number of agents led to a remarkable increase in the concerts and recitals during the spring and autumn seasons, but the artists brought forward, including several "prodigies," did not always exhibit conspicuous ability.

The Important Festivals.

There were several important festivals. That at **Kendal**, April 25th to 28th, was conducted by Henry Wood, and the works performed comprised Goring Thomas's "The Sun Worshippers," Cliffe's "Ode to the North-East Wind," Bach's "O Light Everlasting," and "Messiah."

The **Lincoln triennial festival** was held June 20th and 21st, and the programme, directed by G. J. Bennett, included Hubert Parry's "Voces Clamantium," Brahms's "Requiem," Dvořák's "Te Deum," and "Israel in Egypt."

The **Three Choirs festival at Hereford**, the 183rd meeting, opened Sept. 9th. The principal novelty was Hubert Parry's sacred symphony "The Soul's Ransom," an impressive composition with very effective choruses ; the solos were rendered by Albani and Plunket Greene. Another new work, which unfortunately failed to quite realise expectations, was "Lift up your hearts," by Walford Davies ; this also was described as a sacred symphony. "Elijah," "The Dream of Gerontius," "The Apostles," Bach's Mass in B minor, Berlioz's "Te Deum," "Hymn of Praise," and "Messiah" were given during the festival, which was conducted by George Sinclair.

The **Birmingham festival**, Oct. 2nd to 5th, was notable for the first performance of the new oratorio "The Kingdom," by Edward Elgar ; this proved to be a fine work, and was received with great enthusiasm both by the audience and by the critics. The composer conducted, and the solos were entrusted to Agnes Nicholls, Muriel Foster, John Coates, and William Higley. A spirited setting for chorus and orchestra of Poe's poem "The Bells," by Joseph Holbrooke, aroused considerable interest ; and Granville Bantock's cantata, based on the Omar Khayyam quatrains, was warmly applauded. Christian Ritter's alto cantata "O amantissime sponse Jesu," which had never previously been heard in England, was a welcome feature, and Percy Pitt's clever Sinfonietta in G minor was the orchestral novelty. "Elijah," "The Apostles" (conducted by the composer), "Messiah," Beethoven's Mass in D, Bach's motet for double

chorus "Sing ye to the Lord," and "The Revenge," were also given. The conductor-in-chief was Hans Richter.

On Oct. 24th **a festival**, directed by Henry Coward, was opened **at Southport** ; the principal works were Hubert Parry's "Pied Piper of Hamelin," "The Ode to the North-East Wind," and "Elijah."

The **Handel festival** at the Crystal Palace was an artistic success, thanks to the splendid chorus-singing and the admirable conducting of Frederic Cowen. June 23rd was "Rehearsal Day. "Messiah" was on the 26th, the soloists being Albani, Ada Crossley, Ben Davies, and Charles Santley (who has sung at every festival since 1865). The 28th was "Selection Day," when the programme included several numbers from "Israel in Egypt" and vocal contributions by Ada Crossley, Kirkby Lunn, Agnes Nicholls, Watkin Mills, Charles Saunders, and Kennerley Rumford. The proceedings closed on June 30th with a spirited interpretation of "Judas Maccabæus."

Opera in London.

There were **two opera seasons at Covent Garden**. That in the spring opened May 3rd with a brilliant performance of "Tristan," in which the principal parts were sustained by Marie Wittich and Anton Burger, with Kirkby Lunn as Brangäne. Then came two cycles of "Der Ring des Nibelungen," conducted by Hans Richter. In "Rheingold" Friedrich Braun was heard as Wotan, Josefine Reinl was the Fricka, Desider Zador the Alberich, Wilhelm Raboth the Fafner, and Paul Knüpfer the Fasolt. The presentations of "Die Walküre" were notable for the reappearance of Milka Ternina as Brunnhilde and of Clarence Whitehill as Wotan. In "Siegfried" one saw Georg Anthes in the title *rôle*, Marie Wittich, and at the second performance Johanna Gadsky, as Brunnhilde, and Anton van Rooy the Wanderer. Ternina and Anna von Mildenburg distinguished themselves as Elisabeth in the performances of "Tannhäuser," in which Anthes sustained the title *rôle* ; and in "Die Meistersinger" Gadsky was the Eva, Anthes the Walther, and van Rooy the Hans Sachs. The revival of "Der Fliegende Holländer" met with public approval, especially with Emmy Destinn as Senta and van Rooy as the Dutchman. Gluck's "Armide," which, though composed in 1777, was first given in England on July 6th, was the artistic feature of the season, with Lucienne Bréval as the heroine. Three other works were added to the Covent Garden repertoire. Poldini's "Der Vagabund und die Prinzessin," in which Percy Pitt made his début as an operatic conductor, and Cornelius's "Barbier von Bagdad" were produced May 11th, and later came Jules Massenet's semisacred "Le Jongleur de Notre Dame." Ballet was also revived, André Messager's Parisian success "Les Deux Pigeons" being given June 21st. Tschaikowsky's "Eugene Onegin" was revived, with Destinn as Tatiana, Kirkby Lunn as Olga, Ivan Altchevsky (who made a very successful début in "Faust" on May 10th) as Lenski, and Mattia Battistini in the title *rôle*. "Don Giovanni" was another attractive revival, with Destinn as Anna, Agnes Nicholls as Elvira, Pauline Donalda as Zerlina, Marcel Journet as Leporello, Battistini as the Don, and Enrico Caruso as Ottavio. The **works performed** during the season, which closed July 26th, were "Madama Butterfly" (9 times), "La Bohème" (9), "Faust" (6), "Armide" (4), "Rigoletto" (4), "Tristan" (4), "Eugene Onegin" (3), "Fliegende Holländer" (3), "Le Jongleur" (3), "Pagliacci" (3), "Tannhäuser" (3), "La Tosca" (3), "Die Walküre" (3), "Les Deux Pigeons" (3), "Aida" (2), "Carmen" (2) with Kirkby Lunn in the title *rôle*, "Don Giovanni" (2), "Meistersinger" (2), "Traviata" (2), "Rheingold" (2), "Siegfried" (2), "Götterdämmerung" (2), "Barbier von Bagdad" (1), "Der Vagabund" (1), "Romeo et Juliette" (1). The conductors were André Messager, Hans Richter, Cleofonte Campanini, and Percy Pitt.

The **autumn season** of eight weeks started Oct. 5th with "Rigoletto," directed by Leopoldo Mugnone, in which Melba appeared as Gilda and Mario Sammarco was the hunchback. Fernando Carpi made his début as the Duke in the second performance of this work, Oct. 11th, "Adriana Lecouvreur" was revived Oct. 23rd, with Rina Giachetti, Eleanore de Cisneros, Sammarco, and Giovanni Zenatello in the principal parts. **Umberto Giordano's "Fedora,"** which was produced in Milan in '98, was well received by English opera-goers on Nov. 5th. Giachetti and Zenatello successfully embodied the leading characters. Among the other operas given during the season were "Faust," "Madama Butterfly," "Carmen," "La Tosca," "Traviata," and "Aïda."

At the Lyric from July 21st to Aug. 25th the **Moody-Manners Co.** had a successful English season, during which there were performances of "Faust" (8 times), "Pagliacci" (7), "Cavalleria Rusticana" (7), "Tannhäuser" (7), "Lohengrin" (6), "Trovatore" (3), "Eugene Onegin" (2), "Bohemian Girl" (2), "The Huguenots" (2), "Lucia di Lammermoor" (2), and "The Marriage of Figaro" (1). Richard Eckhold was the conductor. This company produced at Sheffield on March 1st, and introduced to London musicians at the Crystal Palace May 24th, a new one-act opera by Nicholas Gatty, "Greysteel."

Prominent London Societies.

Seven concerts were provided by the **Philharmonic Society** at Queen's Hall during its 94th season, under Frederic Cowen's direction. At the first, Feb. 27th, Teresa Carreno played Rubinstein's concerto in D minor. Emil Sauer, Mischa Elman, Ernst von Dohnanyi, and Raoul Pugno were distinguished soloists at the other concerts. Edwin York-Bowen's piano concerto in D was first performed, with the composer as the soloist, on May 31st; and another orchestral novelty, Coleridge-Taylor's variations on the negro air "I'm troubled in mind," was brought out at the last concert, June 14th.

Some fine performances were given by the **Royal Choral Society** at the Royal Albert Hall, and by the **London Choral Society** at Queen's Hall. The **Handel Society** on May 23rd interpreted Samuel Coleridge-Taylor's setting of Samuel Taylor Coleridge's "Kubla Khan." In April the **Bach Choir** gave two concerts at Queen's Hall under the direction of Walford Davies, the Mass in B minor being rendered at the second. Nine concerts were held at the Portman Rooms under the auspices of the **Mozart Society**, that on Jan. 20th being in commemoration of the 150th anniversary of Mozart's birth. The **Royal Amateur Orchestral Society** opened its thirty-fifth season at Queen's Hall, Nov. 14th, under the direction of Ernest Ford. The soloists were Lady Hallé, Florence Schmidt, and Charles Santley.

Foreign Visits and Visitors.

The **London Symphony Orchestra** gave concerts in Paris, Jan. 10th and 12th, conducted by Charles Stanford and Édouard Colonne. Accompanying this organisation were 300 picked voices from the Leeds Festival chorus. A **Yorkshire Chorus**, consisting of 142 singers from Leeds and 149 from Sheffield, visited Dusseldorf, Cologne and Frankfurt in September, and won warm praise for their artistic interpretation of familiar works. Henry Coward was the conductor.

The **Garde Républicaine band** started on Feb. 17th a series of Promenade Concerts at Covent Garden, directed by Gabriel Parés.

In March, **Giuseppe Creatore** directed in vigorous fashion his Italian band at a series of concerts at Queen's Hall.

Edward Grieg came for two concerts of his own works at Queen's Hall, on May 17th and 24th.

The **Vienna Male Choral Society**, conducted by Edouard Kremser and Richard Heuberger, gave interesting concerts at Queen's Hall on May 25th and 28th, and on the 29th sang at Buckingham Palace by command of the King.

The **Vienna Philharmonic Society** came to London the following month, playing at Queen's Hall on June 26th, and at the Royal Albert Hall on June 30th, the latter concert being given at the King's request.

Camille Saint-Saens appeared at Joseph Hollman's recital at Bechstein Hall, July 12th, and assisted in the first **performance of his** 'cello sonata in F.

The **Joachim Quartet** played at several concerts at Queen's and Bechstein Halls ; and among the **other notable foreign musicians** who appeared during the year were Lady Hallé, Elena Gerhardt (début Bechstein Hall, June 13th), Helène Stagemann (début Æolian Hall, June 19th), Irma Sänger-Sethe, Clothilde Kleeberg, Johanne Stockmarr, Ester de Munsterhjelm, Mary Münchhoff, Pepito Arriolo (aged 10—début Royal Albert Hall, Oct. 14th), the Cherniavsky brothers (début Æolian Hall, Oct. 20th), Miecio Horszowski (aged 12), Leon Delafosse, Jan Mulder, Maurice Dambois, Herman Sandby, Achille Rivarde, Viggo Kihl, Louis Abbiate, Ferencz Hegedus, Ludwig Wullner, Pablo Sarasate, Ferrucio Busoni, Reynaldo Hahn, Emil Sauer, Richard Buhlig, Vladimir de Pachmann, Jean Gerardy, Fritz Kriesler, Michel de Sicard, Franjo Naval, Aldo Antonietti, Joska Szigetti, Wilhelm Backhaus, Leopold Auer, and Arthur de Greef—a formidable list of celebrities.

Other Noteworthy Concerts.

The **London Symphony Orchestra** started another series of symphony concerts at Queen's Hall, that on Jan. 18th being conducted by Charles Stanford, who introduced his sixth symphony, composed "in honour of the life-work of a great artist," G. F. Watts, and inspired by his pictures "Love and Life" and "Love and Death," and by the sculpture "Physical Energy," now a memorial to Cecil Rhodes on the Matoppo Hills. On Nov. 5th a third series of symphony concerts was commenced under the sole direction of Hans Richter.

The symphony concerts of the Queen's Hall Orchestra, conducted by Henry Wood, given between Jan. 1st and May 10th, were very popular. Another series was commenced on Nov. 3rd, when Sarasate was the soloist.

A **Bach concert** was organised by Campbell McInnes on Feb. 23rd, at Æolian Hall, when the programme included "The Peasants' Cantata," and in the same building on May 1st an entertainment was held in aid of the fund for the purchase of Bach's house at Eisenach.

Katie Parker, a talented young violinist, made her début at an orchestral concert at Queen's Hall on Feb. 20th ; and on May 25th **Lionel Ovenden**, a twelve-year old violinist, pianist and composer, gave his first recital at Bechstein Hall.

The **National Union of School Orchestras** gave a concert at the Royal Albert Hall on May 26th, when 800 young violinists played simultaneously under the direction of Walter Hedgcock.

A shorter form of string quartet was introduced at the Phantasy concert at Bechstein Hall on June 22nd, as the result of a competition organised by William Cobbett. Of the 67 MSS. submitted, that by William Hurlstone won first prize ; the composer unhappily died three weeks before the concert.

Boris Hambourg gave five 'cello recitals at Æolian Hall, illustrating the development of 'cello music from the time of Domenico Gabrieli's "Picercara," written in 1689.

The King attended the **British-Canadian** festival at Queen's Hall, June 27th, when works by Alexander Mackenzie, Edward Elgar, Charles Stanford, Hubert Parry and Frederic Cowen were performed under the composers' direction.

Irene Ainsley, a soprano from New Zealand, made her professional début at Bechstein Hall, July 10th, when some of her songs were accompanied by Melba.

The **Promenade Concerts at Queen's Hall** were started on Aug. 18th, and ran until Oct. 26th, under the direction of Henry Wood. Twenty-eight new works were brought forward. Seven were by British composers, these being "A Norfolk Rhapsody," by R. Vaughan Williams ; an overture, "In Springtime," by Norman O'Neill ; a prelude, "Sappho," by Granville Bantock ; a suite for flute and piano by Edwin York Bowen ; an overture, "In Memoriam," by George Halford ; a music-poem, "Epithalamium," by G. H. Foulds ; and a symphony, "Les Hommages," by Joseph Holbrooke.

The **Brass Band festival** at the Crystal Palace, Sept. 29th, aroused great interest ; the principal prize was won by the Wingate Temperance Band, W. Rimmer, conductor.

1907

There was great musical activity in England during 1907. This country, indeed, seems to be becoming **the musical centre of Europe**, judging from the number of concerts given in London and the principal provincial cities during the year by **distinguished foreign soloists**. Several native-born composers won increased popularity by their new works—notably Hubert Parry and Granville Bantock—but no really great composition was brought out during the twelve months under review.

Provincial Festivals.

Three important provincial festivals were held, the first being the 184th meeting of the Cathedral choirs of **Worcester, Hereford, and Gloucester**, which took place at Gloucester. The programme was mainly made up of familiar works — "Elijah," "The Apostles," "The Kingdom," "Messiah," Verdi's "Requiem," Mendelssohn's "Hymn of Praise," and Hubert Parry's "The Love that casteth out Fear ;" the only noteworthy novelty was Granville Bantock's cantata "Christ in the Wilderness," the solos in which were rendered by Agnes Nicholls and Ffrangcon Davies. The principal conductor was Herbert Brewer, whose effective composition "Emmaus" was revived during the week.

No fewer than eight **novelties** were produced at the **Cardiff Festival**, the most prominent being Hubert Parry's symphonic poem "**A Vision of Life**," a work which materially adds to his reputation. This inspiring cantata was splendidly interpreted by the choir and the soloists, Agnes Nicholls and Ivor Foster, and the difficult instrumental passages were well played by the London Symphony Orchestra. Arthur Hervey's tone-poem "Summer," Hamilton Harty's setting of Keats's Ode to a Nightingale, and Frederic Cowen's delicate version of Elizabeth Browning's poem "He giveth His Beloved sleep," were also successfully brought forward. The other novelties were Herbert Brewer's cantata, "Sir Patrick Spens," two orchestral "Norfolk Rhapsodies" by R. Vaughan Williams, David Evans's cantata "The Coming of Arthur," and the second part of Granville Bantock's version of "Omar Khayyam." Familiar works performed during the festival, which was a great artistic success, were "The Kingdom," "The Golden Legend," Bach's "Phœbus and Pan," Schubert's Mass in E flat, Cæsar Franck's 150th Psalm, and Haydn's "Spring."

Six new works were included in the festival programme at Leeds, all by British composers. That which aroused the greatest interest was Charles Stanford's impressive "Stabat Mater," the solos in which were sung by Gladys Honey (a R.C.M. student who deputised for Agnes Nicholls), Kirkby Lunn, Gervase Elwes, and Plunket Greene. There were many commendable points in R. Vaughan Williams's setting of Walt Whitman's "Toward the Unknown Region" and in Granville Bantock's "Sea Wanderers," a work in which a fog-horn is employed in the orchestra. Herbert Brewer, Arthur Somervell and Rutland Boughton were the other composers honoured with commissions. The standard compositions which attracted large audiences were "The Kingdom," Mozart's "Requiem," Bach's Mass in B minor, Beethoven's "Choral" Symphony, and a selection from "Israel in Egypt," in all of which the Leeds choir won well-merited commendation.

Opera in London.

There were **three opera seasons at Covent Garden**. The first, opened on Jan. 14th, was under the direction of Ernest van Dyck, and was devoted to German works. Notably attractive were the representations of "**Die Meistersinger**," with Fritz Feinhals as Hans Sachs, Allen Hinckley as Pogner, and Hans Bussard as David. In "**Tristan und Isolde**" the principal parts were effectively sustained by van Dyck and Felia Litvinne, Marie Brema being the Brangäne. **Interesting revivals** of Weber's "Der Freischutz," of Smetana's "Die Verkaufte Braut," of Nicolai's "Die Lustigen Weiber von Windsor," and of Beethoven's "Fidelio," marked the season. The operas revived were as follows, the number of performances being stated in brackets : "Lohengrin" (6), "Die Meistersinger" (5), "Der Fliegende Holländer" (4), "Die Walküre" (4), "Tristan" (3), "Fidelio" (3), "Der Freischutz" (3), "Die Verkaufte Braut" (3), "Die Lustigen Weiber" (2), and "Tannhäuser" (2). The conductors were Eugene Ysaye, Franz Schalk, Leopold Reichwein, and Arthur Nikisch.

The "**grand**" **season** started on April 30th with "Das Rheingold," the first of a series of "Ring" cycles. In "Die Walküre," Ernst Kraus and Fliescher-Edel were the lovers, and Ellen Gulbranson the Brunnhilde. The performances of "Siegfried" were notable for the fine singing of Ernst Kraus in the part of the young hero, of Clarence Whitehill as the Wanderer, of Hans Bechstein as the Mime, and of Ellen Gulbranson as the Brunnhilde. Anton van Rooy made his reappearance as Hans Sachs in "Die Meistersinger," supported by Carl Jörn as Walther, Frieda Hempel as Eva, Paul Knupfer as Pogner, Hans Bechstein as David, and Joseph Geis as Beckmesser—a brilliant cast. Heinrich Knote distinguished himself as Tannhäuser, and in "Lohengrin" Peter Cornelius sustained the title *rôle*,

Fleischer-Edel was the Elsa, and Kirkby Lunn the Ortruda. There were excellent performances of "Der Fliegende Holländer," with van Rooy and Emmy Destinn in the leading parts. In "Die Lustigen Weiber von Windsor" Frieda Hempel and Cilla Tolli were the "merry wives," Erna Fiebiger the Anne Page, and Paul Knupfer the Falstaff. On June 20th Ponchielli's "La Gioconda" was revived, with Emmy Destinn in the title *rôle*. Catalani's "Die Loreley" was the only novelty given during the season, being produced on July 12th. Melba and Caruso sang several times in "La Bohème," and the Australian prima donna also appeared in a popular revival of "Lucia di Lammermoor," supported by Antonio Scotti as Ashton and Alessandro Bonci as Edgardo. Pauline Donalda sang in the single representation of Gounod's "Faust," with Fernando Carpi as the hero, and Emmy Destinn delighted crowded audiences by her admirable impersonation of the unhappy geisha in "Madama Butterfly." The season's repertoire consisted of the following operas: "La Bohème" (9), "Madama Butterfly" (7), "La Traviata" (5), "Cavalleria Rusticana" (5), "Pagliacci" (4), "Rigoletto" (4), "La Tosca" (4), "Aïda" (3), "Bastien und Bastienne" (3), "Der Fliegende Holländer" (3), "La Gioconda" (3), "Hansel und Gretel" (3), "Lucia" (3), "Die Meistersinger" (3), "Tannhäuser" (3), "Die Walküre" (3), "Götterdämmerung" (2), "Siegfried" (2), "Das Rheingold" (2), "Die Lustigen Weiber" (2), "Loreley" (2), "Lohengrin" (2), "Fedora" (2), "Carmen" (2), "Un Ballo in Maschera" (2), "Andrea Chenier" (2), "Faust" (1). The conductors were Hans Richter, Cleofonte Campanini, Ettore Panizza, and Percy Pitt.

On Oct. 3rd another season was started, the opening performance being a fine interpretation of "Madama Butterfly," with Rina Giachetti in the title *rôle*. Francesca Vignas made his reappearance the following night as Turiddu in "Cavalleria Rusticana"; the second part of the programme consisted of "Pagliacci." Great enthusiasm was aroused by the reappearance of Maria Gay in "Carmen," an opera which was frequently given during the season. In "Faust," Julia Lindsay distinguished herself as Marguerite. Felia Litvinne and Jeanne Paquot represented the principal women in "Aïda," and in "Rigoletto" the Australian prima donna, Lalla Miranda, reappeared as Gilda, after a long absence from England. The revival of "La Tosca" served for the début of Edith de Lis, an accomplished dramatic vocalist, and another interesting first appearance was that of the Irish tenor John McCormack, on Oct. 15th, as Turiddu. Amid considerable enthusiasm Luisa Tetrazzini, who had worthily been described as the "new Patti," made her début on Nov. 2nd in "Traviata," this memorable performance being conducted by Ettore Panizza. This Italian prima donna electrified crowded audiences by her wonderful singing in "Lucia di Lammermoor" and in "Rigoletto." The only new work produced during the season was Alberto Franchetti's spectacular opera "Germania," Nov. 13th, which was favourably received. There were attractive revivals of "La Gioconda," "La Bohème," and "Don Giovanni."

The Moody-Manners Company had a successful season of opera in English at the Lyric, commencing July 15th. One novelty was produced, a one-act work by Hermann Löhr entitled "Sarenna," which achieved a fair success. On July 26th John Coates made his first appearance in England as Lohengrin. The operas performed were: "Faust" (11), "Tannhäuser" (10), "Lohengrin" (10), "Madama Butterfly" (9), "La Bohème" (5), "Cavalleria Rusticana"

(5), "Pagliacci" (5), "Il Trovatore" (4), "Aïda" (4), "Figaro" (3), "Tristan" (2), "Merry Wives of Windsor" (2), "Greysteel" (1), and "Sarenna" (1).

In April Offenbach's "Tales of Hoffmann" was successfully revived at the Adelphi by a Berlin company under the direction of Hans Gregor. The prima donna was Hedwig Franzillo-Kauffmann, and Jean Nadolovitch impersonated Hoffmann. The Komische Oper Orchestra, directed by Fritz Cassirer, was engaged. Of this beautiful work 45 consecutive performances were given.

Prominent Societies.

Interesting programmes were submitted at the various concerts given by the Philharmonic Society. The first, on Feb. 6th, was conducted by Edouard Colonne. On March 13th Christian Sinding, the Norwegian composer, directed a performance of his violin concerto in A, the soloist being Johannes Wolff. Among the other artistes who appeared during the season were Sophie Menter, Teresa Carreno, Vladimir de Pachmann, Johanne Stockmarr, Marie Brema, Clara Butt, Amy Castles, Felix Senius, Kennerley Rumford, Mischa Elman, and Lady Hallé.

Several new works were brought forward by the London Choral Society at Queen's Hall. On Feb. 4th Enrico Bossi's "Paradise Lost" was given for the first time in England, but failed to arouse the enthusiasm with which it had been received in Italy. Dalhousie Young's setting of "The Blessed Damozel" proved more attractive. The general public, however, preferred familiar works such as Saint-Saens's "Samson and Delilah" and Elgar's "The Dream of Gerontius," the latter being performed at the complimentary concert on June 22nd to this Society's enthusiastic conductor Arthur Fagge.

The Royal Choral Society, directed by Frederick Bridge, the Royal Amateur Orchestral Society, conducted by Ernest Ford, the Handel Society, the Bach Choir, the Mozart Society, and the Oriana Madrigal Society, provided attractive concerts during the year.

Various conductors appeared at the concerts given by the London Symphony Orchestra. Hans Richter directed several, and, by way of commemorating his 30 years' association with music in this country, a special programme, devoted to the works of Beethoven, was performed in his honour on June 3rd. Wassili Safonoff conducted two concerts in May, and introduced new works at each. A new violin suite[in]E, Op. 68, by Alexander Mackenzie, was the feature of another concert, and was brilliantly performed under the composer's direction, the soloist being Mischa Elman. The Leeds Philharmonic Chorus and the Sheffield Choir visited London to take part in two programmes arranged by the directors of this enterprising organisation.

Noteworthy Concerts.

The thirteenth season of Promenade Concerts at Queen's Hall commenced on Aug 17th, and lasted for ten weeks. Nearly every evening there was a crowded audience to listen to the attractive programmes arranged by Henry Wood. The performance of Beethoven's symphonies and piano concertos in chronological order proved of great value to earnest musicians, who also welcomed the inclusion in the repertoire of less familiar works, such as Mozart's concerto for three pianos and Beethoven's trio for two oboes and cor anglais. Eighteen novelties by British composers were produced, five being by musicians who were comparatively unknown—Frederic Austin's orchestral rhapsody "Spring," F. C. Barker's violin concerto, Havergal Brain's "English" suite and the overture "For Valour," and Felix White's "Shylock" overture. Of the other British novelties the most important was the piano concerto of Frederic Delius, if only because of the peculiar position of this composer, whose music has attained a great reputation in Germany while at home it is practically unknown. The list also included the fourth of Edward Elgar's "Pomp and Circumstance" marches, Roger Quilter's "Serenade," Hamilton Harty's "Comedy" overture, Frank Bridge's symphonic poem "Isabella," and Walford Davies's "Holiday Tunes." No fewer than 105 soloists took part in the concerts, the pianists including Fanny Davies, Mathilde Verne, Irene Scharrer, Edwin York-Bowen, Percy Grainger, and Edward Isaacs, who introduced his own concerto in C sharp minor.

The **Queen's Hall Orchestra's symphony concerts** attracted large audiences, and among the novelties introduced was a concertstück by Ernst von Dohnanyi, which was brought forward on Feb. 2nd, the soloist being Hugo Becker. Fritz Kreisler, Teresa Carreno, Richard Buhlig and Raoul Pugno also played at these concerts.

Charles Santley's jubilee as a professional singer was commemorated by a festival concert at the Royal Albert Hall on May 1st. A cheque for £2160 was subsequently presented to him, and on the King's birthday he received the honour of knighthood.

The **Upsala Students' Choir** gave three concerts at Queen's Hall directed by J. E. Hedenblad.

Joseph Holbrooke continued his modern English Chamber Concerts at the Salle Erard, and introduced several new works by native-born composers. **Thomas Dunhill** also arranged a series of British concerts on similar lines.

The **Blackpool Glee and Madrigal Society,** conducted by Herbert Whittaker, gave a concert on March 5th at Queen's Hall, when a promising young soprano, Clara Butterworth, a student at the Royal Academy, made her début.

On June 15th there was a **festival performance** of "Elijah" at the Crystal Palace, conducted by Frederic Cowen, the solo-quartet consisting of Agnes Nicholls, Ada Crossley, Ben Davies, and Charles Santley. A fortnight later in the same building the **Tonic Sol-Fa Association** held its jubilee festival.

The **Joachim Quartet** had arranged to give seven concerts devoted to the works of Haydn, Mozart and Beethoven, at Bechstein Hall in April, but owing to the illness, which eventually proved fatal, of the famous violinist, they were postponed until June. Carl Halir then took the first violin parts, Karl Klingler being the second violinist, Emanuel Wirth playing the viola, and Robert Hausmann the 'cello. Among the assistants at some of the concerts were Fanny Davies, Alfred Gibson, Frank Bridge, Manuel Gomez, Wilfred James, and Adolf Borsdorf.

Attractive concerts were also provided by the Walenn, the Wessely and the Hambourg Quartets. The Brodsky Quartet played at Queen's Hall at one of the Grieg Memorial Concerts.

An orchestra of **1000 juvenile violinists** selected from the elementary schools of London played at the Alexandra Palace on June 22nd, conducted by Allen Gill.

Distinguished Visitors.

In addition to the names mentioned above many other distinguished foreign musicians visited England during 1907. The **vocalists** included Rodolfa Lhombino, Julia Culp, Lylli Zachner, Ida Kopetschni, Theodora Salicath, Tilly Koenen, Suzanne Morival, Elena Gerhardt (who made her début on April 11th with Arthur Nikisch as her accompanist), Helène Staegemann, Sven Scholander, and Carlos Ronzevalle. Among the **violinists** were Audrey Richardson, Haidee Voorzanger, Adolf Rebner, Joska Szigeti, Aldo Antonietti, Franz von Vecsey, Floris Ondricek, Oskar Back, Plotenj Worth, Kubelik, Francis Macmillen, and Johann Kruse. The best of the **pianists** were Paderewski (who gave his only recital on June 18th at Queen's Hall), Alice Ripper, Mania Seguel, Marie Bender, Cecile Chaminade, Else Gipser, Gottfried Galston, Julian Pascal, Ludovic Breitner, Basil Sapellnikoff, Bruno Mugellini, Leopold Godowsky, Emil Sauer, and Jacques Pintel. Among other **notable musicians,** whose visit is worthy of record, are Max Fiedler (conductor, début June 25th), Alexander Birnbaum (conductor, début June 27th), Reynaldo Hahn, Sergei Kussewitzky (double-bass soloist), Jean Gerardy, Emil Mylnarski (conductor, début Oct. 19th), Emil Sjögren (Scandinavian composer and pianist), and Charles Harriss (the Canadian conductor, who directed an Empire concert at Queen's Hall on May 24th.

1908

The increasing interest taken by the public in the art of music was shown by the number of concerts given during 1908, and considerable attention was paid to the works of British composers, some by Granville Bantock, Frederick Delius, Hamilton Harty, Joseph Holbrooke, and Montague Phillips being particularly appreciated. Edward Elgar brought forward two orchestral suites based on his juvenile opera "The Wand of Youth," and he also completed his first symphony.

Opera at Covent Garden.

The year opened at Covent Garden with some performances by the **Carl Rosa Company,** the most interesting being the revival on Jan. 3rd of Goring Thomas's "Esmeralda," in which the title-rôle was vivaciously sustained by Elizabeth Burgess, Walter Wheatley representing the Captain of the Guard, Arthur Winckworth the infatuated Priest, and Charles Victor the Hunchback.

On Jan. 27th the **Grand Opera Syndicate** gave two cycles in English (Frederick Jameson's translation) of "Der Ring des Nibelungen," conducted by Hans Richter. The majority of the characters were impersonated by British singers, and among those who distinguished themselves were Maud Perceval Allen, who made her stage début on Feb. 1st as Brunnhilde in "The Twilight of the Gods," Caroline Hatchard, Agnes Nicholls, and Walter Hyde, the last-mentioned having previously won fame in musical comedy. Siegfried was represented by Peter Cornelius, Hans Bechstein was the Mime, and Clarence Whitehill did well as Wotan. The performances throughout were remarkably good and were well patronised.

The "grand" season opened on April 30th and lasted for thirteen weeks. The **conductors** were Hans Richter, Cleofonte Campanini, Ettore Panizza, and Percy Pitt; and the following were the **works performed** with the number of representations: "Aida" (4), "Armide" (2), "Barbiere di Siviglia" (6), "La Bohème" (5), "Carmen" (2), "Cavalleria Rusticana" (4), Gounod's "Faust" (2),

"Fedora" (1), "Der Fliegender Holländer" (2), "Götterdämmerung" (2), "Lucia di Lammermoor" (6), "Madame Butterfly" (5), "Manon Lescaut" (3), "Die Meistersinger" (3), "Otello" (5), "Pagliacci" (4), "I Pescatori di Perle" (3), "Rigoletto" (5), "Tannhäuser" (2), "La Tosca" (2), "Traviata" (7), "Tristan" (3), "Gli Ugonotti" (3), and "Die Walküre" (3). The season was memorable for the vocal triumphs of **Melba** and **Tetrazzini**, and for the artistic efforts of such "**stars**" as Emmy Destinn, John McCormack, Mario Sammarco, Anton Van Rooy, Alessandro Bonci, and Giovanni Zenatello. Among the **new-comers** were Lina Cavalieri, Corinne Rider-Kelsey, Fely Dereyne, Edyth Walker, and Marie Edvina (the *nom de théâtre* of the Hon. Mrs. Cecil Edwardes).

On May 27th there was a **gala performance** in honour of the visit of the President of the French Republic, and the programme consisted of the first act of "I Pescatori di Perle," with Tetrazzini as Leila, and the garden scene from "Faust," in which Melba represented Marguerite.

To commemorate **Melba's 20th anniversary** at Covent Garden, the diva, by permission of the directors, gave an operatic matinee on June 24th, the proceeds of which were devoted to the London Hospital.

There was no season in the autumn.

The Provincial Festivals.

There were four important festivals in the autumn. The first was the 185th meeting of **the Three Choirs,** held in September at Worcester, and directed by Ivor Atkins. The programme included "The Dream of Gerontius," "The Kingdom," "Elijah," "Everyman," "Hymn of Praise," and Stanford's "Stabat Mater," the **chief novelties** being Hubert Parry's motet "Beyond these voices there is peace," and Granville Bantock's delightful orchestral prelude "The Pierrot of the Minute." Henry Wood conducted **the Sheffield Festival,** the features of which were Bach's "St. Matthew Passion," Verdi's "Manzoni Requiem," "Everyman," Franck's "Beatitudes," "Elijah," and Berlioz's "Te Deum"; in these works the splendid choir, trained by Henry Coward, won special distinction. **The 12th Bristol Festival,** directed by George Riseley, was noteworthy for the introduction of Charles Stanford's solemn setting of Alfred Tennyson's "Ode on the Death of Wellington." The familiar items in the programme were "Elijah," "King Olaf," Max Bruch's "Lay of the Bell," and the Choral Symphony. The last **festival** was that given at Norwich, Henry Wood being the conductor, and the works performed comprised "The Dream of Gerontius," Dvorak's "Stabat Mater," Bach's Magnificat in D and "Phœbus and Pan," "King Olaf," Brahms' "Requiem," Hugo Wolf's "Christmas Night," Debussy's "Blessed Damozel," "Elijah," the Choral Symphony, and a new cantata by Julius Harrison on the subject of "Cleopatra," which won the prize in the competition organised by the Committee.

Some Notable Concerts.

Conducted by Hans Richter and Arthur Nikisch, the **London Symphony Orchestra** provided several excellent concerts at Queen's Hall. On May 2nd the programme included the prelude to the 2nd act of Ethel Smyth's opera "**The Wreckers,**" which work was performed in the same building some days later, the leading rôles being sustained by Blanche Marchesi, Anna El-Tour, John Coates, and Hamilton Earle.

At the **London Choral Society's concert** on Feb. 12th, Arthur Fagge introduced a selection

from Henry Waller's opera "Fra Francesco," a work originally produced in Berlin, and a sacred cantata, "The Beatitudes," by Edward Maryon, the pseudonym of Comte d'Aulby de Gatigny, which was repeated on April 1st. No novelty was performed by the Royal Choral Society.

There were seven attractive concerts arranged by the **Philharmonic Society,** and they were directed by Henry Wood, Frederic Cowen, Landon Ronald, and Arthur Nikisch. Among the notable artists to appear were Jeno Hubay and Jean Sibelius. At the fourth concert the programme included a clever viola concerto by Edwin York-Bowen, the soloist being Lionel Tertis.

On March 14th the **Queen's Hall Orchestra** gave the first performance of Haydn's divertimento for wind instruments on the "Chorale Sancti Antonii," the manuscript of which had been discovered in the Royal library at Berlin.

The fourteenth season of **Promenade Concerts at Queen's Hall,** under the direction of Henry Wood, proved extremely attractive. Six new works by native composers were introduced, the most important being Balfour Gardiner's symphony in E flat. Considerable attention was paid during the season to French music, and some concerts were conducted by Edouard Colonne. For the opening of the new **St. James's Hall** in Great Portland Street a series of Promenade Concerts had been arranged, the first taking place on April 25th.

Wilhelm Ganz celebrated his artistic diamond jubilee by a concert at Queen's Hall on May 26th, at which Patti sang. The diva reappeared at the Albert Hall on Nov. 4th, at a concert given "in aid of poor children."

Two performances of Gluck's "Iphigenia in Tauris" were given in June by the students of the **Guildhall School of Music** in their own theatre. On Jan. 21st the **Royal College of Music** students revived at His Majesty's Verdi's "Falstaff."

Interesting **chamber concerts,** mainly devoted to English compositions, were provided by Joseph Holbrooke and Thomas Dunhill. The former composer's setting of Herbert Trench's poem "On Human Immortality" was performed in darkness at Queen's Hall on Jan. 20th, the work being entitled "Apollo and the Seaman."

Alys Lorraine, a gifted operatic soprano, gave an unconventional recital at Bechstein Hall on June 10th, the programme being confined to the compositions of Royal musicians, those represented including Henry VIII., Charles I., Henri IV., Marie Antoinette, the German Emperor, Duke Ernst II., the Prince Consort, and Princess Henry of Battenberg.

The famous German choir, **the Kölner Männer Gesangverein,** visited London in June for two concerts at Queen's Hall, which were conducted by Joseph Schwartz, and which aroused considerable interest.

Sergei Kussewitzky, the double-bass virtuoso, conducted an orchestral concert at Queen's Hall on May 26th, at which Sergei Rachmaninoff made his début in England as a pianist and composer. The programme included the first symphony of the deceased Russian musician Basil Kalinnikoff.

On Nov. 15th Georg Szell, a native of Buda-Pesth, where he was born in 1897, appeared at the Albert Hall both as a pianist and as a composer, his work in the latter capacity being an overture in E, which was well received and brilliantly performed by the London Symphony Orchesta, conducted by Landon Ronald.

Among the **other musical visitors to England** during the year who either gave recitals or assisted at concerts were : **conductors,** Camille Saint-Saens, Emil Mylnarski, Moritz Moszkowski (who on Feb. 19th gave an entertainment

Sir Augustus Harris

Emmy Destinn as Tess

Enrico Bevignani   Alberto Randegger   Luigi Mancinelli

devoted to his own compositions), and Claud Debussy; **pianists**, Ignaz Paderewski (whose only recital took place on June 23rd), Vladimir de Pachmann, Wassily Sapellnikoff, Ferrucio Busoni, Emil Sauer, Raoul Pugno, Archy Rosenthal, Ossip Gabrilowitsch, Richard Buhlig, Sigismond Stojowski, Leopold Godowsky, Alma Haas, Tina Lerner, Sofie Menter, Teresa Carreno, and Jolanda Mero; **violinists**, Leopold Auer, Mischa Elman, Fritz Kreisler, Ephrem Zimbalist, Willy Burmester, Ferencz Hegedus, and Kathleen Parlow; **singers**, Tilly Koenen, Clara Clemens (a daughter of "Mark Twain"), Elena Gerhardt, Helene Staegemann, Julia Culp, Antonio Dolores, Charles Clark, Hugo Heinz, Ludwig Wullner, Emile Engel, and Fery Lulek.

1909

There was remarkable musical activity in this country during 1909, especially in the domain of grand opera. Early in the year efforts were made to establish **English Opera** on a firm basis; but so far these schemes have made little progress, the projectors recognising that there are few British composers of the day who have won distinction in this branch of work—a fact which may, of course, be attributed to the lack of opportunity to exhibit their talent in this direction. It was particularly gratifying to note the increasing interest taken by continental audiences in several home-trained vocalists and instrumentalists; their tours in Europe were not only artistic but financial successes.

Opera at Covent Garden.—The year opened at England's only opera-house with some performances in English, commencing on Jan. 16th with three cycles of "Der Ring des Nibelungen," under the direction of Hans Richter. Nearly all engaged in the four works were of British nationality; but having failed to find a satisfactory Siegfried in London, the management secured the services of Peter Cornelius. On Jan. 27th the Grand Opera Syndicate produced E. W. Naylor's "The Angelus," a work which met with a fair amount of success, thanks in no small measure to the excellent singing of Florence Easton, Francis Maclennan, and Robert Radford in the leading rôles. The performances during this short season were "Rheingold" (3 times), "Siegfried" (3), "Die Walküre" (4), "Götterdämmerung" (3), "Die Meistersinger" (4), "The Angelus" (2), and "Madame Butterfly" (4).

On April 26th the "grand" season was auspiciously opened with the first stage performance in England of Saint-Saëns's **"Samson et Dalila,"** a delightful work which had not previously received the Censor's licence owing to its Biblical story, but which had become familiar to musicians through its frequent interpretation in cantata form. This opera, in which Kirkby Lunn and Charles Fontaine sustained the leading rôles, was most picturesquely presented, and was a great attraction. The following month, on May 21st, the management brought forward Claude Debussy's **"Pelléas et Mélisande,"** another novelty which now the favour of the public, and which would have been more frequently performed had it been possible to keep all the artistes in town. In this delightful "dream-drama" Rose Feart was the Mélisande, Emma Trentini the boy Yniold, Vanni Marcoux the garrulous but good-natured Arkel, Jacques Bourbon the Goulaud, and Edmond Warnery the Pelléas. The composer specially travelled to this country to assist at the rehearsals, and the general pro-

duction was cordially eulogised by him. The third new work was Charpentier's "Louise," first performed on June 18th, with Marie Edvina (the Hon. Mrs. Cecil Edwardes) in the title-rôle, Charles Dalmores as the lover Julien, Anna Berat as the heroine's mother, and Charles Gilibert as the father. Another novelty was "Tess," by Frederic d'Erlanger, which proved to be a melodious musical version of Thomas Hardy's novel. The composer was fortunate in having Emmy Destinn to represent the chief character, the other prominent parts being sustained by Giovanni Zenatello as Angel Clare, Mario Sammarco the Alec, Charles Gilibert the Jack, and Edith de Lys as Aby. During the season Luisa Tetrazzini was heard in several "classics," including "Sonnambula," "Rigoletto," "Traviata," and "Lucia," and there were crowded audiences whenever she sang. The **new-comers** who made their mark were Marie Kousnietzoff, a Russian prima donna whose singing in "Faust" and "La Bohème" pleased the patrons; Mary Beral, for whom "Armide" was specially revived, with Kirkby Lunn as La Haine and Charles Fontaine as Renaud; and Leo Slezak, a magnificent tenor, who made his rentrée as Otello in Verdi's opera, the Desdemona being Marie Edvina. The following is a list of the **works performed during the season**—which was extended to July 31st—with the number of representations of each: "Samson et Dalila" (9), "Madame Butterfly" (7), "Aida" (6), "Il Barbiere di Siviglia" (6), "La Bohème" (6), "Rigoletto" (6), "Traviata" (6), "Faust" (5), "Louise" (5), "Sonnambula" (4), "La Tosca" (4), "Cavalleria Rusticana" (3), "Lucia di Lammermoor" (3), "Otello" (3), "Pelléas et Mélisande" (3), "Pagliacci" (3), "Tess" (3), "Gli Ugonotti" (2), "Don Giovanni" (2), "Die Walküre" (2), and "Armide" (1). The conductors were Cleofonte Campanini, Ettore Panizza, Maurice Frigara, Percy Pitt, and Hans Richter, the last-mentioned directing the performances of "Die Walküre," the only work given in German, the revival being in honour of Minnie Saltzmann-Stevens, a superb Brunnhilde. Mention must also be made of the exhibition of solo dancing which was provided at the close of several performances by Marie Preobrajenska, the star of the ballet at the St. Petersburg opera-house.

In the autumn the **Carl Rosa Company** had a season at Covent Garden, starting on Oct. 18th with "Lohengrin," in which John Coates sustained the title-rôle. The conductors were Walter van Noorden and Eugene Goossens; and among the singers who assisted in the other revivals were Ina Hill, Doris Woodhall, Marie Alexander, Gertrude Vania, Arthur Winckworth, E. C. Hedmondt, and Edward Davies.

Other Opera Performances.—Thanks to the enterprise of Sir Herbert Tree, Londoners had an opportunity of hearing Ethel Smyth's opera "The Wreckers," a work which had previously been performed in Germany. The first representation at His Majesty's was on June 22nd, and the cast then included Clementine de Vere-Sapio as the heroine Thirza, Elizabeth Amsden as Avis, Lewys James as Laurence, and John Coates as Mark, Thomas Beecham directing the orchestra.

Joseph Holbrooke's two-act opera, "Pierrot and Pierrette," words by Walter Grogan, was produced here, also in connection with the Afternoon Theatre, on Nov. 11th, the cast consisting of Albert Archdeacon, Esta d'Argo, Katherine Jones, and Leon de Sousa.

The **Moody-Manners** annual season at the Lyric started on Aug. 14th with "Carmen," in which Zelie de Lussan sustained the title-rôle, Joseph O'Mara was the Don José, and Charles

Royal Opera   Covent Garden

Proprietors   THE GRAND OPERA SYNDICATE, LIMITED.

WINTER OPERA SEASON, 1909

General Manager   ...   ...   Mr. NEIL FORSYTH.
Musical Director   ...   Mr. PERCY PITT.

The Management earnestly request those who are unable to remain until the close of the last Act to leave during the interval immediately preceding it, and thus avoid disturbing the Artistes and the Audience while the Performance is actually proceeding.

NOTICE.

In order to facilitate the setting-down and taking-up of vehicular traffic it is requested that Cabs will draw up at the Two Outer Doors in Bow Street.

Friday, February 5th, at 8.15

THE ANGELUS

In a Prologue and Four Acts

(IN ENGLISH)

Music by E. W. NAYLOR, Mus. Doc.

Libretto by WILFRID THORNELY

Abbot Tunstall	...	Mr. ROBERT RADFORD
Francis	...	Mr. FRANCIS MACLENNAN
Beatrice	...	Miss FLORENCE EASTON
Lutteral	...	Mr. CLAUDE FLEMMING
Catherine	...	Miss EDITH CLEGG
Death	...	Mme. EDNA THORNTON
Sylvia	...	Mme. GLEESON-WHITE
A Nymph	...	Miss ALICE PROWSE
1st Monk	...	Mr. CHARLES KNOWLES
2nd Monk	...	Mr. ALBERT GARCIA
1st Villager	...	Mr. CAMPBELL-CARR
Conductor	...	Mr. PERCY PITT

Synopsis of Scenery :   Approximate times :
PROLOGUE. Interior of a Monastery.—Evening   8.15 to 8.50
ACT I.   A Village Green during a Feast-day   9.10 to 9.50
ACT II.   Interior of Catherine's Cottage.—A Week later   9.50 to 9.55
ACT III. Sacred Grove of the Temple of the Fates   10.10 to 10.50
ACT IV.   Interior of Catherine's Cottage. Winter   10.45 to 11

Produced by Mr. W. WIRK.

"The Ring of the Niblung"

By RICHARD WAGNER (1813-1883)

THIRD PERFORMANCE OF 3rd SERIES

Saturday, February 6th, at 7

THE VALKYRIE

In Three Acts

(IN ENGLISH)

English Version by Mr. FREDERICK JAMESON

The poem was written in 1852. The score was finished at Zurich, in 1856. The Pianoforte score was published in 1865. "Die Walküre" was first performed (at Munich) June 26th, 1870.

Mesdames SALTZMANN-STEVENS, GLEESON-WHITE, HATCHARD, EVANS, ROBERTS, YELLAND, PROWSE, CLEGG, ALEXANDER, JONES and FREASE-GREEN

Messrs. WALTER HYDE, RADFORD and WHITEHILL

Conductor   ...   Dr. HANS RICHTER

ACT I. 7 to 8   ACT II. 8.30 to 9.50   ACT III. 10.15 to 11.15

"The Ring of the Niblung"

By RICHARD WAGNER (1813-1883)

FOURTH PERFORMANCE OF 3rd SERIES.

Monday, February 8th, at 6.30

SIEGFRIED

In Three Acts

(IN ENGLISH)

English Version by Mr. FREDERICK JAMESON

The poem was written in 1851. The music took twelve years (1857—1869) to complete. "Tristan and Isolde" and "The Meistersinger" being also composed during the same period. "Siegfried" was first performed (at Bayreuth) August 16th, 1876.

Mesdames SALTZMANN-STEVENS, HATCHARD, and EDNA THORNTON

Messrs. CORNELIUS, BECHSTEIN, MEUX, HARFORD and WHITEHILL

Conductor   ...   Dr. HANS RICHTER

ACT I. 6.30 to 7.50   ACT II. 8.20 to 9.35   ACT III. 10 to 11.20

FIFTH PERFORMANCE OF 2nd SERIES.

Tuesday, February 9th, at 6.30

THE MASTERSINGERS

In Three Acts

(IN ENGLISH)

English Version by Mr. FREDERICK JAMESON

"Die Meistersinger von Nürnberg" was produced at Munich, under one flebow, June 21st, 1868 : in England, at Drury Lane, under Dr. Richter, May 30th, 1882.

Mesdames FREASE-GREEN and EDNA THORNTON

Messrs. WALTER HYDE, MEUX, RADFORD, D'OISLY, KNOWLES, GARCIA, DAWSON, HARFORD, FLEMMING, ROYD, BYNDON-AYRES, ROBERTS, MAXWELL and NISSEN

Apprentices :—Messrs. May, Twemlow, Aulchrook, Baker, Messrs. Knox, Alcanto, Potts, Butcher, Dawson, Tucker, Kilson-Green, Reynolds

Conductor   ...   Dr. HANS RICHTER

ACT I. 6.30 to 7.45   ACT II. 8.5 to 9   ACT III. 9.15 to 11.15

Wednesday, February 10th, at 8.15

MADAME BUTTERFLY

In Three Acts

(IN ENGLISH)

By GIACOMO PUCCINI (Born 1858)

The Opera is based on the Story of Madame Butterfly written by the American author, JOHN LUTHER LONG. It was dramatised by him and Mr. DAVID BELASCO and was seen at the Duke of York's Theatre, in London, on April 28th, 1900. The Italian version is by LUIGI ILLICA and GIUSEPPE GIACOSA ; it was produced at Covent Garden, on July 10th, 1905.

Madame Butterfly (Cio-Cio-San)		
	...	Miss FLORENCE EASTON
Suzuki	...	Miss EDITH CLEGG
Kate Pinkerton	...	Miss C. HATCHARD
F. B. Pinkerton	...	Mr. F. MACLENNAN
Sharpless	...	Mr. FREDERIC AUSTIN
Goro	...	Mr. BYNDON-AYRES
Prince Yamadori	...	Mr. ALBERT GARCIA
The Bonze	...	Mr. CHARLES KNOWLES
The Imperial Commissioner	Mr. FRANCIS HARFORD
The Official Registrar	Mr. H. TREADAWAY
Cio-Cio-San's Mother	Miss VITO
The Cousin	...	Miss G. TREVITT
Conductor	...	Mr. PERCY PITT

Synopsis of Scenery.   Approximate times :
ACT I.   A House near Nagasaki   ... 8.15 to 9.10
ACT II.   Interior of Butterfly's House   9.35 to 10.20
ACT III. The Same   ... ... 10.40 to 11.15

"The Ring of the Niblung"

By RICHARD WAGNER (1813-1883)

FIFTH PERFORMANCE OF 3rd SERIES.

Thursday, February 11th, at 6

The TWILIGHT of the GODS

In Three Acts

(IN ENGLISH)

English Version by Mr. FREDERICK JAMESON

The poem was begun as "Siegfried's Tod," June, 1848. The music was begun at Lucerne, 1870, and completely finished November, 1874. "Götterdämmerung" was first performed (at Bayreuth, under Dr. RICHTER) August 17th, 1876, on the day after the first performance of "Siegfried."

Mesdames SALTZMANN-STEVENS, EVANS, PROWSE, HATCHARD, JONES and EDNA THORNTON

Messrs. CORNELIUS, MEUX, KNOWLES and AUSTIN

Conductor   ...   Dr. HANS RICHTER

ACT I. 6 to ...   ACT II. 8.50 to 9.55   ACT III. 10.15 to 11.30

SEASON OF
GRAND OPERA IN ENGLISH

Prices for Single Performances of the Series : Pit and Grand-Tier Boxes, £4 4s. ; First-Tier Boxes, £2 12s. 6d., £2 2s. ; Second-Tier Boxes, £1 10s. ; Orchestra Stalls, 17s. 6d. ; Grand Circle, 1st Row, 17s. 6d., other Rows, 15s. ; First Circle, 1st Row, 17s. 6d., other Rows, 15s. ; Balcony Stalls, 12s. 6d. ; Amphitheatre Stalls, Rows 1—2, 9s., Rows 3—7, 6s. ; Gallery (Reserved), 5s.

Prices for Other Performances : Pit and Grand-Tier Boxes, £4 4s. and £3 3s. ; First-Tier Boxes, £1 11s. 6d. ; Second-Tier Boxes, 16s. ; Orchestra Stalls, 12s. 6d. and 10s. 6d. ; Grand Circle, 10s. 6d. and 7s. 6d. ; First Circle, 10s. 6d. and 7s. 6d. ; Balcony Stalls, 6s. ; Amphitheatre Stalls, 5s. and 4s. ; Amphitheatre (Unreserved), Admission, 1s. 6d.

No Performance on Friday, February 12th, when the Theatre will be required for the Fancy Dress Ball.

Sandwiches and Consommé supplied by the RITZ HOTEL, Piccadilly, on sale in the Theatre.

Acting Manager   -   Mr. PERCY EALES

Stage Manager, Mr. W. WIRK
Assistant Stage Manager, Mr. H. G. MOORE

Musical Staff on Stage :
Messrs. S. P. WADDINGTON, EMIL KREUZ, H. GRUNEBAUM, R. CHELAS and W. WILTSHIRE.

Chorus under direction of Mr. E. KREUZ.

Organ supplied by the "Positive" Organ Co. Ltd. 44, Mornington Crescent, London, N.W.
Pianos exclusively by C. BECHSTEIN, Bechstein Hall, Wigmore Street, London, W.

Costume Designer M. COMELLI   Scenic Artist, Mr. HARRY BROOKE
Machinist, Mr. R. AFFLECK   Electrician, Mr. WM. CRAWSHAW
Properties, Mr. W. CLARKSON

Doors Open Half-an-Hour before the Performance commences.

Box Office Open from 10 to 10.
Telephones : 463-4 Gerrard.   2105 Gerrard.

Moorhouse the Escamilio. Subsequently came interesting revivals of "Die Meistersinger," "Madame Butterfly," "Faust," "Lohengrin" (with Philip Brozel as the Knight), "Aïda," "Tannhauser," and "Rienzi." The only new work introduced was a one-act opera by Alick Maclean, entitled "Ma tre Seiler." The libretto of this is based on the Erckmann-Chatrian story of "The Unterwald Wedding," and the music is bright and effective. At the first performance, Aug. 20th, Lewys James appeared as the elderly lawyer, Seth Hughes as the gallant lover Wilhelm, Raymonde Amy as his sweetheart Lotte, and Charles Magrath as her father.

Herold's "Pré aux Clercs" was revived by the students of the Guildhall School of Music in May, and in the performances at that institution Lilian Allen appeared as Marguerite and Alfred Steed as Mergy.

On June 21st The City of Rome Children's Company commenced a short season at Terry's, during which the talented juveniles gave "La Sonnambula," "Lucia," Strauss's "Primavera," and "The Geisha."

Castellano's opera company, assisted by Maria Galvany and Maria Gay, visited Drury Lane Theatre, and opened the season on May 31st with "Trovatore." Later came revivals of "Rigoletto," "Don Pasquale," "Ernani," "Dinorah," "Norma," "L'Elisir d'Amore," "Orfeo," and "Il Barbiere." A few weeks previously the company appeared at the Coronet, where on April 30th Leoncavallo's "Zaza" was given for the first time in this country. On May 10th came the first representation of Domenico Monleone's "Cavalleria Rusticana," a work that suffers by comparison with Mascagni's version of the same story.

Four important festivals were held in the autumn. The first was that at Hereford, the 186th meeting of the cathedral choirs of Gloucester, Hereford, and Worcester, which took place on Sept. 5th, 7th, 8th, 9th, and 10th. The conductor, G. R. Sinclair, was fortunate in being able to include in the programme a beautiful unaccompanied part-song by Edward Elgar, entitled "Go, song of mine," a setting of a little poem by Guido Cavalcanti which had been "translated" by Rossetti. The other choral novelties were Schubert's unfinished oratorio "Lazarus," and H. Walford Davies's cantata "Noble Numbers." Among the familiar works performed were "Elijah," "Messiah," "The Apostles," "Job," the first part of "Creation," and selections from "Die Walküre" and "Parsifal."

The Musical League's festival at Liverpool on Sept. 24th and 25th was directed principally by Mr. Harry Evans, and nearly all the works heard at the three concerts were by British composers, among them Arnold Bax, Havergal Brian, R. Vaughan Williams, Joseph Holbrooke, Joseph Hathaway, and Frederic Austin.

Hans Richter conducted the Birmingham festival, Oct. 5th, 6th, 7th, and 8th, at which the chief novelties were Rutland Boughton's chorus "A Song at Midnight," and the third part of Granville Bantock's "Omar Khayyám," the first section of which was introduced at the 1906 festival, while the second was heard at the Cardiff gathering in 1907. Among the well-known works presented were "Elijah," "Judas Maccabeus," "The Dream of Gerontius," Dvořák's "Stabat Mater," Brahms's "Song of Destiny," Berlioz's "Faust," and Cherubini's Mass in C.

On Oct. 20th, 21st, and 22nd an attractive festival was held at Newcastle-on-Tyne, and was directed by Henry Coward and Wassily Safonoff. Haydn's oratorio "The Return of Tobias" was given for the first time in this country, and the other novelties comprised Rutland Boughton's "The Invincible Armada," Edgar Bainton's overture-phantasy "Prometheus," and Henry Hadley's tone-poem "Salome." "Elijah" and "The Kingdom" were the leading choral works.

The Handel-Mendelssohn festival was held at the Crystal Palace on June 19th, 22nd, 24th, and 26th, under the direction of Frederic Cowen. "Elijah" and "Messiah" attracted the largest audiences, and on the "selection day" the programme included the "Hymn of Praise" and excerpts from "Israel in Egypt," in which the fine chorus was heard to the best advantage.

Mention must also be made of the National Eisteddfod, held for the first time in London at the Royal Albert Hall in June. In the chief choral competition the first prize was awarded to the Pembroke Dock Choral Society.

Apart from the new compositions mentioned above, many others were brought forward by various organisations at Queen's Hall. On Feb. 15th Alick Maclean's "The Annunciation" was successfully introduced by the Sheffield Musical Union, with Agnes Nicholls, Edna Thornton, Gervase Elwes, and Robert Barnett as the soloists. A brilliant composition, "A Mass of Life," by Frederick Delius, won favour on June 7th at a concert directed by Thomas Beecham. Two days later Charles Stanford's whimsical setting of C. L. Graves's "Ode to Discord" proved entertaining to a crowded and expectant audience, the soloists being Cicely Gleeson-White and Plunket Greene. In commemoration of the death of Haydn and the birth of Tennyson, this distinguished composer wrote a choral overture, "Ave atque Vale," which was impressively performed at a Bach Choir concert on March 2nd. The new Queen's Hall Choral Society made its début on March 30th, when, conducted by Franco Leoni, the members sang a clever work by Hubert Bath, "The Wedding of Shon Maclean." At Joseph Holbrooke's concert on June 25th the programme included an excerpt from his new opera "Dylan," the libretto of which has been written by T. E. Ellis, a name that represents Lord Howard de Walden. Various other novelties by British composers were also introduced by the Philharmonic Society, by the New Symphony Orchestra (conducted by Landon Ronald), and at the Promenade Concerts, which ran from Aug. 14th to Oct. 23rd.

Several concerts were given in commemoration of the centenary of Mendelssohn's birth, the best being that provided by the London Choral Society on Feb. 3rd, when "Elijah" was performed under the direction of Arthur Fagge.

Sergei Kussewitzky conducted two interesting concerts devoted to Russian composers. At the first, May 11th, Scriabine's Symphony in C minor was played by the London Symphony Orchestra. The second, held on May 25th, was noteworthy for the début in this country of the famous Russian tenor, Leonid Sobinoff.

At the London Symphony Orchestra Concert on April 7th, directed by Hans Richter, Bach's triple pianoforte concerto in C was played by Leonard Borwick, Donald Francis Tovey, and York Bowen.

On New Year's Day Edward Elgar conducted for the first time his symphony at the Queen's Hall Orchestra's concert. This work was frequently played during the year, especially during January and February.

Distinguished Visitors.—Many famous musicians visited England during 1909. The composers included Jean Sibelius, Vincent d'Indy, Claude Debussy, Max Reger, and Charles Widor; while among the conductors were Camille Chevillard, Luigi Mancinelli, Bruno Walter, Arthur Nikisch, Emil Mlynarski, and

FACING PAGE: *Covent Garden programme for* The Angelus, *February 5th, 1909.*

Wassily Safonoff. The vocalists comprised Emma Calvé (who reappeared on June 16th), Lilian Nordica (who gave a farewell concert June 17th), Selma Kurz, Signe von Rappe, Elena Gerhardt, Alice Verlet, Schumann-Heink, Anita Rio, Jeanne Darlays, Helene Stylianides, Anton van Rooy, Reinhold von Warlich, and Georg Henschel. Among the foreign instrumentalists were Teresa Carreno (whose farewell recital was held on March 11th), Jolanda Mero, Katherine Ruth Heyman, Vera Jachles, Irene Gorainoff (début May 26th), Pepita Arriola, Ferrucio Busoni, Leopold Godowsky (who only appeared on May 15th), Vladimir de Pachmann, Moritz Rosenthal, Gottfried Galston, Emil Sauer, Basil Sapellnikoff, and Richard Buhlig; Erna Schulz, Fritz Kreisler, Jan Kubelik (farewell recital July 10th), Efrem Zimbalist, Francis Macmillen, and Jacques Thibaud; Serge Barjansky, a fine 'cellist, and Bokken Lasson, a popular lutenist.

1910

The most remarkable feature of the musical year was the extraordinary activity displayed in London in the domain of opera. At Covent Garden alone no fewer than three seasons were carried out. Of two of these the organiser and manager was **Mr. Thomas Beecham**, who, moreover, extended his enterprise by entering the field of light opera with a summer campaign at His Majesty's Theatre. His first season at Covent Garden was held from Feb. 19th to March 19th, and opened with the first performance in England of Richard Strauss's "**Elektra**." The production excited considerable interest, and was attended by their Majesties the late King Edward and Queen Alexandra. Mr. Beecham himself conducted an orchestra of 115, and the leading parts were sustained with notable skill by Edyth Walker (Elektra), Frances Rose (Chrysothemis), and Frau Mildenburg (Clytemnestra). The work was given nine times, two of the performances being conducted by Dr. Strauss. Another novelty brought to a hearing was Delius's "**The Village Romeo and Juliet**," the other operas staged being Sullivan's "Ivanhoe" (revived very elaborately after nineteen years), "Tristan und Isolde," Ethel Smyth's "The Wreckers," "Carmen," "Hänsel and Gretel," and "L'Enfant Prodigue," an early work of Debussy. Several native artists appeared during the season, including Perceval Allen, Edith Evans, Ruth Vincent, John Coates, Walter Hyde, Frederic Austin, and Harry Dearth.

Several interesting features marked **Mr. Beecham's subsequent venture** at His Majesty's Theatre, which lasted from May 12th to July 30th. The most popular work, judging by the number of representations it received, was Offenbach's "Tales of Hoffmann." A French opera, " Muguette," by the late Edmund Missa, was produced, but, despite its graceful music, failed to create any particular impression. Massenet's "Werther" was given once, and there was a revival of Stanford's "Shamus O'Brien." A noteworthy feature was a Mozart festival, admirable performances being given of "Il Seraglio," "Le Nozze di Figaro," and "Cosi fan Tutte." These works were rendered in English, as were all the other operas mounted during the season. Johann Strauss's merry comic opera, "Die Fledermaus" ("The Bat"), was virtually a novelty, as it had never previously been performed in this country according to the composer's intentions; and July 9th witnessed the production of Richard

Strauss's "Feursnot," this so-called "comic" opera, the music of which is most elaborately wrought, dating from 1901. The remaining novelty was a clever one-act work by George H. Clutsam, the Australian composer, entitled "A Summer Night." Several of the artists who had appeared under Mr. Beecham's banner at Covent Garden were again heard at His Majesty's, together with Zélie de Lussan, Maggie Teyte, Caroline Hatchard, Joseph O'Mara, Lewys James, Robert Radford, and others.

In the course of the "grand" season at Covent Garden, which opened on April 23rd and concluded on July 30th, only one actual novelty was produced. This was "La Habanera," the work of a young French composer, Raoul Laparra, and it was introduced on July 18th. An exceedingly gruesome story militated against the success of the opera, although its music was acknowledged to be interesting and appropriate. Hélène Demellier, a singer new to London, made a favourable impression in the chief rôle. Melba (who returned after an absence of two years), Tetrazzini (for whom primarily Delibes's "Lakmé" was added to the répertoire), and Destinn were the season's foremost stars; and the principal newcomers were Zerola and Riccardo Martin, a young American singer, among the tenors, and George Baklanoff, a Russian baritone. Two cycles were given of **Wagner's** "**Ring**," under the direction of Hans Richter, who, however, owing to a breakdown in his health, was unfortunately unable to complete his duties as conductor. The operas performed, and the number of representations of each, were as follows: "Aïda" (5), "Barbiere di Siviglia" (6), "La Bohème" (6), "Faust" (5), "Götterdämmerung" (2), "La Habanera" (2), "Lakmé" (5), "Louise" (4), "Madama Butterfly" (5), "Manon Lescaut" (2), "Otello" (1), "Pelléas et Mélisande" (3), "Rheingold" (2), "Rigoletto" (5), "Siegfried" (2), "La Sonnambula" (2), "Samson et Dalila" (6), "Tess" (3), "La Tosca" (3), "La Traviata" (7), "Tristan und Isolde" (2), "Gli Ugonotti" (3), "Die Walküre" (2).

On Oct. 3rd **Mr. Thomas Beecham**, resuming away at Covent Garden, opened a three months' season of "grand" opera. In the first week was produced D'Albert's "Tiefland," a work which has enjoyed immense popularity all over Germany. Other novelties, as well as several of the "standard" operas, classic and modern, were presented during the season, many of the performances being in English. Mr. Beecham's company was a very strong one.

Interesting events during the year in the operatic world were also a revival, remarkable for its artistic perfection and the beauty of its *mise en scène*, of Gluck's "Orpheus," by Miss Marie Brema—who appeared herself in the title-part—at the Savoy Theatre; and the first production in this country, outside of London, of Wagner's "Ring," of which two complete cycles were given at the King's Theatre, Edinburgh, beginning on Feb. 28th, by Ernst Denhof, in conjunction with the Carl Rosa Opera Company. On Feb. 19th students of the Royal College of Music revived Gluck's "Iphigenia in Tauris," at His Majesty's Theatre, Viola Tree undertaking the title-rôle.

Some Notable Concerts.—Considerable activity was displayed in the concert world, although the death of King Edward naturally brought a lull at the very time when musical entertainments would have been most numerous. Of the older organisations, the **Royal Choral Society** maintained its reputation for conservatism, among other works performed under Sir Frederick Bridge's direction at the

Albert Hall being "Messiah," "Acis and Galatea," Berlioz's "Faust," Brahms's "Triumphlied," and Elgar's "Dream of Gerontius."

At the **London Choral Society's Concert** in Queen's Hall on Feb. 15th Granville Bantock's fine setting of "Omar Khayyám" was given in its entirety, under Arthur Fagge. Later in the season this energetic society also performed Bach's "St. Matthew" Passion. The Bach Choir's rendering, on March 15th, of the great Mass in B minor also deserves mention, as does the singing on another occasion of the Edward Mason Choir. Modern works of interest were brought forward at the concerts given by the newly formed Queen's Hall Choral Society, the novelties conducted by Franco Leoni including Hubert Bath's "Look at the Clock" and Moellendorff's "The Night Mail."

The present high standard of orchestral playing in London was upheld by all the leading organisations. The venerable **Philharmonic Society**, which on May 19th brought its 98th season to a close, numbered among its conductors Nikisch, Landon Ronald, and Mancinelli. Chopin's centenary was duly observed by this organisation, which performed, among quasi-novelties, Parry's Symphony in E minor (a revised version), Holbrooke's "Queen Mab," and Ronald's "Lament of Shah Jehan," besides giving Rachmaninoff's E minor Symphony for the first time in England.

A memorable feature of the series of Symphony Concerts given by the **Queen's Hall Orchestra**, under Henry Wood's command, was the appearance on April 9th of **Richard Strauss**, who secured one of the finest performances of Mozart's "Jupiter" Symphony probably ever heard in London. César Franck's highly individual Symphony in D minor was given with so much success at one of the concerts that it had to be repeated later in the season. Among the soloists who appeared at different times were Elena Gerhardt, Moriz Rosenthal, Pugno, Sauer, and Zimbalist. On May 19th a Memorial Concert for the late King was given by the Queen's Hall Orchestra in the presence of a vast audience, Henry Wood conducting.

Some admirable performances were listened to at the London Symphony Orchestra's series of Symphony Concerts, the conductors comprising Richter, Nikisch, Wassili Safonoff, and Sergius Kussewitzky. At the concert on Feb. 14th Dr. Coward's famous Sheffield Musical Union took part in an impressive rendering of Beethoven's Mass in D, under Richter. The season's novelties embraced Ahn Carse's clever Symphony in G minor, originally produced at the Newcastle Festival, and a new work by the Russian composer, Scriabine.

Excellent progress continued to be made by the **New Symphony Orchestra**, under their brilliant young conductor, Landon Ronald. Attention was paid to British works, Nicholas Gatty, who contributed skilful Variations on "Old King Cole," Coleridge-Taylor, and Norman O'Neill being among the composers represented. On June 8th Busoni's Pianoforte Concerto, a work of fresh design and very large scope, proved a notable attraction. It was conducted by the composer, the soloist being Mark Hambourg.

In the domain of chamber music interesting concerts were given, among other organisations, by the London Trio, the New String Quartet, the Grimson Quartet, the Solly String Quartet, the Walenn Quartet, the Russian Trio, and the Classical Concert Society, who devoted three programmes to Schumann's works, in commemoration of the centenary of the composer's birth.

At Æolian Hall Messrs. Chappell gave a series of matinées with the object of introducing little-known British artists of talent. In the list of **singers who gave concerts** or recitals in London during the season were Melba, Donalda, Clara Butt, Gerhardt, Ida Reman, Mrs. George Swinton, Maggie Teyte, Edith Kirkwood, Susan Strong, Jean Waterston, Edith Miller, Janet Spencer (an American contralto), John Coates, Theodore Byard, Campbell McInnes, and Plunket Greene. Pianoforte recitals were given, among others, by Godowsky (who commemorated the 100th anniversary of Chopin's birth on Feb. 22nd), Rosenthal, Pachmann, A. Cortot, Backhaus, Buhlig, E. Schelling, Benno Moiseiwitsch, Katharine Goodson, Polyxena Fletcher, Percy Grainger, John Powell, Johanne Stockmar, Herbert Fryer, Frank Merrick, Vernon Warner, Maria Seguel, and Fanny Davies (whose Schumann centenary concert on June 8th was an interesting event). A notable visitor was **Saint-Saëns**, the distinguished French musician devoting three concerts at Bechstein Hall to the performance of Mozart's pianoforte concertos; while Pugno and Ysaye were associated in a series of recitals in Queen's Hall, at which they played Beethoven's piano and violin sonatas in a faultless manner. Among **violinists** heard during the season were May Harrison (the clever young English artist being warmly welcomed back after her studies on the continent), Elman, Kathleen Parlow, Zimbalist, Szigeti, Eddy Brown, and Robert Pollak; while among **'cellists** Joseph Hollman (who gave a concert at Queen's Hall on June 7th to mark the 25th anniversary of his first appearance in this country), Pablo Casals, Boris Hambourg, Jean Gerardy, Felix Salmond, and Livio Boni especially distinguished themselves.

Mention should also be made of Henry Bird's Jubilee Concert in Queen's Hall on April 26th, at which the veteran accompanist received the support of a large number of popular singers.

The sixteenth season of **Promenade Concerts**, under the management of Mr. Robert Newman, opened at Queen's Hall on Aug. 13th, and continued until Oct. 22nd. As in previous years the Queen's Hall Orchestra was conducted by Henry J. Wood, who introduced several novelties during the season. Among them were works by Vaughan Williams (a "Fantasia on English Folk-Songs"), Walford Davies (Festival Overture), Arnold Bax, W. J. Hurlstone, Ernest Austin, and Percy Pitt.

Provincial Festivals.—The first festival of the year was that at **Brighton**, held in the first week of February, under the direction of Joseph Sainton, who had under him the Municipal Orchestra. The novelties produced were Coleridge-Taylor's cantata "Endymion's Dream," and Arthur Hervey's "Life's Moods," a clever piece of programme music. Sinding, the Norwegian composer, conducted a performance of his D minor Symphony. In July, for the first time since 1835, **York** held a festival, its revival being due to the efforts of T. Tertius Noble. A suite of dramatic dances by Granville Bantock was one of the new works performed, and altogether the meeting proved a great success. Three important festivals marked the early autumn. That of the **Three Choirs** took place at Gloucester, and introduced a new short oratorio, "Gethsemane," by Bantock, laid out for baritone solo and chorus ; and, among other novelties, an organ concerto by Basil Harwood, an orchestral work by Vaughan Williams, and a suite by Herbert Brewer. The **Cardiff Festival** had as its conductor-in-chief Frederic Cowen, whose setting of Buchanan's "The Veil" was one of the most interesting of the works brought to a first hearing. Another was Mackenzie's "The Sun-God's Return." A symphonic poem by Hamilton Harty, "With the Wild Geese," and a new choral work by David Thomas, were also produced; while a quasi-novelty was Strauss's "Wanderer's Storm Song." "Messiah," "Elijah," "Hymn of Praise," and Dvorák's "Stabat Mater" were also in the scheme. The **Leeds Triennial Festival** opened on Oct. 12th with a performance of "Elijah," under Sir Charles Stanford. The novelties comprised Vaughan Williams's "**Sea Symphony,**" for soli, chorus, and orchestra; a new symphony by Rachmaninoff, which the composer conducted; and Stanford's "Songs of the Fleet"; while among more or less familiar works were Bach's "St. Matthew" Passion, Brahms's German Requiem, Parry's "Pied Piper of Hamelin," Elgar's "Variations," Wallace's "Villon," Hubert Bath's "Wedding of Shon Maclean," and some Wagner selections, including the first act of "Die Walküre."

1911

Undoubtedly the feature of the "grand" season at **the Royal Opera, Covent Garden,** which opened on April 22nd, and concluded on July 31st, was the appearance of **the Russian Imperial Ballet,** whose performances, it is no exaggeration to say, created a furore. London opera-goers had been prepared for the rare accomplishments of this company, and the striking beauty of the ballets they presented, by the sensation they had made in Paris shortly before their arrival in this country. But the success achieved by the troupe at Covent Garden probably exceeded anticipations, and led to their re-engagement by the syndicate for the autumn season. Tamar Karsavina, who had previously visited London, was the *première ballerine,* and Vaslav Nijinsky the *premier danseur,* and although the other leading performers were of high merit, the two artists mentioned, by their remarkable graces, outshone the rest. A striking feature, moreover, of these performances was the beauty and excellence of the ensemble, while both musically and pictorially the ballets reached a high and exceptional artistic level. Among the works presented were "Le Pavillon d'Armide" (with music by M. Tcherepnine, who conducted all the ballets); "Scheherazade," composed by Rimsky-Korsakoff; "Les Sylphides" and "Le Carnaval," the last two deriving particular charm from the music respectively of Chopin and Schumann, as scored for orchestra by various well-known Russian composers. In its general scheme the opera season hardly offered any features of surpassing interest. **The chief novelty** was Puccini's "La Fanciulla del West" ("The Girl of the Golden West"), which had been produced at the Metropolitan, New York, in the previous autumn. Although the work contained a good deal of skilfully wrought music, characteristic in its idiom of the italian composer, the latter's inspiration was found to have served him far less well than in "Madama Butterfly" and the previous operas from his pen. The production, indeed, was chiefly remarkable for Emmy Destinn's fine embodiment of the heroine. The only other novelties were Massenet's "Thaïs"—of which the original Paris production occurred in 1894—and Wolf-Ferrari's "Il Segretto di Susanne" ("The Secret of Suzanne"), a pleasing little work in one act, of which the music—simple, graceful, and fluent—proved very much better than the trivial "plot." Massenet's opera was produced on a scale of lavishness hardly justified by the intrinsic merits of the work, which does not represent the French com-

poser at his best. Melba and Tetrazzini again appeared during the season in rôles long identified with them.

On July 26th a gala performance took place "in honour of the Coronation of King George V. and Queen Mary," and, attended by their Majesties and a brilliant company, proved a picturesque function, the house being beautifully decorated. Excerpts were given from "Aïda," "Roméo et Juliette," and "Il Barbiere di Siviglia," and the Russian Ballet appeared.

The operas mounted during the season, and the number of representations of each, were as follows : " Aïda " (5), " Barbiere di Siviglia " (3), " La Bohème " (5), " Carmen " (1), " Ballo in Maschera " (2), " Faust " (2), " Girl of the Golden West " (5), " Lakmé " (3), " Louise " (7), " Madama Butterfly " (6), " Pagliacci " (3), " Pelléas et Mélisande " (3), " Rigoletto " (6), " Roméo et Juliette " (4), " La Sonnambula " (1), " Samson et Dalila " (6), " Thaïs " (3), " La Traviata " (6), " Gli Ugonotti " (3), " Il Segretto di Susanne " (3). Twelve performances, including matinées, were devoted exclusively to the Russian Ballet.

In the autumn the Grand Opera Syndicate held a season of **German Opera** and Russian Ballet at Covent Garden. Beginning on Oct. 19th, three complete cycles of Wagner's "Ring" were given, conducted by Franz Schalk, of the Imperial Opera House, Vienna. The list of artists included several who have won distinction in Wagner's music-dramas, among them being Borghild Langaard-Bryhn, Minnie Saltzmann-Stevens, Kirkby Lunn. Peter Cornelius, Hans Bechstein, and Anton van Rooy. Other operas from the Wagnerian repertory were also mounted. Humperdinck's "Königskinder," which had proved one of the successes of the last season at the Metropolitan Opera House, New York, was also produced for the first time in this country. Alternately with the opera performances, the Russian Ballet, reinforced by Mlle. Pavlova, appeared, having been re-engaged on the strength of the signal success they achieved on the same stage during the summer. The season lasted eight weeks.

The well-known American impresario Mr. Oscar Hammerstein, who had shown so much enterprise in connection with opera-giving at the New York Manhattan, fulfilled his promise of erecting **a new Opera House** in London. The site chosen was Kingsway, and here a building was set up—at a cost, it was stated, of over £200,000—in accordance with every modern advance in comfort, stage equipment, etc. Seating accommodation was provided for 2,700, the holding "capacity" of the house representing £2,000. Mr Hammerstein had drawn up a repertory of thirty-two operas, and inaugurated a twenty weeks' season on Nov. 13th with "Quo Vadis," a work, composed by Jean Nouguès, which had met with considerable success both in Paris and New York.

The Concert Season.—Although in respect of the number of concerts and recitals given the season of 1911 proved a very busy one, it brought no little disappointment to artists and entrepreneurs who had based hopes of financial success on the expected invasion of visitors to London for the Coronation festivities. As a matter of fact, the latter interfered appreciably with nearly all public amusements, since they practically monopolised attention. Moreover, the protracted spell of exceptionally hot weather made the public disinclined for indoor entertainments.

An interesting feature of the season was **the London Musical Festival,** held at Queen's Hall in the latter part of May. No such festival had been organised in London for a good many years, the previous one having been given, under Mr. Robert Newman's management, in 1899. The week's music began on May 22nd, and at the concert on the 24th occurred the first performance of **Edward Elgar's second Symphony, in E flat**. The event excited a good deal of interest, and the work, which was conducted by the composer, received an enthusiastic welcome. Critical opinion was divided, however, on the relative merits of the symphony and its predecessor. That the novelty contained many passages of considerable beauty, as well as of characteristic energy and vigour, was nevertheless acknowledged on all hands. The same evening witnessed the production of of Bantock's symphonic poem, "**Dante and Beatrice**"—a fine work—while two other English novelties were Walford Davies's little suite, "Parthenia," and Percy Pitt's "English Rhapsody." Sir Henry Wood also afforded the festival's patrons opportunities of hearing the Norwich, Sheffield, and Leeds Festival Choirs.

There was no lack of choral and orchestral concerts, but the season brought with it little that was striking in the way of novelties. **The Royal Choral Society**, for instance, relied in the main, as usual, upon works in their established repertory, Sir Frederick Bridge conducting performances of "Messiah," Coleridge-Taylor's "Hiawatha," Elgar's "King Olaf" and "Dream of Gerontius," and other works for which the Society's patrons possess an abiding affection. Under Arthur Fagge **the London Choral Society** continued to make satisfactory progress, although, contrary to its usual custom, it brought forward nothing new. Performances given by this organisation in Queen's Hall of Bach's "St. Matthew" Passion and Beethoven's great Mass in D were marked by a fine spirit of endeavour. But the lack of fresh material already mentioned indicated a dearth in the supply of promising new works—a regrettable fact emphasised by the announcement made during the season of the discontinuance of the concerts of **the Queen's Hall Choral Society**, owing to the difficulty of finding novelties of sufficient attractiveness. Early in the year this enterprising Society produced a new sacred work by Franco Leoni, entitled "Golgotha," which excited some discussion by reason of its unconventional musical treatment of a solemn subject. **Other choral concerts** were given by the Bach Choir, the Edward Mason Choir, and the Smallwood Metcalfe Choir.

The conductors who directed **the Philharmonic Society's Concerts** during its 99th season were Nikisch, Albert Coates, and Chessin. Among the soloists who appeared were Maggie Teyte, Mignon Nevada, Rosenthal, Alfred Cortot, and Katherine Goodson. For their series of **symphony concerts** the London Symphony Orchestra engaged the services, as conductors, of Richter, Nikisch, Safonoff, Mlynarski, and Elgar. A memorable occasion was the farewell appearance of Richter, upon his retirement, at the concert given on April 10th. The Leeds Philharmonic Choir, the Hallé (Manchester) Choir, and the Hanley Glee and Madrigal Society appeared during the season; while the soloists who came forward in the course of it, under the same auspices, included Donalda, Susan Strong, Walter Hyde, Kreisler, Bronislaw Huberman, Ernest Schelling, Percy Grainger, Tina Lerner, and Eleanor Spencer. In the ranks of the soloists who took part in the symphony concerts of the Queen's Hall Orchestra were Jacques Thibaud, Casals, and Sauer. At the concert on Feb. 4th Wagner's Symphony in C, an early work from his pen, was revived, its performance, however, exciting more curiosity than enthusiasm. The New Symphony Orchestra, conducted by Landon Ronald, continued its series of symphony con-

certs. Melba sang at the concert given by the organisation in Queen's Hall on Feb. 14th, and the programme on May 2nd was devoted to works by British composers.

In the department of **chamber music** a good many concerts and recitals claimed attention, among them those given by the Classical Concert Society, Broadwood's, the London Trio, the London Quartet (a new and admirably equipped organisation), the Walenn Quartet, Thomas Dunhill, Joseph Holbrooke, and, from the Continent, the Brussels, Rosé, and Sevcik Quartets.

The 17th season of **Promenade Concerts** was held at Queen's Hall, under the management of Mr. Robert Newman, from Aug. 12th to Oct. 21st. Sir Henry Wood, who conducted all the concerts with the exception of a few of which Dr. George Henschel took charge, added several works to the repertory of the Queen's Hall Orchestra. Among the novelties produced were compositions by Hamilton Harty, Balfour Gardiner, Norman O'Neill, Raymond Roze, Georges Enesco, and Ravel.

Among **the singers who gave concerts** or recitals during the season were Melba, Elena Gerhardt, Clara Butt and Kennerley Rumford, Alice Verlet, Julia Culp, Maggie Teyte, Beatrice La Palme, Jomelli, Susan Metcalfe, Lilla Ormond, Mysz-Gmeiner, Ida Reman, Mrs. Elsie Swinton, Eugénie Ritt, Palgrave Turner, Alice Mandeville, Evangeline Florence, Rhoda von Glehn, Irene Ainsley, E. van Dyck, Paul Reimers, Theodore Byard, Daniel Beddoe, George Henschel, Enrico Tiberio, Leon Rains, Reinhold von Warlich, Ernest Groom, Lorne Wallet, Denis Byndon-Aires, and Hugo Heinz. **The season's pianists** numbered, among others, Paderewski, Rosenthal, Harold Bauer, Pachmann, Godowsky, Emil Sauer, Max Pauer, Leonard Borwick, Frederic Lamond, A. Cortot, Backhaus, Percy Grainger, York Bowen, Jules Wertheim, Ernst Lengyel, Edw. Goll, Paul Goldschmidt, E. Schelling, Moiseiwitsch, Howard Jones, Robert Lortat, Schönberger, Vianna da Motta, Paolo Martucci, Carreño, Katherine Goodson, Fanny Davies, Adela Verne, Leginska, Myra Hess, Marie Novello, Gertrude Peppercorn, Myrtle Meggy, Tora Hwass, Augusta Cottlow, Myrtle Elvyn, and Susanne von Morvay, the last named, a young Hungarian pianist, being the most remarkable of the season's new-comers. **Violinists** who came forward included Ysaye (who gave a series of Beethoven sonata recitals with Pugno); Kreisler, Hubermann, Thibaud, Kubelik, Albert Spalding, Sigmund Beel, John Dunn, Arrigo Serato, Fritz Hirt, Philip Cathie, Achille Rivarde, Petschnikoff, Leila Doubleday, and May Harrison. Among the season's **'cellists** who gained distinction were Pablo Casals, Hans Bottermund, Livio Boni, Serge Barjansky, Gerardy, Paulo Gruppe, Hugo Oushoorn, Herbert Withers, Beatrice Harrison, May Mukle, and Gustav Havemann, who at Queen's Hall, on June 6th, introduced a "Concertstück" for 'cello and orchestra, by the veteran Max Bruch.

It should be noted that special music was composed for **the Coronation service** in Westminster Abbey by Hubert Parry (a Te Deum), Stanford (a Gloria), Elgar, Alcock, and Sir Frederick Bridge, who directed the musical arrangements. The solo in an anthem composed by him for the occasion was sung by Edward Lloyd.

From May 29th to June 3rd was held the **International Musical Congress**, the meetings of which had never previously taken place in London. King George granted his patronage to the Congress, which was inaugurated with a meeting presided over by Mr. Balfour. Distinguished musicians from all parts of the world came to London to take part in the re-union. Sir Alexander C. Mackenzie acted as President of the Congress, at the sittings of which a large number of papers dealing with various subjects connected with the art were read and discussed.

The Festival of Empire was inaugurated at the Crystal Palace on May 12th by a concert which was attended by their Majesties the King and Queen. An Imperial Choir organised for the occasion by Charles Harriss numbered some four thousand voices, and was said to be the largest body of the kind ever brought together. An "all-British" programme was carried out, several representative native composers conducting performances of their own works.

Early in the autumn the **Royal Academy of Music**, which was founded in 1822, moved from its old premises in Tenterden Street, Hanover Square, to a new and commodious building, erected at a cost of some £60,000, in Maryle-bone Road.

In succession to W. H. Cummings, Landon Ronald was appointed Principal of the **Guild-hall School of Music.**

The honour of knighthood was conferred during the year on Frederic H. Cowen, the well-known composer, and Henry J. Wood, conductor of the Queen's Hall Orchestra.

Provincial Festivals.—The first of the year's Musical Festivals was that held at **Sheffield**, whose triennial meeting occurred on April 26th, and the two following days. For the first time in the history of the festival the chorus had been trained by Sir Henry J. Wood, who thus assumed greater responsibilities in connection with the music performed than on any previous occasion. The conductor of the Queen's Hall Orchestra—whose services were also requisi-tioned—directed all the performances, and the festival was opened with a rendering of "Messiah" which challenged criticism in more than usual measure by reason of its unortho-dox character. The only novelty introduced was Professor Georg Schumann's cantata, "Ruth," which had obtained considerable success in Germany. Although the work was found to contain a good deal of effective choral writing, and not a few picturesque passages, its obvious reminiscences in parts of Wagner's music-dramas robbed it of any particular claim to freshness of inspiration. It was finely per-formed, the soloists being Agnes Nicholls, Kirkby Lunn, Thorpe Bates, and Robert Rad-ford. The other works given included Bach's Mass in B minor and "St. Matthew" Passion, Brahms's "Song of Destiny," and Bantock's "Omar Khayyám" (Part I.), while excerpts from the "Ring" and "Parsifal" were also comprised in the scheme.

On Sept. 12th the **Three Choirs Festival** was opened at Worcester Cathedral, four days being devoted to the meeting, which enlisted the services, as conductor, of Sir Henry Wood. The chief works performed on the classical side were "Messiah," "Elijah," and Bach's "Passion" according to St. Matthew. Several novelties were introduced, none of them, how-ever, being of very important dimensions. Walford Davies provided a setting of words taken from Thomas à Kempis's "Imitation of Christ," in which the solos were sung by Gervase Elwes; W. H. Reed a new set of Variations for string orchestra; Granville Bantock an "Overture to a Greek Tragedy"; and Vaughan Williams "Five Mystical Songs." The latter, which were interpreted by J. Camp-bell McInnes, proved on the whole the most impressive of the new works. Parry's "Te Deum" and Elgar's "Coronation March," both of which had been heard at the Coronation service in Westminster Abbey, were also per-formed at the Festival.

The Norwich Festival was held from Oct. 25th to 29th under the conductorship of Sir Henry Wood. No new works were brought forward.

1912

Exceptional activity in operatic domains was a feature of the first half of the musical year. Between January and the end of July there were three **opera seasons** in London. That is to say, Mr. Oscar Hammerstein, in the early part of the year, continued the campaign he had opened at his London Opera House, Kingsway, in November 1911, while the summer months found him conducting an enterprise there in rivalry, as it were, with Covent Garden. The continuance of the American manager's inaugural venture witnessed the production on the stage of the Kingsway house principally of works in the modern French répertoire, including Massenet's "Hé-rodiade" and "Le Jongleur de Notre Dame," and Charpentier's "Louise." The season ended on March 2nd.

The Royal Opera season at Covent Garden was the longest ever held in the annals of that theatre. It opened on April 20th, and did not conclude until Aug. 1st, the date originally fixed for the closing—July 29th—being altered in order to enable the **Russian Ballet**, whose performances were a feature of the season (as of that of 1911) to make three extra appear-ances. It may be mentioned here that Mlle. Karsavina and Nijinsky were again the chief "stars" of Serge de Diaghilew's troupe, and that unfamiliar works produced by the Rus-sian dancers were "Thamar," with music by Balakireff, "Narcisse" (Tcherepnin), and "L'Oiseau de Feu," the last-named a singu-larly beautiful ballet, composed by Stravinsky, a young Russian musician of remarkable talent and individuality. Some of these performances were conducted by Thomas Beecham. Two cycles of **Wagner's** "**Ring**" marked the early stages of the season, Dr. Rottenberg, from the Frankfort Opera, being the conductor. In connection with these German series two re-presentations were also given of "Tristan und Isolde." Minnie Saltzmann-Stevens, Gertrud Kappel, Kirkby Lunn, Peter Cornelius, Hein-rich Hensel, and Anton van Rooy were among the artists who bore a prominent part in the Wagner performances. The remainder of the season was devoted to the **Italian and French répertoire.** Only two novelties were staged—"Giojelli della Madonna" ("Jewels of the Madonna") and "Conchita." The opera first mentioned, composed by Wolf-Ferrari, met with considerable favour, its success being due in no small measure to the melo-dramatic effectiveness of a somewhat lurid story, and the rare picturesqueness of its Neapolitan setting. The music was melo-dious, in a rather conventional way, and revealed the skilled hand of the practised musician. But far greater originality of treat-ment was found in the score of "Conchita," the work of a young and almost unknown Italian, Zandonai, which came from Milan. Nevertheless the music was lacking in direct-ness of expression, and this deficiency, coupled with the ineffectiveness of the "book"—founded upon Pierre Louy's "La Femme et le Pantin"—militated against the popularity of the opera. A newcomer, Tar-quinia Tarquini (who also appeared during the season as Carmen), achieved some dis-tinction as the heroine. Melba was absent from the list of the season's "stars," but

Tetrazzini again figured in the company, as did Emmy Destinn; and it was generally agreed that the latter had never sung or acted so finely before. A young Italian tenor new to London, Giovanni Martinelli, made a striking impression by the beauty, freshness, and power of his voice. John McCormack, the Irish tenor, ran him close in favour, and another artist who greatly increased his reputation was Vanni Marcoux, who gave notably an extremely fine performance as Scarpia in Puccini's "La Tosca." All told, the operas staged numbered twenty-two, the list, with the number of performances given of each, being as follows: "Aïda' (5), "Barbiere di Siviglia" (2), "Bohème" (7), "Carmen" (3), "Conchita" (2), "Giojelli della Madonna" (6), "Girl of the Golden West" (3), "Segreto di Susanna" (3), "Louise" (4), "Madama Butterfly" (6), "Manon Lescaut" (2), "Pagliacci" (5), "Rigoletto" (4), "Samson et Dalila" (3), "Tosca" (6), "Traviata" (3), "Gli Ugonotti" (4), "Rheingold" (2), "Walküre" (2), "Siegfried" (2), "Gotterdämmerung" (2), "Tristan" (2).

Mr. Hammerstein opened his summer season at the London Opera House on Monday, April 22nd, and brought it to an end on Saturday, July 13th. The most interesting feature of his campaign was the production of a music-drama, entitled "**Children of Don**," and composed by Joseph Holbrooke, the "book," based upon ancient Cymric legends, being by T. E. Ellis (Lord Howard de Walden). Unfortunately, notwithstanding the enormous amount of serious effort manifestly lavished upon the production, the work, which it had been hoped might advance the cause of native opera, proved far from satisfactory. The story, as set forth by the librettist, was vague, undramatic, and difficult to unravel, while the score, although indisputably clever and showing wonderful orchestral resource, was too obviously modelled upon the modern German pattern to carry conviction as a "British" product. Three performances of the novelty were given, the first two being conducted by Nikisch. The only other unfamiliar opera staged by Mr. Hammerstein was Massenet's "Don Quichotte," which, however, failed to make any deep impression. A French baritone, Lafont, gave a strikingly fine performance in the name-part. During the season Felice Lyne and Orville Harrold, the chief "stars" of the company, made frequent appearances. Appended is the list of the operas mounted, with the number of performances each obtained: "Tales of Hoffmann (12), "Romeo and Juliet" (8), "Faust" (9), "Don Quichotte" (8), "Les Cloches de Corneville" (8), "Il Trovatore" (6), "Rigoletto" (6), "Mignon" (3), "Barber of Seville" (3), "Children of Don" (3), "La Favorita" (2), "William Tell' (2), "La Traviata" (1). On the last night of his season Mr. Hammerstein, in a speech from the stage, mentioned that he had lost on his two undertakings over £45,000; and a few weeks later, on returning to New York, he announced that he had no intention of renewing his attempts to popularise opera in London.

The Concert Season.—Concert and recital-givers displayed hardly less activity than in previous seasons. Outstanding features of the year were the centenary of the Philharmonic Society, and the celebration, at the Crystal Palace, of the **Handel Triennial Festival**, of which this one was rumoured to be probably the last. It opened on June 22nd, the choral and orchestral forces numbering upwards of 3,000, and the works, given under the direction of Frederic H. Cowen, included "Israel in Egypt," "Messiah," and excerpts from "Samson" and other of the master's oratorios. **The Philharmonic Society** entered upon its cen-

tenary in March, having come into existence on March 8th, 1813. In fulfilment of a promise to mark its centenary season by the production of new works by British composers, the Society brought to a hearing, among other novelties, a Symphony in D minor by Charles Villiers Stanford, Arthur Hervey's "Life-moods," and an "Invocation" by Alexander Mackenzie. At the final concert, on May 22nd, Beethoven's "Choral Symphony" was given, Nikisch being the conductor.

Lovers of orchestral music were again liberally catered for. An interesting feature of the series of concerts given by the **New Symphony Orchestra**, under Landon Ronald, was the production of the so-called "Jena" Symphony, ascribed to Beethoven. Its performance, however, hardly persuaded all the experts present that the work had really come from that composer's pen, and, in any case, it could only claim interest as a "youthful indiscretion." On Feb 1st the same organisation introduced, at Queen's Hall, a cleverly wrought symphony by York Bowen.

Henry J. Wood conducted another season of symphony concerts given by the **Queen's Hall Orchestra**. Noteworthy features of the series were the appearances of the Manchester Orpheus Male Voice Choir, and of Mme. Myszgmeiner, Carreño, Kreisler, Casals, and Pugno. Later in the summer the Queen's Hall Orchestra gave a novel and interesting series of "Shakespeare" concerts in the Empress Hall, Earl's Court, the programme being made up of compositions inspired by the dramatist's works. **The London Symphony Orchestra**, which paid a visit to the United States in April, with Nikisch in command, numbered among its conductors in a series of symphony concerts at Queen's Hall the *chef d'orchestre* just mentioned, Safonoff, Mengelberg, Steinbach, and Elgar. The artists who appeared at these concerts included Paderewski, Franz von Vecsey, Adolf Busch, and Paula Hegner.

On May 12th **Siegfried Wagner**, who had not visited London for a number of years, conducted a concert at the Albert Hall, the programme consisting of excerpts from his own and his father's works.

Under Frederick Bridge **the Royal Choral Society** gave their customary number of performances at the Albert Hall. In addition to the works in their usual repertory, there were heard Bach's "St. Matthew" Passion, Cowen's "The Veil" (conducted by the composer), and extracts from Wagner's "Parsifal." Following their approved custom, the **London Choral Society**, under the conductorship of Arthur Fagge, included novelties in the scheme of their concerts at Queen's Hall, not the least successful work brought to a hearing in the course of their last season being Coleridge-Taylor's "A Tale of Old Japan"—a fresh and melodious composition which met with considerable favour. Good work was also done, among other organisations, by the Smallwood Metcalfe Choir, the Edward Mason Choir, the Handel Society, the Bach Choir (which, on Jan. 31st, gave the first London performance of César Franck's "Beatitudes"), and the Stock Exchange Choral and Orchestral Society.

Among the most interesting of the season's concerts were those given at Queen's Hall by Balfour Gardiner, with the object of bringing forward works by native composers. The first concert of the series took place on March 13th. New works were produced by Delius, Percy Grainger, Arnold Bax, W. H. Bell, G. von Holst, Cyril Scott, Balfour Gardiner, and others.

Mention should be made of the Patrons' Fund Concert, which was given at Queen's Hall on July 23rd, and was attended by their

Majesties the King and Queen.

Interest in **chamber music** was well sustained, among the organisations and concert-givers ministering to lovers of this art-form being the Classical Concert Society, Broadwood's, Thomas Dunhill, J. Holbrooke, the Strings Club, Donald Tovey, the Motto Quartet, the Walenn and Wesseley Quartets, the London Trio, the Parisian Quartet, and the St. Petersburg Quartet. At Æolian Hall, Mathilde Verne gave a successful series of "Twelve O'clocks."

Vocalists who came forward during the season as recital-givers included Elena Gerhardt, Nordica, Julia Culp, Clara Butt and Kennerley Rumford, Maggie Teyte, Kirkby Lunn, George Henschel, Mysz-Gmeiner, Theodore Byard, William Pitt Chatham, Doris Woodall, Theo. Lierhammer, Jean Waterston, Christine d'Almayne, Edith Kirkwood, Paul Reimers, Bessie Mark, Tamini, Gervase Elwes, Campbell McInnes, Eva Katharine Lissmann, Hélène Martini, Leon Rains, Gertrude Lonsdale, Fraser Gange, Vernon d'Arnalle, Ernest Groom, Marie Oléline d'Alheim, Sonia Darbell, Daker-Fletcher, **Speranza** Calo, Leila Duart, and Gregory Hast, whose farewell occurred at Queen's Hall on May 20th. Tetrazzini made two appearances at the Albert Hall.

In the ranks of **the season's pianists** were Busoni, Godowsky, Buhlig, Pugno, Egon Petri, Emil Sauer, Backhaus, Ernst Lengyel (whose playing astonished all hearers), F. S. Kelly, Frederic Lamond, Max Pauer, Arthur Rubinstein, Norman Wilks, Deszo Szánto, David Levine, Alex Raab, Herbert Fryer, Percy Grainger, Frank Merrick, Rumschiysky, Frederick Dawson, James Friskin, the boy Solomon, Marcan Thalberg, Schelling, Wm. Murdoch, Cernikoff, Robert Lortot (who, at a series of recitals in Bechstein Hall performed the whole of Chopin's works for the pianoforte), Carreño, Susanne Morvay, Fanny Davies, Winifred Christie, Winifred Purnell (an Australian prodigy), Marjorie Wigley, Mania Seguel, Gabrielle Leschetizky, Auriol Jones, Hilda Saxe, Gertrude Peppercorn, Tina Lerner, and Guiomar Novaer (a young girl pianist who created a deep impression).

Recitals were given by the following, among others, **violinists**: May Harrison, Franz von Vecsey, Kreisler, Mischa Elman, Bronislaw Hubermann, Jacques Thibaud, Paul Kochchanski, Audrey Richardson, Joan Manen, Zimbalist, Hegedus, Godfrey Ludlow, Louis Persinger, Marian Jay, Armida Senatra, and Leila Doubleday; while among 'cello-players who appeared were Casals, Beatrice Harrison, Paul Grummer, May Mukle, Luiz Figueras, **Georges** Pitsch, Arrigo Provvedi, Rubio, Joseph Malkin, Arnold Trowell, and Pàulo Gruppe.

The eighteenth season of **Promenade Concerts,** under the management of Robert Newman, was held at Queen's Hall from August 17th to Oct. 26th. Henry J. Wood, in command of the Queen's Hall Orchestra, introduced some twenty-two novelties, among the composers represented being Georges Enesco, Glazounoff, Sinigaglia, Arnold Schönberg, Erich Korugold, Coleridge-Taylor, Weingartner, Julius Harrison, Algernon Ashton, Paul Juon, Alfred M. Hale, J. Dale, Edgar Bainton, Frank Bridge, and Roger Quilter.

Early in the year the old premises of the **Royal Academy of Music**, in Tenterden Street, were vacated, the staff and students entering into possession of a new and handsome building erected for them in Marylebone Road. The opening ceremony was performed by the Duke of Connaught in June.

On Sept. 1st occurred the death, after a short illness, of **Samuel Coleridge-Taylor**, the well-known Anglo-African composer, whose "Hiawatha" has obtained such widespread popularity. The decease of so accomplished a musician, at the age of thirty-seven, excited deep sympathy in the musical world.

Provincial Festivals.

The first of the provincial festivals was that of the **Three Choirs**, which was held at Hereford from Sept. 8th to 13th inclusive. Among the classical masterpieces performed were Handel's "Messiah," Bach's "St. Matthew" Passion, and a motet of Palestrina, and—on the modern and quasi-modern side—Mendelssohn's "Elijah," Brahms's "German Requiem," Dvořák's "Stabat Mater," and Elgar's "Dream of Gerontius." Novelties were contributed to the scheme by Hubert Parry ('Ode to the Nativity'), Vaughan Williams ("Choral Fantasia on Christmas Carols") Edward Elgar, and Granville Bantock (both of whom were represented by an orchestral work). The conductor of the festival was G. R. Sinclair.

Several important works figured in the scheme of the **Birmingham Triennial Festival,** held from Oct. 1st to 4th. The most interesting of the novelties was a choral and orchestral work, "We are the Music Makers," by Elgar, in which the solo part was sung by Muriel Foster. Other novelties were Walford Davies's "The Song of St. Francis," Granville Bantock's "Fifine at the Fair," and Sibelius's Symphony (No. 4) in A. Bach's "St. Matthew" Passion, Handel's "Messiah," and Mendelssohn's "Elijah," as well as Elgar's "Apostles," were also performed, Henry J. Wood being the conductor.

The most important feature in the scheme of the **Bristol Festival,** which opened on Oct 23rd and continued for three days, was the performance in concert-form of the four dramas of Wagner's "Nibelungen Ring." Agnes Nicholls, Perceval Allen, Marion Beeley, Edith Clegg, Peter Cornelius, Lloyd Chandos, Morgan Kingston, Hans Bechstein, Clarence Whitehill, and Robert Radford were among the singers engaged for the cycle and for the other works presented, which included Saint-Saëns's "Samson and Delilah" and Elgar's "Caractacus." Paderewski and Kreisler appeared at the festival, and the conductor was George Riseley.

1913

Quite early in the year Covent Garden threw open its doors to opera-lovers, under the auspices of Thomas Beecham, who inaugurated a season of grand opera and Russian ballet on Jan. 29th. The season, which lasted six weeks, was made particularly interesting by the production of Richard Strauss's "Rosenkavalier"—its first performance in England. The work, which achieved a brilliant success, attracting a crowded audience to each of the eight representations, was given with a fine cast, Margarette Siems and Eva von der Osten—a charming mezzo-soprano—appearing in the rôles they had created at Dresden, while Paul Knupfer and other artists of distinction supported them. The orchestral performance, under Thomas Beecham, was also on a high plane. The repertory included two other Strauss operas—"Salome" and "Elektra"—while Wagner was drawn upon for "Tristan" and "Die Meistersinger," the revival of the last-named work, in particular, being a memorable achievement. "L'Après-midi d'un Faune," the curious ballet fashioned by Nijinsky to

Debussy's music, and "Pétrouchka," a clever and fantastically conceived work composed by Igor Stravinsky, a young Russian, of revolutionary musical ideas, were among the novelties introduced during the brief but eventful season by the Russian Ballet.

The centenary of Wagner's birth, which occurred in May, was duly commemorated at the Royal Opera, Covent Garden, in the "grand" season which opened on April 21st and closed on July 28th. The enterprise was ushered in with a performance of "Tannhäuser," and afterwards three cycles, made memorable by the presence of Nikisch at the conductor's desk, were given of "Der Ring des Nibelungen." This was the first time London had heard the tetralogy under this famous conductor, and his readings of the great work proved nothing short of a revelation by reason of their extraordinary lyrical character. The orchestral playing was magnificent, but it was never allowed to overshadow the voices, with results that brought to light many unsuspected beauties in Wagner's score, familiar though it was. As will be seen from the list of works performed, other of the master's music-dramas were staged in the early part of the season. Saltzmann-Stevens, Gertrud Kappel, Perard-Petzl, Peter Cornelius, Heinrich Hensel, and Anton van Rooy were among the well-known artists who took part in the "Ring."

It was hoped that Charpentier's new opera "Julien"—his sequel to "Louise"—would be produced during the season. But it was not found possible to introduce the work, the production of which at the Paris Opéra Comique was only witnessed tardily, after many postponements. Of the two novelties brought to a hearing at Covent Garden neither made any particular impression. "Oberst Chabert," the work of a young German composer, W. von Waltershausen, was founded upon Balzac's "Le Colonel Chabert," and the story, treated concisely and not undramatically, had some effective moments. The score, however, while clever enough of its kind, and modern in feeling, was lacking in inspiration and "grip." But both musically and in respect of its book this novelty proved more satisfying than "La Du Barry," produced later in the season. Its composer, Ezio Camussi, is a young Italian, who obtained with the work some success in Milan. Those who heard it at Covent Garden, however, seemed agreed that the music was insipid and colourless, and wholly deficient in individuality.

A distinguishing feature of the campaign was the reappearance of Caruso, who had not sung here in opera for some six years. In "Aïda," "La Tosca," "Pagliacci," and other operas the famous tenor again made a deep impression, even if his voice was hardly found to possess all its old volume and ring. On the night of his return the house was "sold out" at greatly enhanced prices. Melba was also among the season's "stars," and upon one evening she sang in "La Bohème" together with Caruso, the audience including the King and Queen. The superb singing of Emmy Destinn on many occasions was a noteworthy feature, as in previous years; and a newcomer who made a fine impression was the Italian conductor, Giorgio Polacco. Twenty-five operas were sung in German, forty-nine in Italian, and fifteen in French.

The works mounted, and the number of representations given of each, were as follows : "Aïda" (7), "Du Barry" (2), "Bohème" (7), "Cavalleria Rusticana" (2), "Don Giovanni" (3), "Faust" (2), "Gioielli della Madonna" (5), "Fliegende Holländer" (2), "Königskinder" (2), "Lohengrin" (2), "Louise" (4), "Madama Butterfly" (6), "Oberst Chabert" (2), "Pagliacci" (4), "Pelléas et Mélisande" (3), "Rigoletto" (1), "Roméo et Juliette" (2), "Samson et Dalila" (4), "Segreto di Susanna" (2), "Tannhäuser" (3), "Tosca" (8), "Traviata" (2), "Rheingold" (3), "Walküre" (3), "Siegfried" (3), "Götterdämmerung" (3), "Tristan" (2).

Concurrently with the latter part of the Covent Garden season a very remarkable enterprise was carried out by Sir Joseph Beecham at Drury Lane Theatre. It was the means of introducing to London the Imperial Opera Company from St. Petersburg, and of enabling the public to renew acquaintance with the wonderful Russian Ballet. Chief interest centred in the performances of the Russian singers, who included the famous basso, Chaliapine, whose début created as great a sensation here as it had in Paris and elsewhere. Three operas were staged : Moussorgsky's "Boris Godounow" and "La Khovantchina," and Rimsky-Korsakow's "Ivan le Terrible," all of them new to London. Of the three the most striking was the first-named, whose composer, an indubitable genius, did not live to enjoy the fruits of his strangely original gifts. The folk-song idiom predominated in all these Russian operas, and the freshness of their atmosphere, in conjunction with the wonderfully vivid quality of the performances they received, produced a very striking impression.

Both as actor and singer, Chaliapine, in particular, revealed himself as an artist of unsurpassable attainments and a magnetic personality, while the beautiful singing of the Russian chorus excited the utmost admiration.

Karsavina and Nijinsky were again the chief "stars" of the Ballet, and the repertory on this side of the enterprise included three novelties : Debussy's "Jeux," Florent Schmitt's "La Tragédie de Salome," and Stravinsky's "Le Sacre du Printemps." Æsthetic beauty was evidently not aimed at in any of these productions, and the work last-mentioned gained for its composer—Igor Stravinsky—the distinction of having written the most deliberately and repellently ugly music ever heard in a London theatre.

Earlier in the season music-lovers were indebted to Mr. Thomas Beecham for the opportunity of hearing Richard Strauss's "Ariadne auf Naxos," of which a few special performances, beginning on May 27th, were given at His Majesty's Theatre, with the co-operation of Sir Herbert Tree, who assumed the title-part in a version of "Le Bourgeois Gentilhomme," which preceded the opera. In the adaptation of Molière's comedy the incidental music composed by Strauss for Hofmannsthal's version of the play was used, so that the two linked works were heard as in the production a few months previously at Stuttgart. In the comedy and the opera forming a pendant to it Strauss revealed a rather baffling blend of musical styles, a simplicity at times almost Mozartean characterising some of the numbers he wrote for "Le Bourgeois Gentilhomme," while in "Ariadne" the composer's personal idiom often asserted itself. In it an extraordinary coloratura air was sung very cleverly by Madame Bosetti ; another accomplished singer, Eva von der Osten, appearing as Ariadne. The performances were conducted by Thomas Beecham.

The Concert Season.—Although activities in the concert-room were not of the exceptional character which marked operatic history in 1913, no lack of enterprise was displayed by the leading musical organisations ; and lovers of orchestral performances, in particular, found their needs amply provided for. Following its comparatively recent practice of engaging various well-known conductors, for its 101st season the Royal Philharmonic Society enabled its supporters to listen to some fine orchestral playing under such distinguished foreign *chefs d'orchestre* as Safonoff and Mengelberg, while at one of the concerts command was taken by Landon Ronald. Busoni and Kathleen Parlow were among the soloists who appeared between January and the end of the Philharmonic season. The Queen's Hall Orchestra's 17th season of Symphony Concerts, under Henry J. Wood, was marked by two features that made it memorable. On Jan. 18th the first performance in London of Gustav Mahler's 7th Symphony—a work of colossal length, and certainly of less beauty than technical cleverness—excited considerable discussion ; while at the concert on Feb. 1st something of a sensation was created by the production of a so-called "Poem of Fire," by the young Russian composer Scriabine, entitled "Prometheus." The harmonic eccentricities of this strange and baffling work were hardly of a kind to obtain for it a sympathetic hearing, and although it was played twice on the same afternoon—with a view to its better understanding by the audience—the public was manifestly perplexed by the composer's deliberate and far-fetched avoidance of the conventional. The soloists who appeared at these concerts included Godowsky, Frederic Lamond, Busoni, Kreisler, Carl Flesch, and Jacques Thibaud ; and on March 1st the Birmingham Festival Choir took part in a performance of Beethoven's "Choral" Symphony.

Another successful series of Symphony Concerts was given at the Queen's Hall by the London Symphony Orchestra, the conductors who directed that fine organisation including Nikisch (who conducted on one occasion a new Symphony by Arthur Somervell), Steinbach, Safonoff, Mengelberg, and Hamilton Harty. In the list of the singers and solo instrumentalists who appeared were Muriel Foster, Herbert Heyner, Paderewski, Josef Lhevinne, Tina Lerner, Donald Tovey, and Paul Kochanski. The Leeds Philharmonic Chorus made an appearance at one of the concerts, and at the last of the series, on June 23rd, some new works by Ethel Smyth obtained a hearing. Further progress was made by the New Symphony Orchestra, under the able conductorship of Landon Ronald, and at their concert in Queen's Hall on Feb. 6th Phyllis Neilson-Terry made her début as a concert singer. It should be noted that the New Symphony Orchestra, with Landon Ronald in command, also took part in a long series of Sunday afternoon concerts at the Royal Albert Hall. An enterprise of considerable interest and importance was a series of orchestral concerts given at Queen's Hall by Balfour Gardiner, with a view to the encouragement of British composers. Thereat new works were produced by, among other native musicians, Vaughan Williams, Percy Grainger, B. J. Dale, Gustav von Holst, Norman O'Neill, Arnold Bax, Delius, and Frederic Austin (a Symphony in E major). Among other events deserving mention were the Bach Choir's performance, for the first time in London, of Vaughan Williams's "Sea" Symphony, originally produced at the Leeds Festival of 1910 ; two concerts (on April 15th and 16th) by the famous Colonne Orchestra (from Paris), conducted by Gabriel Pierné ; and three concerts of Slavonic music directed by Emil Młynarski, all these events taking place at Queen's Hall. Here, too, concerts were given during the season by the Royal Amateur Orchestral Society (conductor, Arthur Payne), the Stock Exchange Choral and Orchestral Society, (Hamish MacCunn and George Kitchin), the Strolling Players (Joseph Ivimey), and the Wilhelm Sachse Orchestra.

On May 22nd, the anniversary of his birth, a concert was given at the Albert Hall in celebration of Richard Wagner's centenary. Excerpts from the master's music-dramas were performed by the London Symphony Orchestra, under Mengelberg, and an address was delivered by Louis N. Parker, President of the Wagner Society.

Another interesting celebration was that organised by an influential committee to mark the jubilee of Camille Saint-Saëns's entry into musical life. The veteran French composer and pianist played a Mozart Concerto, as well as works from his own pen, and in the course of the proceedings—which occurred at Queen's Hall on June 2nd—received an address, the presentation being made by Alexander Mackenzie. The Beecham Symphony Orchestra bore part in the programme. On the following evening Saint-Saëns attended a "gala" performance of his opera, "Samson et Dalila," at Covent Garden

Choral Concerts.—In the domains of choral music the Royal Choral Society, under Frederick Bridge, sustained its reputation, and the support accorded its concerts at the Royal Albert Hall was no less substantial than in previous years. On Ash Wednesday the Society revived Gounod's "Redemption," other works performed during the season including "Messiah," Elgar's "Dream of Gerontius," and Coleridge-Taylor's "Hiawatha" and "A Tale of Old Japan." The London Choral Society, under Arthur Fagge, continued to make satisfactory progress. A Beethoven programme on Feb. 12th (Queen's Hall) was composed of the Mass in C, the Choral Fantasia, and the 9th Symphony. On April 9th the Society produced Wolf-Ferrari's "La Vita Nuova," also performing the Grail Scene from "Parsifal." Record should also be made of Thomas Beecham's revival of Delius's "A Mass of Life," which took place at the Covent Garden Opera House on March 10th, the North Staffordshire District Choir taking part ; and of the Handel Society's performance at Queen's Hall on April 29th of Henschel's "Requiem," the composer conducting. In the same hall interesting performances were given by a splendidly equipped Finnish Choir—Suomen Laulu—and by the Edward Mason Choir and the Smallwood Metcalfe Choir.

The annual series of Promenade Concerts by the Queen's Hall Orchestra opened on August 16th. The season, which lasted until Oct. 25th, was again under the management of Robert Newman, the conductor being Henry Wood.

In the ranks of the **singers** who gave recitals during the season were Elena Gerhardt, Julia Culp, Maggie Teyte, Muriel Foster, Lula Mysz-Gmeiner, Agnes Nicholls, Julia Hostater, Helen Henschel, Jean Waterston, Edith Clegg, Betty Callish, Yvette Guilbert, Carmen Hill, Muriel von Raatz, Mrs. Hazzard Peacock, Mrs. George Swinton, Mme. d'Onyskiewicz, Felia Dorio, Lena Maitland, Mme. Munthe-Kaas, Gertrude Lonsdale, Arnolde Stephenson, Christine d'Almayne, Ethel Maas, Mme. Sobrino, Nina Jaques-Dalcroze, Gladys Mogen, Alma Gluck, Florence Macbeth (a young American soprano, whose début was very successful), George Henschel, J. Campbell McInnes, Theodore Byard, Robert Pitt, Cecil Fanning, Tamini, Paul Reimers, Fraser Gange, Whitney Mockridge, Arthur Alexander, Robert Chignell, and Sven Scholander.

Pianoforte recitals were given by, among others, Busoni, Pachmann, Eugen d'Albert, Harold Bauer, Backhaus, Frederic Lamond, Dohnányi, Mark Hambourg, Fanny Davies,

Katherine Goodson, Ernest Schelling, Egon Petri, Guiomar Novaes, Leonard Borwick, Georg von Lalewicz, Louis Edger, Mathilde and Adela Verne, Bruno Moiseiwitsch, Alexander Raab, Hélène Morsztyn, Percy Grainger, Herbert Fryer, J. Lhevinne, Gertrude Peppercorn, James Friskin, Howard Jones, Edith Walton, Myra Hess, Vianna da Motta, Jules Wertheim, Sidney Rosenbloom, Cyril Scott, W. Morse Rummel, Susanne Morvay, Max Darewski, Myrtle Meggy, T. Perceval Fielden, Aurelio Giorni, F. S. Kelly, York Bowen, Wesley Weyman, Arthur Rubinstein, Hans Ebell, Carl Friedberg, Hilda Saxe, Wladimir Cernikoff, Vernon Warner.

Violinists who claimed a hearing as recital-givers included Mischa Elman, Daniel Melsa (a remarkably gifted young Pole), Alexandre Sébald (another successful newcomer), Isolde Menges, Bronislaw Huberman, Daisy Kennedy, Joan Manen, Paul Kochanski, Zacharewitsch, Marcel Bonnemain, Isoline Harvey (also a vocalist), Maurice Warner, Marjorie Hayward, Dorothy de Vin, Mary Dickenson, Hans Neumann, Ibolyka Gyarfas (aged 13), and Duci Kerekjarto (another prodigy, from Hungary, whose playing created a deep impression).

Violoncellists who appeared at recitals included Beatrice Harrison (who proved herself one of the finest artists of the day), Boris Hambourg, G. Wille (a newcomer, from Dresden, whose playing was greatly admired), Joseph Hollman, Belooussof, Kolni-Belozky, Felix Salmond, May Fussell, Percy Such, Arnold Trowell, and Paul Ludwig. In the realms of chamber-music memorable performances were given in association by Thibaud, Casals, and Bauer, and no less memorable were the performances given at Bechstein Hall by the Rosé Quartet. In the same hall a favourable impression was made by the Geloso Quartet (of Paris), and among other concerts of chamber-music deserving mention were those given by the Wessely Quartet, the London Trio, the English String Quartet, the Rotterdam Trio, the London String Quartet, Brodsky Quartet, J. Holbrooke, T. F. Dunhill —both of whom devoted attention to native works—and Donald Tovey, who assumed control of the "Chelsea" Concerts at the Æolian Hall.

Provincial Festivals.

The Three Choirs' Festival, held at Gloucester from Sept. 8th to 13th, was chiefly remarkable for the production of a new work from the pen of Camille Saint-Saëns. This was an oratorio bearing the title "The Promised Land," the text of which, taken from Scripture, was provided by Hermann Klein. The novelty failed to realise expectations. most of the critics finding the music old-fashioned and uninspired. The composer conducted in person, and the soloists were Ruth Vincent, Phyllis Lett, John Coates, and Robert Radford. Hubert Parry directed the performance of a revised version of his "Te Deum," and another novelty was Sibelius's tone-poem "Luonnotar," the solo part in which was sung by Madame Ackté. Dr. Brewer was the conductor-in-chief of the festival.

An important feature of the Leeds Triennial Festival, which occurred in the first week of October, was the production of a new orchestral work by Edward Elgar, described as a "Symphonic Study with two Interludes," and entitled "Falstaff." A choral and orchestral work, "Song of May Morning," by Basil Harwood, and "The Mystic Trumpeter,' a setting of Whitman's poem by Hamilton Harty, were also heard for the first time. Nikisch and H. P. Allen were the principal conductors, the services of the London Symphony Orchestra

were retained, and the vocalists included Edyth Walker, Carrie Tubb, Muriel Foster, Phyllis Lett, John Coates, Gervase Elwes, Van Rooy, R. Radford, and Thorpe Bates. The solo pianist was Carreño, and the violinist Mischa Elman.

1914

A year of extraordinary operatic activities was rendered noteworthy almost at the beginning by the first stage production in this country of Wagner's "Parsifal," of which the copyright had expired on Dec. 31st, 1913, so enabling the work to be performed in any part of the world. Previously, save for a few "unauthorised" performances in America, and one or two in Amsterdam, Cosima Wagner had contrived to preserve for the Bayreuth Festspielhaus a monopoly of her husband's "sacred festival play"—his last music-drama. The lapse of the copyright gave rise to performances in rapid succession all over the continent, and the Covent Garden production, which occurred on Feb. 2nd, followed quickly upon the heels of that at the Paris Opera. Immense interest was manifested in the venture, and its success on the artistic side—as to which Wagner-lovers who thought that only Bayreuth could do justice to the work had been sceptical—was complete. Artur Bodanzky, from Mannheim, conducted the initial representation, and the fine cast included Heinrich Hensel (Parsifal), Paul Bender (Amfortas), Paul Knüpfer (Gurnemanz), August Kiess (Klingsor), and Eva von der Osten (Kundry). The singing of the artist last named was on an extraordinarily high plane. At subsequent hearings of "Parsifal" the title-rôle was taken by Johannes Sembach and Carl Burrian, among other artists, while the representatives of Kundry included Melanie Kurt and Cäcilie Rüsche-Endorf. All told, some twelve performances were given of the work, each to a crowded audience. In the course of the same season, which was of five weeks' duration, "Tristan und Isolde," "Die Meistersinger," and "Die Walküre" were also staged, while, in addition, a work wholly unfamiliar in this country, Méhul's Biblical opera, "Joseph," was mounted, but failed to prove attractive. A fine impression was made at many of the Wagner performances by Albert Coates, a young English conductor attached to the St. Petersburg Opera.

For opera-lovers the season proper was one of unexampled attractiveness by reason of the fact that for two months Covent Garden and Drury Lane Theatre were engaged simultaneously in operatic enterprise. At the former the "grand" season opened on April 20th and lasted till July 28th. The scheme was of a comprehensive kind, drawing as it did upon the German, French, and Italian repertories. The former element was provided by two complete series of Wagner performances, comprising the "Ring," "Parsifal," and "Die Meistersinger," in addition to two representations of "Lohengrin." "Parsifal" exercised an appeal hardly less potent than on the production of that work earlier in the year, and was given five times. As in the season of 1913, the Nibelungen dramas were conducted by Arthur Nikisch, whose readings of the scores were again superlatively fine. Among the Wagnerian singers an artist new to London was Madame Matzenauer, a contralto of rare gifts, histrionic as well as vocal, whose dramatic embodiment of Kundry and Ortrud ("Lohengrin") revealed dramatic qualities of a compelling order. Maude Fay's beautiful singing as Elsa in the latter opera was another noteworthy feature, while, as in previous seasons, Peter Cornelius and Gertrud Kappel were among the artists who distinguished themselves in the "Ring."

Two new operas were staged during the season. The first was "L'Amore dei tre Re," by a young Italian composer, Montemezzi. This novelty, which came with high credentials from New York, where it had achieved remarkable success a few months earlier, hardly proved epoch-making, although the music was worthy of serious and respectful consideration as being evidently the work of a sincere composer of lofty aims and impeccable refinement. Its freedom from commonplace utterance lent the score a certain distinction, but the unrelieved gloom of the story militated against the opera's chances of a popular success. The other novelty hailed also from Italy, being the work of Riccardo Zandonai (the composer of "Conchita," produced in a previous season). For his "book" he had turned in this instance to D'Annunzio's well-known tragedy, "Francesca da Rimini." The opera, with Martinelli and Louise Edvina in the two leading rôles, proved a stronger work in some respects than the novelty presented earlier in the season, and, like it, showed that modern musical influences have laid hold of the younger school of Italian composers. Zandonai's score was wholly free from anything blatant or puerile, reticence and poetic feeling being its predominant characteristics, but it proved to be somewhat lacking in authentic inspiration.

Boïto's "Mefistofele," with an entirely new setting designed by Bakst, was revived after a long interval; and a particularly welcome revival was that of Verdi's "Falstaff," which had not been heard at Covent Garden for some two decades. Among the season's familiar "stars" were Melba, Destinn, and Caruso, who was in full possession of his wonderful powers and drew crowded houses; while in the ranks of the newcomers a notably good impression was made by Claudia Muzio, whose acting in "La Tosca" was singularly striking. A gala performance on May 11th, in honour of the visit of the King and Queen of Denmark, was a brilliant function.

The operas staged, and the number of representations given of each, were as follows: "Aïda" (8), "Un Ballo in Maschera" (5), "La Bohème" (6), "Die Meistersinger" (2), "Don Giovanni" (3), "Falstaff" (2), "Francesca da Rimini" (3), "L'Amore dei tre Re" (3), "Lohengrin" (3), "Louise" (5), "Butterfly" (6), "Manon Lescaut" (4), "Mefistofele" (3), "Nozze di Figaro" (2), "Otello" (4), "Parsifal" (5), "Pelléas and Mélisande" (2), "Rigoletto" (2), "Samson et Dalila" (4), "La Tosca" (5), "Rheingold" (2), "Walküre" (2), "Siegfried" (2), "Götterdämmerung" (2).

The Drury Lane season, carried out, like that of the previous summer, by Sir Joseph Beecham, was of unique interest and variety, and its success equalled its deserts. Beginning on May 20th, the enterprise continued until July 25th, and to nearly all the performances the public flocked in large numbers, the house being frequently sold out at very high prices. The nights of Russian opera upon which the famous Chaliapine appeared proved the foremost attraction. The greater part of the season was devoted to Russian opera and ballet. But there were also memorable performances of German opera, the works chosen on this side of the repertory being Strauss's "Der Rosenkavalier," with a cast, on the opening night, including Margarete Siems, Charlotte Uhr, Claire Dux, Paul Knüpfer, and Hans Bechstein —Thomas Beecham conducting—and Mozart's "Die Zauberflöte," which had not been heard

in London within the memory of the younger generation. In this masterpiece Claire Dux's singing in the part of Pamina was remarkably beautiful.

Moussorgsky's "Boris Godounow" and "Khovantchina," and Rimsky-Korsakoff's "Ivan le Terrible," in all of which Chaliapine again covered himself with glory, were found, as in the previous season, to be of potent attractiveness. Several novelties, however, were added to the list of Russian operas, including Borodin's "Prince Igor" (a wonderfully picturesque production), Rimsky-Korsakoff's "Nuit de Mai" and "Le Coq d'Or" (an extraordinarily original work which was given in the novel form of an "opera-ballet," with a most striking *mise en scène*), and Stravinsky's "Le Rossignol," a novelty as fantastic in its setting as it was bizarre in its music, the young Russian composer therein exhibiting a defiance of musical conventions as daring almost as those that baffled the public a year before in his "Le Sacre du Printemps." In their several ways all these works, which were seen for the first time in England, proved uncommonly interesting. Once again the Russian Ballet constituted an all-important feature of the Drury Lane season, and of chief interest among the novelties they presented was Strauss's "La Légende de Joseph," which had only been produced a few days earlier in Paris. A novel version of the Bible story, framed in a fanciful Renascence setting, it was wondrously sumptuous as a production, but did little or nothing to enhance its composer's reputation. Strauss himself conducted the first performance, receiving a great ovation. Other new works staged by the Russian Ballet (of which Karsavina and Michael Fokine were the chief "stars") were Maurice Ravel's "Daphnis et Chloé," a charming production, and Steinberg's "Midas."

Before the season closed Sir Joseph Beecham produced a music-drama by Josef Holbrooke (composed to a libretto by Lord Howard de Walden), entitled "Dylan," a sequel to "Children of Don," the Celtic opera by the same author and composer which saw the light during Oscar Hammerstein's régime at the London Opera House. "Dylan," which was sung in English, possessed greater musical interest and value than its predecessor, but the undramatic character of the "book" proved a powerful factor against its achieving any lasting success.

The Concert Season. Although less memorable than events in the domain of opera, the concerts of the year were hardly less numerous than those of previous seasons—at any rate up to the outbreak of the war—and London was visited, as usual, by the leading vocalists and instrumentalists of the day, whose recitals made collectively a very formidable list. Orchestral music played an important part in the musical life of the metropolis, and there was no falling-off in the quality of the performances for which London's permanent organisations were responsible. The programmes drawn up for the 102nd season of the Royal Philharmonic Society contained much that was interesting, and were noteworthy for the number of works by British composers brought forward. First performances were accorded to Stanford's Fourth Irish Rhapsody, and to two picturesque and characteristic tone-poems by Delius. A "Dance Poem" by Frank Bridge was so ultra-modern in its cacophony as to excite some signs of disapprobation. Another novelty was Strauss's "Festliches Præludium," a *pièce d'occasion* which proved chiefly interesting for the immense orchestra required for its performance. Mengelberg conducted most of the concerts of the series, and the soloists engaged for it were Muriel Foster (who, after the final concert, on March 31st, was awarded the Society's gold medal), and the following pianists: Joseph Lhevinne, Sapellnikoff, Leonard Borwick, Alfred Cortot, and Frederic Lamond.

The 18th season of Symphony Concerts given by the Queen's Hall Orchestra (from Oct. 18th, 1913, to April 25th, 1914) was marked by the production of several interesting novelties. The concert on Jan. 17th—the first in the new year—provided something of a sensation in the appearance of that much-discussed composer, Arnold Schönberg, who came over from Germany to conduct his "Five Orchestral Pieces," which had been soundly hissed on the occasion of their performance under Sir Henry Wood at a Promenade concert in 1912. The composer himself received a very cordial welcome, though it was doubtful whether the audience really grasped the meaning of music so strange and outlandish. At the next concert of the series Henry Wood produced Gustav Mahler's so-called symphony, "Das Lied von der Erde," an interesting work fashioned upon unaccustomed lines; while a subsequent novelty was Stravinsky's brilliant little orchestral fantasia, "Fireworks." On March 14th the distinguished Russian composer and pianist, Scriabine, appeared as the soloist in his own "Prometheus," as well as an early pianoforte concerto from his pen. The Sheffield Musical Union took part in a performance of Beethoven's "Choral" Symphony, and other works, on March 25th. Among the soloists who appeared during the season were Carrie Tubb, Phyllis Lett, Gervase Elwes, Ernst von Dohnányi, Guiomar Novaes, Adela Verne, Elly Ney, Alfred Cortot, F. Lamond, Mischa Elman, and Pablo Casals. Unlike those directed by Henry Wood, the series of Symphony Concerts—the 10th—carried out at Queen's Hall by that fine organisation, the London Symphony Orchestra, was devoted wholly to familiar works, those of the classical masters predominating. This policy was justified by the presence of very large audiences. The season lasted from Oct. 27th, 1913, to June 22nd, 1914. Five of the concerts were conducted by Fritz Steinbach, two by Mengelberg, three by Arthur Nikisch, and one each by Wassili Safonoff and E. F. Arbos. At one of the concerts Paderewski played his Concerto in A minor, the other soloists who appeared during the series including Agnes Nicholls, Mark Hambourg, and the following violinists: Isolde Menges, Paul Kochanski, and Bronislaw Huberman. Another similar series of concerts in Queen's Hall was that given by the excellent New Symphony Orchestra, under Landon Ronald. An important novelty brought to a hearing was Elgar's symphonic poem "Falstaff," which had been produced first at the Leeds Festival. Familiar programmes were framed for the remainder of the series, at which appeared in turn as soloists, Elena Gerhardt, Kirkby Lunn, Mark Hambourg, Isolde Menges, and Daniel Melsa.

Other events that should not pass unrecorded were the Beethoven Festival held at Queen's Hall in April under the conductorship of Henri Verbrugghen; the concerts of Slavonic music given there in June under Emil Mlynarski; those organised in the interests of British music by T. E. Ellis, at one of which was produced Vaughan Williams's "London Symphony"; and the concert of the Queen's Hall Orchestra conducted on June 26th by Richard Strauss. Something of a "sensation" was created by a seven-year-old Italian boy, Willy Ferrero, who conducted the New Symphony Orchestra at some concerts in the Albert Hall.

Choral Concerts.—Under the direction once again of Frederick Bridge the Royal Choral Society amply sustained its reputation in the course of its 43rd season at the Albert Hall. In accordance with almost invariable custom, the Society appealed to its supporters mainly with works in the established repertory. The only novelty of the season was Saint-Saëns's oratorio, "The Promised Land," which first came to a hearing at the Gloucester Festival in September 1913, the other works performed being "Messiah," "Elijah," "The Dream of Gerontius," Gounod's "Redemption," and Coleridge-Taylor's "Hiawatha" and "A Tale of Old Japan." A spirit of enterprise continued to be displayed by the London Choral Society under their enthusiastic conductor, Arthur Fagge. In addition to Beethoven's "Missa Solennis" and a revival of that master's "Mount of Olives," this organisation gave, in the course of its 11th season at the Queen's Hall, several works by British composers, among the novelties being a melodious cantata, "The Eve of St. Agnes," by the veteran John Francis Barnett, a symphonic poem, "King Arthur," by Charlton Speer, and Balfour Gardiner's cantata, "April." A concert performance was also given (on April 1st) of "Parsifal." Among other choral concerts should be noted those of the Edward Mason and Smallwood Metcalfe Choirs, the Bach Choir, the Oriana Madrigal Society, and the Handel Society, while a striking impression was made by the singing of the Swedish National Choir and the Orfeo Catala (from Barcelona), which both paid brief visits to London.

The annual series of Promenade Concerts by the Queen's Hall Orchestra opened on August 15th, and was carried on until Oct. 24th. The season was again under the management of Robert Newman, the conductor being Henry Wood.

Among vocalists the list of the season's concert- and recital-givers included Vernon d'Arnalle, Nathalie Aktzéry, Clara Butt, Theodore Byard, Bertram Binyon, Ilona Durigo (a newcomer who created an exceptional impression as a lieder singer), Murray Davey, Donalda, Felia Dorio, Elena Gerhardt, Plunket Greene, Alma Gluck, Yvette Guilbert, George Henschel (whose farewell as a singer occurred at Bechstein Hall on April 29th), Frieda Hempel, Carmen Hill, Eva Katharine Lissmann, T. Lierhammer, Brabazon Lowther, Lula Mysz-Gmeiner, Blanche Marchesi, Florence Macbeth, Alice Mandeville, Campbell McInnes, Agnes Nicholls, Helga Petri, Kennerley Rumford, Tetrazzini, and Jean Waterston.

In the ranks of **pianists** who came forward were Leonard Borwick, Vera Brock, York Bowen, Lonie Basche, Cernikoff, Dohnányi, Max Darewski, Fanny Davies, Leon Eustration, Louis Edger, Hans Ebell, Herbert Fryer, Polyxena Fletcher, Rudolph Ganz, Percy Grainger, Aurelio Giorni, Howard-Jones, Tora Hwass, Myra Hess, F. S. Kelly, Tina Lerner, Joseph Lhevinne, Frederic Lamond, Robert Lortat, Rosamond Ley, Marguerite Melville, Benno Moiseiwitsch, Dorothy Moggridge, Susanne Morvay, Henriette Michelson, Marie Novello, Leo Ornstein (a young Russian whose extraordinary performances as an exponent of "Futurist" music excited more ridicule than admiration), Egon Petri, Max Pauer, John Powell, Pachmann, Arthur Rubinstein, Sidney Rosenbloom, Scriabine, Cyril Scott, Irene Scharrer, and the clever boy Solomon.

Violin recitals were given by, among others, Sascha Culbertson, Henri Etlin, Frederic Fradkin, Frank Gittelson, Bronislaw Huberman, May Harrison, Kreisler, Lena Kontorowitsch, Kubelik, Paul Kochanski, Daisy Kennedy, Anton Maaskoff, Daniel Melsa, Isolde Menges, Amy Emerson Neill (one of the most successful of the season's débutantes), Albert Spalding, Jacques Thibaud, and Zimbalist. Violoncellists who gave recitals included Livio Boni, Luis Figuéras, Beatrice Harrison, Boris Hambourg, Ioseph Hollman, Enrico Mainardi, Engelbert Röntgen, Felix Salmond, and Arnold Trowell. In the domain of chamber music there were numerous events. Among concert-givers in this branch of music were the Brussels Quartet, the Classical Concert Society, T. F. Dunhill, Geloso Quartet, J. Holbrooke, London Trio, London String Quartet, De Lutece Trio, Rosé Quartet and Wessely Quartet.

In consequence of the war, nearly all the concerts and recitals arranged for the autumn were cancelled.

Provincial Festivals.

A two-days' musical festival was held at Torquay in April, the conductors being Thomas Beecham and Basil Hindenburg. An early symphony by Stravinsky, and new orchestral compositions of an unambitious character by Percy Pitt and G. H. Clutsam, were among the works performed. Owing to the war, the Three Choirs Festival, which should have taken place in September at Worcester, the Norwich and Cardiff Festivals, both due in October, and the Sheffield Festival, announced for November, were all cancelled. Arrangements were made, however, to carry through the scheme of the Brighton Musical Festival in November.

1915

During 1915 there was an enormous range of musical activity. At the end of May, Sir Henry Wood indicated he had conducted 112 concerts in the previous 9 months. The great choral festivals were in abeyance, yet choral music was performed throughout the year. In Manchester on 7 January, Thomas Beecham, a recurring name synonymous with quality and enterprise, conducted the Hallé Orchestra and choirs in Berlioz' "Te Deum" as well as Arnold Bax's "Fatherland", Delius's "Paris" and the last scene from Stravinsky's "Petroushka", and on 21 January Beecham deputised for Bantock at three days' notice to conduct a complete "Omar Khayyam". Beecham's later novelties included Ethel Smyth's choral works "Hey Nonny No" and "Sleepless Dreams" on 4 November.

The Ladies Night of the Bristol Madrigal Society on January 14 celebrated the fiftieth concert conducted by Mr D W Rootham, Stanford ("Ode on Time") and Parry ("La Belle Dame Sans Merci") producing new works. Provincial choral societies continued, "Messiah" being most popular, though "Gerontius" also enjoyed many performances. As an example of local enterprise the Central Croydon Choral Society gave Bantock's "The Fire-Worshippers" on February 13. On April 10, Worcester Cathedral hosted 725 voices from across Worcestershire for Bach's "Christmas Oratorio" in Ivor Atkins' 75-minute version excluding all but one aria.

In Birmingham the spring season was the poorest in memory and the Festival Choral Society and Theatre Royal Promenade concerts were abandoned. Although there was only one concert anywhere during September, a full range of activities were later promoted, including Sullivan's "Golden Legend" on October 16. Yet Clara Butt, returning from her World Tour, chose to make her debut in Birmingham Town Hall on 1

February, and hundreds were turned away. Butt's appearance in London on 27 February marked her first assumption of the role of the angel in Elgar's "Gerontius". Elgar appeared in Birmingham with the LSO. Dvorak's "New World Symphony", the eminent Belgian pianist Arthur de Greef in Saint-Säens' G minor Piano Concerto and his own "Fantasia on Old Flemish Folksongs", as well as Elgar's "Carillon" recited by Constance Collier, were heard. Sir Edward and the LSO were in Liverpool on March 2 and Glasgow on 5 March.

There were notable Delius performances; Beecham repeated "Paris" in London at a Royal Philharmonic Society concert on 26 January, and accompanied young Benno Moiseiwitsch in Delius' Piano Concerto at the LSO's Queen's Hall concert on 8 February.

On January 12, Albert Sammons made his solo debut in Beethoven's Concerto in Glasgow (repeated at Queen's Hall on 12 April), while in Liverpool Ysaÿe appeared for the first time in public since his adventurous escape from Belgium, losing all except his Strad, on which he played Viotti's Violin Concerto No 22. At Liverpool, Sir Henry Wood included Brahms' Third Symphony, and the great German composers, including Wagner, continued to be supported by the public, as at the Bach-Beethoven-Brahms Festival at Queen's Hall in April. Recent Teutonic works were embargoed, but Strauss's "Tod und Verklärung" was heard in Belfast on 26 March.

Many organisations were active: the Committee of Music in War-time; the persistent efforts of Mr Isidore de Lara, especially for British composers; Broadwood's Camp Concerts, and many others, found support. Longstanding series, such as Thomas Dunhill's Chamber Concerts and the Royal Philharmonic Society, contrived to keep going, a typically interesting programme being the second Dunhill Concert of works by women, including Miss Katherine Eggar's Piano Quintet. De Lara's concert on 25 March heard John Ireland's new Trio for Piano, Clarinet and Cello, while that on 10 June featured the Piano Quartet in A minor by Arthur Bliss. At the Edgbaston Botanical Gardens on June 5 a finished performance of Grieg's Sonata Op 8 was given by Master Paul Beard. Concerts ended much earlier than hitherto, and the Royal Choral Society pioneered Saturday afternoon concerts.

At the colleges of music, young artists continued to make a mark, such as A L Benjamin, whose performance of the Cesar Franck "Symphonic Variations" was conducted by Stanford on 16 February at the RCM. At the Academy, students gave Frederick Corder's fine "Elegy" for 24 violins and full orchestra in memory of the RAM's late secretary, Mr F. W. Ranat.

New music included the works of Debussy, Stravinsky and Ravel. March 17 saw the first English performance of Ravel's "Trois Poèmes de Stéphane Mallarmé"; Madame Jane Barthori-Engel sang the ungrateful vocal part most artistically and Beecham conducted. The Société des Concerts Français at Aeolian Hall on June 18 presented Casella in the first performance of Ravel's new trio which was much enjoyed. The Music Club at the Grafton Galleries on 25 January included Carrie Tubb in Stravinsky's "Three Japanese Songs" with orchestra and Albert Sammons introduced Delius's "Legende" with three of Delius' songs newly orchestrated. At Bournemouth the first provincial performance of Vaughan Williams' "A London Symphony" on 11 February, the score recently reconstructed from the orchestral parts after its loss in Germany, was well received; a first provincial performance, too, was Miss Mary Mackenzie's recitation of Elgar's "Carillon".

Arthur Nikisch

Sir Henry Wood and his first wife Olga

Sir Thomas Beecham

Sir Landon Ronald

Sir Granville Bantock

Percy Pitt

Leonard Borwick

Arnold Trowell

Crystal Palace

May Harrison

Beatrice Harrison

Mark Hambourg

Tamara Karsavina as the Firebird

Saint-Saëns

Sinding

Safonov

Mlynarski

Ivor Atkins   Herbert Brewer   George Sinclair

Rosina Buckmar

Marie Hall

The closure of Covent Garden allowed opera in English to flourish. During the Spring, London's Shaftesbury Theatre had a remarkable success with a fourteen-week run including "The Tales of Hoffmann", "Madame Butterfly", "La Bohème" and "Rigoletto" under the batons of Hubert Bath and Hamish MacCunn. But in May, Vladimir Rosing's season of French and Russian repertoire at the London Opera House in Kingsway failed for want of public support for Tchaikovsky's "Pique Dame", Puccini's "Madame Butterfly" and Delibes' "Lakme", the latter two with a Japanese Mimi and a Hindu singer respectively. Benefit concerts were held on 15 and 17 July to relieve the distress of the performers, included the first UK performance of Rachmaninov's opera "Aleko". A second season at the Shaftesbury Theatre started with Gounod's "Roméo et Juliette" on October 2. The season was long-running, four other conductors taking over from Beecham. The London season saw the Carl Rosa Company at the Marlborough Theatre, Moody-Manners at Croydon, and D'Oyley Carte at Hammersmith.

Out of London, Moody-Manners (who premiered Colin McAlpin's prize-winning one-acter "The Vow") were in Nottingham in May; Carl Rosa and the O'Mara Opera Company at Manchester's Gaiety Theatre. At Bournemouth, four concert performances of Rutland Boughton's opera "The Immortal Hour" made a great impression in January with the Bournemouth Municipal Orchestra and Frederick Austin as Eochaidh, Arthur Jordan as Midir and Marjorie Ffrancon Davies as Etain. Charles Kennedy-Scott conducted. The newly-formed Harrison-Frewin Opera Company appeared in Birmingham's Alexandra Theatre with popular operas plus Halévy's "La Juive" and Alfred Bruneau's "The Attack on the Mill", but its biggest success was "The Bohemian Girl". Later came Moody-Manners with a week at the Bordesley Palace Theatre, where Balfe's "The Puritan's Daughter" was followed by Saint-Säens' "Samson and Delilah", plus "The Lily of Killarney", "The Bohemian Girl", "Carmen", "Rigoletto" and "The Daughter of the Regiment" conducted by Aylmer Buest.

That the Glastonbury Festival should survive says much for the untiring energy of Mr Rutland Boughton, who gave Edgar Bainton's opera "Oithona", the orchestral part being played on the piano by Mr Clarence Raybould. The composer, a prisoner at Ruhleben Camp in Germany, was perforce unable to be present.

In Liverpool, Mr Adrian C. Boult promoted his popular orchestral concerts aimed at the growing working audience, in the Sun Hall, but they were not well attended, receipts being less than half the costs, causing Mr Boult to have to make a full call on the guarantee fund established to underwrite them. Later a series of six fortnightly orchestral concerts were announced by Mr Boult from 6 October at the David Lewis Club Theatre.

In Manchester, Mr R. J. Forbes, besides the Delius Piano Concerto at the Hallé Pension Fund Concert, appeared with Mr Arthur Catterall, violin, in the new Violin Sonata by Delius, who was present on 24 February to hear it twice. The sonata was repeated at the Music Club concert in London on 29 April and at an Adela Maddison concert on 30 April.

During May, considerable attention was paid to British composers, firstly with de Lara's series of three concerts of British music, commencing on 29 April. Holbrooke's "Queen Mab Scherzo" and "Auld Lang Syne Variations" were featured in the first two, Frank Bridge conducted his tone poem "Isabella", and Solomon played Stanford's "Down Among the Dead Men". The LSO presented British works in mixed programmes including Delius' new "North Country Sketches" and

Ethel Smyth's "The Wreckers" overture. Beecham, with Mlynarski, Ronald and the LSO, presented a Festival of three concerts of British Music at Queen's Hall, high points being Delius' "Sea Drift", Bantock's "Fifine at the Fair", Holbrooke's "The Bells", Elgar's Violin Concerto (with Albert Sammons), Cyril Scott's new Piano Concerto, Vaughan Williams' "In the Fen Country" and Bax's "In the Faery Hills". The end of May saw the production of Donald Francis Tovey's Symphony under the baton of Henri Verbruggen.

Second Lieutenant Edward Mason, cellist and conductor of the choir that bore his name, was killed on active service on 9 May in his 37th year; he was unfortunately soon followed by William Denis Browne, who was killed at the Dardanelles on 7 June.

Stanford's Second Piano Concerto was played by Harold Bauer at Norfolk (Connecticut) in June, Stanford travelling to the USA for it. On 6 July a Polish benefit concert at Queen's Hall featured Elgar's new symphonic prelude "Polonia" conducted by the composer.

Sir Henry Wood was active throughout the year, and on 17 April his own orchestration of Moussorgsky's "Pictures from an Exhibition" was heard. The Promenade Concerts opened at Queen's Hall on August 14 (the Queen's Hall Orchestra now the New Queen's Hall Orchestra). Sir Henry eschewed living Germans but played the classical composers and Wagner, as a compromise in the debate which flared up on the announcement of the programmes. Sir Arthur Markham, MP, strongly attacked the inclusion of German music and Hubert Bath attempted to start a boycott. The first programme drew an immense audience, and the novelties included the Alsace composer Loeffler's "The Death of Tintagiles" (17 Aug); Debussy's "Fragments Symphoniques" from "Le Martyre de St-Sébastien", and Haydn Wood's Piano Concerto played by Miss Auriol Jones (26 Aug). Of the special "Allies programmes", the Russian night on 12 September had an overwhelming audience for Tchaikovsky but also Stravinsky's "Fireworks" and Sibelius' "Finlandia". A Wagner night on 6 September drew a large audience. Moiseiwitsch played the Delius Concerto, and a substituted programme on 15 September was mainly Italian but included Frank Bridge's heartfelt "Lament".

1916

As in the previous year, the war inevitably cast its shadow over the musical world during 1916. Yet, taking all the circumstances into account, the record of activities in one sphere and another afforded ground for congratulations and for confidence in the future. Enterprise was by no means at a standstill, and if little was attempted upon venturesome lines—concert-givers, in particular, showing a disposition to rely upon proved attractions rather than tempt the public with the unfamiliar—it stands to the credit of the leading musical organisations that they one and all contrived a national times to " keep the flag flying."

To Sir Thomas Beecham opera-lovers were placed under a considerable debt. For, with the doors of Covent Garden closed since the summer season of 1914, it was left to that enthusiastic musician to supply their needs. Wisely he turned his energies in the direction of opera in English, and with such admirable and encouraging results that there is good reason to hope that a permanent public has now been created in London for the support of similar enterprises. Starting in association with Robert Courtneidge, he carried through a season at the Shaftesbury of which the tale, begun in the autumn of 1915, was continued in the New Year. Apart from familiar works of the established repertory, such as the Puccini operas ("Manon Lescaut," among them, being staged for the first time in English), "Il Trovatore," "Tales of Hoffmann," etc., Sir Thomas Beecham devoted particular attention to the production of new native works. First of them (on Jan. 14) was an "operatised" version of "The Critic" by Sir Charles Stanford, who, with the assistance of Cairns James, had arranged Sheridan's text for the purpose. No small measure of success attended the experiment. The satiric spirit of the famous comedy was well preserved, and reflected at moments in the music, even if the score as a whole may have been found lacking in humour. But in tokens of ripe musicianship it was strong, and the opera proved welcome, moreover, for its typically British flavour. Among the artists who particularly distinguished themselves in a performance of uncommon excellence were Frank Mullings (Don Whiskerandos), Caroline Hatchard (Tilburina), Lena Maitland, and Herbert Langley, Frederick Ranalow, Percy Heming, and Albert Chapman.

Another notable production was that, on Jan. 28, of Ethel Smyth's "The Boatswain's Mate," founded upon W. W. Jacobs's well-known story. The composer, her own librettist, had turned the characteristic humours of that tale to capital account, although her score, in this respect, was less successful than might have been hoped. Apparently she was unable to resist the temptation to exploit the strength of her musical resources, and there were scenes, accordingly, of which the effect and appropriateness would have been greater had she seen fit to adopt simpler methods. Incidentally the composer drew very cleverly upon the airs of native folk-song, and, apart from the over-elaboration referred to, her work was a notable addition to the limited repertory of British operas. In the three leading characters Courtice Pounds, F. Ranalow, and Rosina Buckman achieved remarkable success. Another novelty staged, but of a wholly different order, was a little work entitled "A Voice in the Desert," the music of which, by Elgar, was designed to accompany and illustrate a poem by Emile Cammaerts, who drew his inspiration from the anguish caused by the war in his native Belgium. The music showed the composer to be in perfect sympathy with his theme. At the Aldwych a further season of opera under the same auspices was opened on April 15 with a performance in the vernacular of Mozart's "Magic Flute," the principal parts being sustained by Miriam Licette, Sylvia Nelis, Maurice D'Oisly, Alfred Heather, F. Ranalow, and Robert Radford. Other works given included "La Bohème," "Madame Butterfly," "Tales of Hoffmann," "Cavalleria," "Pagliacci," and "The Critic." Interrupted by a season carried out by Beecham in Manchester, the enterprise was resumed on June 13, with a remarkably fine revival of Verdi's "Otello," sung in Italian by, among other artists, Auguste Bouilliez (a singularly gifted Belgian baritone), Mignon Nevada, and Webster Millar. The season was notable also for performances of Moussorgsky's extraordinarily impressive music-drama, "Boris Godounov," given in French for the reason, no doubt, that the rôle of the protagonist was assigned to the Belgian singer mentioned above. All the other operas staged were performed in English. They included "Tristan and Isolde," of which, with Frank Mullings and Rosina Buckman in the title-parts, and Robert Radford as King Mark, performances of quite memorable excellence were witnessed ; a delightful operatic version of Bach's "Phœbus and Pan," Mozart's "Il Seraglio," Gounod's "Faust" and "Romeo and Juliet," and "The Boatswain's Mate." All the works were mounted in first-class style, and rendered in a way that proved a revelation to those who had been sceptical of the adaptability of British singers to the needs of opera. In addition to those already mentioned, the artists who appeared during the Shaftesbury and Aldwych seasons comprised Jeanne Brola, Doris Woodall, Edith Evans, Edith Clegg, Juliette Autran, Olive Townend, Bessie Tyas, Ethel Toms, D. Erlinger, Frederick Blamey, William Samuell (a rarely-gifted young Welshman whose premature death was a real loss to native opera), Gerald O'Brien, Arthur Wynn, Powell Edwards, and Frederic Austin, by all of whom admirable work was accomplished. As conductors there appeared Thomas Beecham, Percy Pitt, Julius Harrison, and Eugene Goossens, junr. The season concluded on Aug. 5, and a further one was opened under the same auspices in October, with Saint-Saëns's "Samson and Delilah."

CONCERTS

At the head of the established musical organisations that "kept the flag flying" was the Royal Philharmonic Society, which carried through its 104th season, giving eight concerts at Queen's Hall under the conductorship of Sir Thomas Beecham. The programmes were admirably varied and refreshingly unhackneyed. Features of particular interest were the suites, etc., from the ballets of Stravinsky and other Russian composers. British music was represented in works by Balfour Gardiner, Arnold Bax, Frank Bridge, Mackenzie, F. Corder, Sterndale Bennett (the centenary of whose birth was observed), and Norman O'Neill ; while the soloists who appeared during the season were : vocalists—Mignon Nevada, Elsa Stralia, Ben Davies ; pianoforte : Fanny Davies, Myra Hess, Pachmann, Arthur Rubinstein, Kumschisky, Sapellnikov ; violin : Renée Chemet, John Saunders, Ysaye ; viola : Lionel Tertis ; flute : A. Fransella, Daniel Wood.

The London Symphony Orchestra's twelfth series of concerts in Queen's Hall opened on Oct. 25, 1915, and concluded on May 29, twelve concerts in all being given. Five were conducted by Beecham, three by Mlynarski, two by Safonoff, one by Arbos, and one by Sir Henry Wood. In the programmes framed for the season there was a discreet blending of the classical, the quasi-modern, and the modern. Thus Bach, Handel, Mozart, Haydn, Gluck, Beethoven, Schubert, and Weber were found in company with Berlioz (whose "Romeo and Juliet" Symphony was revived), Schumann, Brahms, and Wagner, while Tchaikovsky (who had a programme to himself), Rimsky-Korsakov, Moussorgsky, Borodin, Dvořák, Grieg, Saint-Saëns, César Franck, Parry, Elgar, Delius, Bantock, and Ethel Smyth stood for modern art. The season's soloists included Madame Réjane (who recited the text of Elgar's fine "Carillon "), Carrie Tubb, Miriam Licette, Doris Woodall, Ethel Toms, Frank Mullings, Alfred Heather, A. Bouilliez, Fanny Davies, May and Beatrice Harrison, Pachmann, Arthur de Grief, Albert Sammons, and Arthur Catterall.

Under Sir Henry Wood an excellent season's work stood to the credit of the New Queen's Hall Orchestra. Some twelve Saturday afternoon symphony concerts were given, the programmes being designed to make a wide appeal to lovers of the familiar, as represented by the works of the classical masters and popular examples of the established modern repertory. A fine performance of Franck's Symphony in D minor was an outstanding feature of the season, as was Albert Sammons's splendid playing of Elgar's Violin Concerto. Among other soloists who came forward under these auspices were Clara Butterworth, Mark Hambourg, Irene Scharrer, Guilhermina Suggia (a highly accomplished 'cellist), Sapellnikov, Tita Brand Cammaerts, William Murdoch, Benno Moiseiwitsch, Solomon, and A. Rubinstein. Sir H. Wood's Orchestra also gave 26 Sunday-afternoon concerts in Queen's Hall. The usual season of Promenade Concerts began there on Aug. 26, and lasted eight weeks.

At the Albert Hall the popular Royal Choral Society gave some eight concerts, relying upon the performance of such long-enduring works as " Messiah," " The Creation," and " Elijah," and, on the modern side, Verdi's " Requiem," Elgar's " Gerontius," and Coleridge-Taylor's " Hiawatha." Sir Frederick Bridge was once again in control as conductor, and, notwithstanding the depletion of the ranks of his male singers owing to the war, the Society well maintained its reputation.

A memorable feature of the musical season was an Elgar Festival at Queen's Hall organised by Clara Butt on behalf of the British Red Cross Society. As the result of six performances of his " Dream of Gerontius," which the composer conducted, a large sum was handed over to that organisation. Among established institutions, the Chappell " Ballads " at Queen's Hall and the London Ballad Concerts at the Albert Hall received support, a welcome innovation at the former being the appearance of a small orchestra conducted by Alick Maclean. The Albert Hall Sunday concerts also continued to enjoy favour under the conductorship of Landon Ronald. Recitals were considerably fewer than in normal times, but hearings were claimed, among other pianists, by Pachmann, Mark Hambourg, Fanny Davies, Adela Verne, Moiseiwitsch, A. Rubinstein, York Bowen, and William Murdoch (whose recitals in association with Albert Sammons proved particularly interesting), and by a fair number of vocalists, etc. ; while in the field of chamber-music excellent work was achieved, notably by the London String Quartet, the London Trio, the Philharmonic Quartet, J. Holbrooke, and T. F. Dunhill. The " All-British " concerts at Steinway Hall (in connection with the War Emergency scheme organised by Isidore de Lara) were the means of introducing some admirable examples of native chamber-music.

1917

The musical season of 1917 was chiefly remarkable for Sir Thomas Beecham's activities in the domains of opera. In most other spheres of enterprise music remained under the adverse influence of the war, which necessarily restricted the efforts of concert-givers and the opportunities of artists. Covent Garden Theatre having been closed since July 1914 (in the course of the year under notice it was " commandeered " by the Government and used by them as a furniture repository), opera-lovers would have fared but badly had it not been for Beecham's continued endeavours to popularise the performances of opera in English, setting as his aim a high artistic standard and a completeness of ensemble and detail previously unattained in London by any manager working upon similar lines.

Having concluded a winter season at the Aldwych on Feb. 10, Beecham, on May 30, entered into possession of Drury Lane, starting his enterprise with a memorable revival (in English) of Verdi's " Otello," in which Frank Mullings displayed notable power as the Moor, Frederic Austin appearing as Iago, and Mignon Nevada in the rôle of Desdemona. This was followed by the first performance in English of Puccini's " Girl of the Golden West," with Robert Parker (an American artist who achieved singularly fine work in a variety of parts, including that of Boris Godounov), Walter Hyde, and Jeanne Brola in the chief characters. In " Tristan and Isolde," Mullings and Rosina Buckman repeated the uncommonly fine impression they had created in previous seasons ; as also, in " Louise," did Miriam Licette, Maurice D'Oisly, Frederick Ranalow, and Edith Clegg. " Samson and Delilah " was splendidly sung by Edna Thornton, Hyde, and others, and a very interesting production brought with it the first London

performance of Bizet's fifty-year-old opera, " The Fair Maid of Perth," the suave, graceful melodiousness of which made pleasant hearing. Other operas mounted were " Madame Butterfly," " Boris," " La Bohème," " Aïda," " Cavalleria," " Pagliacci," " Il Trovatore," " La Tosca," " Faust," and " The Marriage of Figaro." Of the last-named there was an extraordinarily picturesque and most successful revival, in an entirely new setting, the opera being staged and dressed in accordance with the fashions of Beaumarchais' period. The season, during which Beecham, Percy Pitt, and Eugène Goossens, jun., were the chief conductors, lasted till the end of July.

On Sept. 22 another Beecham campaign was opened at Drury Lane with an impressive performance of Rimsky-Korsakov's " Ivan the Terrible," a work—then sung for the first time in English—characteristic of the composer's rare sense of rich orchestral colouring and containing a wealth of beautiful Russian folk-melody. Robert Parker's impersonation of Ivan (a rôle recalling the triumphs of Chaliapin on the same stage in 1913) was of notable strength and excellence, while Jeanne Brola, Walter Hyde, Ethel Toms, and Powell Edwards also acquitted themselves ably in other parts. Moussorgsky's " Khovantchina " was among the operas subsequently staged.

After many years' absence from central London the Carl Rosa Company also unfurled the banner of opera in English at the Garrick, where, beginning on May 3, they held a season—subsequently transferred to the Shaftesbury—which lasted till July 7. A revival of Bruneau's " The Attack on the Mill " was an interesting feature, as also was Ben Davies's return to the stage in " Maritana " and " The Bohemian Girl." The other operas performed were " Tales of Hoffmann," " Carmen," " Butterfly," " Faust," " The Magic Flute," " Cavalleria," " Pagliacci," " The Marriage of Figaro," " Aïda," " Rigoletto," " Tannhäuser," " Il Trovatore," " Mignon," " The Lily of Killarney," and " The Merry Wives of Windsor."

CONCERTS AND RECITALS

With its 792nd concert the Royal Philharmonic Society entered upon its 105th season. Of the six functions held, five were conducted by Thomas Beecham, and the concluding one by Landon Ronald, while Elgar appeared on one occasion to conduct his second symphony. The only absolute novelties brought forward during the season were Frederic Austin's symphonic poem " Palsgaard," and a song, " Have you news of my boy Jack ? " composed by Edward German for Clara Butt, who introduced it. Other British composers represented in the programmes were Bantock, Delius, Elgar, Percy Pitt, and Ethel Smyth ; there were eight French works—the composers being Chabrier, Debussy, Franck, Ravel, and Saint-Saëns ; while Russia was represented by Balakirev, Glinka (from whose opera " A Life for the Tsar " scenes were performed), Gretchaninov, Rachmaninov, Rimsky-Korsakov, and Tchaikovsky. Of German composers only those whose names stand for the classics, old and modern, appeared in the list. In addition to Clara Butt, the soloists who came forward during the season were Miriam Licette, Kirkby Lunn, Frederick Blamey, Frederick Ranalow ; Eugène Ysaye and Pachmann.

The record of the New Queen's Hall Orchestra's activities in their 21st season (1916–17) was a busy one, and included fourteen symphony concerts and twenty-six Sunday-afternoon programmes, all conducted by Sir Henry Wood. At each of the symphony concerts a novelty was introduced. The list included two interesting examples of the modern Spanish school—the late Granados's symphonic poem " Dante," and Turina's picturesque " La Procession du Rocio," while Albeniz's folk-suite " Catalonia " was given in a revised version. Other novelties comprised four French works, two inspired by the war—" Les Cathédrales," by Gabriel Pierné, and Th. Dubois's " In Memoriam Mortuorum "—the remaining two being Henri Rabaud's symphonic poem " La Procession Nocturne," and a curious work of the " atmospheric " type, " Les Dieux dans l'ombre des Cavernes," by Albert Roussel. Unfamiliar British scores were W. H. Reed's orchestral caprice " Will o' the Wisp," and Two Poems for orchestra by Frank Bridge, quite modern in feeling and treatment. Four Russian works were added to the repertory : a Suite based by Rimsky-Korsakov upon his opera " The Legend of Tsar Saltan " and Kalinnikov's overture " Tsar Boris " typifying the older generation ; and Ostroglazov's " Illustration from the Apocalypse " and Tcherepnin's new Pianoforte Concerto (splendidly played by Moiseiwitsch) being representative of the younger school. Several classical works were also performed in the way of symphonies and so forth, and among the artists heard during the season were: instrumentalists—Albert Sammons, Adela Verne, Guilhermina Suggia, Pachmann, Kathleen Parlow, Irene Scharrer, Myra Hess, de Greef, May and Beatrice Harrison, Melsa, and Wm. Murdoch ; vocalists—Marguerite d'Alvarez, Doris Manuelle, Carrie Tubb, Rosina Buckman, and Gervase Elwes.

On Aug. 25 the New Queen's Hall Orchestra entered upon the annual season of Promenade Concerts, with Henry Wood again as conductor. The programmes were of an attractively varied character, and in the list of new and unfamiliar works British composers drawn upon were Joseph Speaight, the late Lt. George Butterworth, John Ireland, H. Waldo Warner, Percy C. Buck, Norman O'Neill, Montague F. Phillips, Dora Bright, and Howard Carr.

For the most part the programmes carried out by the London Symphony Orchestra in the course of their 13th series of concerts at Queen's Hall were made up of familiar music. Of the first two Safonov took charge, the opening concert being dedicated to Beethoven, and the three remaining were conducted by Hamilton Harty who, at the final concert, on March 19, directed the first London performance of Granville Bantock's " Hebridean " Symphony, an interesting, somewhat complex work based largely upon folk-song, and requiring more than one hearing for a complete understanding. On the same evening (March 19) Arthur de Greef was the soloist in a Pianoforte Concerto of his own, then heard for the first time in England.

Under the direction of Sir Frederick Bridge a successful season was carried through at the Albert Hall by the Royal Choral Society, all the concerts taking place in the afternoon. " Elijah " was the opening attraction, and, in addition to standard works such as " Messiah," Verdi's " Requiem," " The Dream of Gerontius," and ' Hiawatha," there were given Elgar's " For the Fallen " and Parry's " Chivalry of the Sea " (both war-inspired compositions), Stanford's " Songs of the Fleet," Coleridge-Taylor's " Kubla-Khan," and a selection of Christmas carols. Among the artists who took part in the concerts were Ruth Vincent, Agnes Nicholls, Clara Butterworth, Carrie Tubb, Stralia, Muriel Foster, Dilys Jones, Ada Crossley, Phyllis Lett, Kirkby Lunn, Ben Davies, Walter Hyde, Alfred Heather, Gervase Elwes, John Coates, Thorpe Bates, Plunket Greene, George Parker, Herbert Brown, Robert Radford, Bertram Mills, and Frederick Ranalow.

At the Royal Albert Hall Landon Ronald again conducted a successful series of Sunday-afternoon concerts.

In the ranks of recital-givers were : vocalists—Clara Butt, Marguerite d'Alvarez, Doris Manuelle, Kirkby Lunn, Jeanne Jouve, Jean Sterling Mackinlay, Zoia Rosowsky, Olga Haley, Muriel Foster, Helen Henschel, Alys Bateman (who gave various concerts for war charities), Emilia Conti, Vladimir

Rosing, Hugh Marleyn, Austen Carnegie, Constantin Stroesco, Boris Lensky, Boris Bornoff, Lecomte, and Julian Bonell ; pianists—Pachmann, Moiseiwitsch, Leonard Borwick, Wm. Murdoch, Mark Hambourg, Victor Benham, Budden-Morris, Archy Rosenthal, Solomon, Fanny Davies, Adela Verne, Gertrude Peppercorn, Myra Hess, Lily Henkel, Teresa Carreño, Bert Berthe, Mania Seguel, Rhoda Backhouse, and Ethel Hobday ; violinists—Daisy Kennedy, Sybil Eaton (a rarely-gifted newcomer), Yvonne Yorke, Constance Izard, Rhoda Backhouse, Stella Ambrose, and Tessie Thomas (a young Welsh girl who made a remarkable impression).

1918

Activities in the musical world were again considerably restricted by the continuance of war. Of a kind there was no lack of musical entertainments, and concerts, perhaps, were quite as numerous, having regard to the circumstances, as could reasonably be expected. But, for the majority of them, no particular interest could be claimed, and, save for a few exceptional enterprises, the record of the year's music was chiefly remarkable for what was accomplished in the domains of opera. And, in this matter, the public were once again very largely indebted to Sir Thomas Beecham, who, notwithstanding the heavy obstacles that had to be faced, pluckily carried through two important seasons at Drury Lane. The first opened on March 2 and lasted five weeks, and in connection with both ventures the manager adhered to his previous policy of giving only performances of opera in the vernacular and enlisting for them the services exclusively of native artists. And, as most of the latter had served under his banner in several previous seasons, the performances derived all the advantages that come of a well-ordered and thoroughly experienced ensemble.

For the most part, moreover, the admirably disciplined company was called upon to display its quality in works with which every member had long been upon familiar terms. Thus, in the spring season, singers now as well known and deservedly appreciated as Rosina Buckman, Miriam Licette, Jeanne Brola, Sylvia Nelis, Edna Thornton, Edith Clegg, Frank Mullings, Maurice D'Oisly, Webster Millar, Alfred Heather, Frederick Ranalow, Frederic Austin, Robert Parker, Powell Edwards, Norman Allin, Foster Richardson, and Robert Radford, were heard in such popular works of the established repertory as " The Marriage of Figaro," " The Magic Flute," " Seraglio " —in all which the Beecham artists again showed how well they had mastered the difficult art of Mozart-singing; Verdi's " Aïda," " Othello," and " Trovatore," Wagner's " Tristan and Isolda " (the composer's early opera, " Tannhäuser," which formed an addition to the repertory, being staged afterwards in very elaborate fashion) ; and modern favourites like Puccini's " Bohème," " Madame Butterfly " (in which Desirée Ellinger, one of the younger members of the company, made an excellent impression by her charming singing and acting), and " Tosca." " Cavalleria " and " Pagliacci " completed the list of Italian operas ; while " Faust," " Samson and Delila," " Louise," and " Carmen " were the French works represented in the scheme, the last-named revived with Doris Woodall in the title-part. Russian opera was again exemplified in Moussorgsky's " Boris Godounov " and Rimsky-Korsakov's " Ivan the Terrible." From the financial standpoint the season proved more successful than any similar enterprise for which Sir Thomas Beecham had been responsible in London.

The summer season under the same management was opened on June 3, and was continued until the end of July. The repertory was substantially the same as that drawn upon earlier in the year. A very noteworthy addition, however, took the form of a revival of "The Valkyries," which had not been staged in London since the outbreak of war. In English, moreover, the public had not heard it sung since the memorable performances of "The Ring" conducted at Covent Garden by Richter some ten years previously. Wagner-lovers manifested extraordinary interest in the revival and packed the vast spaces of Drury Lane at each representation of the famous music-drama. As at the Covent Garden performances just referred to, Walter Hyde (the Siegmund), Robert Radford (a magnificent Hunding), Agnes Nicholls (Brünnhilde), and Edna Thornton, appeared in the cast, and, in greater or lesser degree, these artists brought to their task a measure of skill and sympathy that earned for them warm tributes. Miriam Licette was the Sieglinde, her singing being characterised by sweetness rather than power, and Robert Parker sang Wotan's music sonorously, his portrayal of the part being deficient only in dignity of bearing. On the whole, however, the performance of the work maintained a high level, and reflected immense credit upon all concerned; more especially on Sir Thomas Beecham, who conducted it and obtained from the orchestra a vivid reading of the wonderful score.

Two other features of the season call for special mention. One was a welcome revival of Ethel Smyth's clever opera, "The Boatswain's Mate," which, founded upon W. W. Jacobs's amusing story of that title, had dropped out of the repertory shortly after its production at the Shaftesbury by the same company a few years ago. The work made a better impression than at the original hearing. The other feature came late in the season and served to introduce the public to Rimsky-Korsakov's extraordinarily quaint opera "The Golden Cockerel" ("Coq d'Or") in the form in which it was written. In the bizarre garb of a "ballet-opera" it was staged at Drury Lane in 1914, during a memorable Russian season. Whether a work so unconventionally fanciful and far-fetched in its humours (which in the original Russian version bore a satirical significance that, for political reasons, led to its immediate withdrawal) is ever likely to command much popularity in this country is more than doubtful. Nevertheless, if only for the charm and cleverness of much of the music, which, like everything from the same pen, is beautifully coloured and touched with rare fancy, the production of Rimsky-Korsakov's whimsically conceived work proved very interesting.

It should be added that, in addition to Beecham himself, the two seasons of opera brought forward, as conductors, Percy Pitt, Eugene Goossens—senior and junior—Julius Harrison, and Wynn Reeves, and that, as regards completeness of detail, in staging as in all else, both ventures were characterised by the high standard of artistic taste that had marked those previously carried out by the same organisation.

On May 6 the Royal Carl Rosa Company opened a season at the Shaftesbury, which concluded on June 15. In addition to the established repertory, the works performed included a novelty in the shape of a short opera, by Stephen Philpot, entitled "Dante and Beatrice," of which the music proved conventional after a well-worn pattern. Another native opera, the late Hamish MacCunn's "Jeanie Deans," a clever and interesting work, was revived on May 10; and on June 10 the Company's jubilee was commemorated by a special performance.

CONCERTS AND RECITALS

Yet another season (the 106th) was carried through at Queen's Hall by the Royal Phil-

harmonic Society, under the control of Sir Thomas Beecham, who conducted all the concerts save one, at which Landon Ronald assumed command. The orchestral works performed, apart from classical examples, included Bantock's "Fifine at the Fair," Chabrier's "Espana" Rhapsody, Debussy's "Three Nocturnes," an excerpt from Delius's "A Village Romeo and Juliet," Dukas's "L'Apprenti Sorcier," Elgar's "Enigma" Variations, Julius Harrison's "Rapunzel," Holbrooke's "Queen Mab" Scherzo, Schumann's "Carnaval" (as scored for the Russian Ballet), Ethel Smyth's "On the Cliffs of Cornwall," Tchaikovsky's "Francesca da Rimini," and Wm. Wallace's "Villon." The soloists who appeared were: Vocalists—Bessie Tyas, Edna Thornton, Frank Mullings, and Norman Allin; Pianoforte—Arthur de Greef, Benno Moiseiwitsch; Violin—Albert Sammons; Viola—Lionel Tertis; 'Cello—Beatrice Harrison. During the season the Society gave its 800th concert.

The New Queen's Hall Orchestra held their 22nd season of symphony concerts under the conductorship of Sir Henry J. Wood. For the most part familiar works were drawn upon, but the following novelties were introduced: Frederick Converse's symphonic-poem "Ormazd," Rimsky-Korsakov's "Symphoniette on Russian Themes," Glazounov's "Two Preludes" for Orchestra, Roger-Ducasse's scherzo, "Le Joli Jeu de furet," Nicolas Kasanli's fantasia "Nuit de Carnaval," Florent Schmitt's etude symphonique "Le Palais Hanté"; Gustave Samazeuilh's orchestral poem "Le Sommeil de Canope." Among the soloists whose services were enlisted during the season were Marguerite D'Alvarez, Zoïa Rosowsky, Kirkby Lunn, Gervase Elwes; Pianists—De Greef, Moiseiwitsch, W. Murdoch, Leonard Borwick, Adela Verne, Myra Hess, Irene Scharrer; Violin — Albert Sammons; Violoncello — Guilhermina Suggia and Beatrice Harrison.

At the Albert Hall Sir Frederick Bridge conducted the 47th season of the Royal Choral Society. In addition to the works in the usual repertory, performances were given of Elgar's "The Spirit of England," Vaughan Williams's "Sea Symphony," Stanford's "Songs of the Fleet," and Parry's "Chivalry of the Sea." The soloists comprised Agnes Nicholls, Carrie Tubb, Ruth Vincent, Olga Haley, Elsa Stralia, Dilys Jones, Phyllis Lett, Ben Davies, Gervase Elwes, Walter Hyde, W. Boland, Thorpe Bates, Plunket Greene, Robert Radford, Herbert Brown, Frederick Ranalow, Norman Allin, and Bertram Mills. On Aug. 10 the 24th season of Promenade Concerts was opened at Queen's Hall, under the management of Robert Newman and the conductorship of Sir Henry Wood.

Among other regular features of the musical season were the Chappell Ballad Concerts at Queen's Hall (with Alick Maclean as the conductor of the orchestra). In the same building Adrian Boult conducted a series of concerts whereat the London Symphony Orchestra performed several British works, including Vaughan Williams's fine "London" symphony. At the Æolian Hall the Oriana Madrigal Society (C. Kennedy Scott, conductor), helped as in past seasons to keep up interest in old-time unaccompanied vocal music; and the London Trio (Sammons, Amina Goodwin, and W. E. Whitehouse) gave a number of chamber concerts. There, too, several series of admirable "Pop" concerts were given by the London String Quartet—who also appealed to lovers of chamber music at a series in Queen's Hall. Native works by, among others, J. B. McEwen, J. Holbrooke, Cyril Rootham, J. D. Davis, Eugene Goossens, jun., and Murray Davey, were performed by these gifted players. There were also chamber concerts by the Philharmonic Quartet, the Catterall Quartet, and at Leighton House; while at the Grafton Galleries a new series was started, Fanny Davies, William Murdoch, G.

Suggia, and Marjorie Hayward appearing at the first concert. At Steinway Hall the "All-British" concerts were continued by Isidore de Lara, who also organised an Italian Festival (three concerts) in Queen's Hall during the summer season. Rene Ortmans conducted a small orchestra at some concerts in Wigmore Hall where Gwynne Kimpton directed a few performances by her Amateur War Orchestra.

Sunday concerts were conducted at the Royal Albert Hall by Landon Ronald, who, on one occasion, produced Stanford's "Verdun"; and in Queen's Hall by Henry Wood. Special events that should be recorded were a concert given in the hall just mentioned, on Jan. 31, in honour of Major J. Mackenzie Rogan, the doyen of British military bandmasters on the attainment of his jubilee; and a notable function at which L'Orchestre de l'Armée Belge appeared in the Albert Hall (July 10), which was honoured by the presence of the King and Queen as well as the King and Queen of the Belgians. The band of the famous Italian Carabinieri gave a memorable concert there on Sept. 25.

Among recital-givers were the following: Singers—D'Alvarez, Felice Lyne, Carrie Tubb, Muriel Foster, Rosowsky, Doris Manuelle, Olga Haley, Gladys Moger, Evelyn Arden, Phyllis Lett, Raymond Collignon, Annabel McDonald, Margaret Cooper, Van der Beeck, Patuffa and Marjory Kennedy-Fraser, Gervase Elwes, Vladimir Rosing, Constantin Stroesco, Yves Tinayre, Plunket Greene, Fraser Gange; Pianists—Moiseiwitsch, Pachmann, Herbert Fryer, W. Murdoch, Victor Benham, Lloyd Powell, Claude Biggs, Archy Rosenthal, Myra Hess, Dorothea Vincent, and Gertrude Peppercorn; Violinists—Daisy Kennedy, Jessie Snow, Tessie Thomas, Lena Kontorovitch, Margaret Fairless, Rhoda Backhouse, Murray Lambert, Phyllis Allan, Albert Sammons, Zacharewitsch, Vigliani; Viola—Lionel Tertis; Violoncello—Felix Salmond.

1919

Operatically the year was notable for the re-opening of Covent Garden, where a season—the first held since the summer of 1914—was run from May to the end of July by the Grand Opera Syndicate in connection with Sir Thomas Beecham. The difficulties attending a renewal, at short notice, of an enterprise involving such heavy preparations and the bringing over of artists from all parts of the Continent at a time when travel facilities were still considerably restricted made it impossible for the opera authorities to soar to any great heights. For the most part they had to rely on the established repertory. But two or three novelties, or quasi-novelties, were added thereto, the most interesting of the new works being Ravel's "L'Heure Espagnole," a one-act opera which owed not a little of its piquant attractiveness to the unaccustomed humours of its libretto. Isidore de Lara's "Naïl" (sung in English) proved a rather wearisome exercise in the Oriental; while Mascagni's twenty-two-year-old Japanese opera, "Iris," failed to prove attractive, despite some music decidedly above the commonplace level of his "Cavalleria." Nor was any particular impression made by Massenet's "Thérèse."

Melba was the chief of the pre-war "stars" who returned to the operatic firmament, while a welcome hardly less enthusiastic awaited the still incomparable Emmy Destinn, who now appeared under her Czechish name of Destinnova. Edvina advanced her reputation, and familiar faces were those also, among others, of Donalda, Mignon Nevada, Rosina Buckman (enrolled under the Beecham banner), Louise Bérat, Kirkby Lunn, Martinelli (who returned with his powers greatly developed), Sammarco, Huberdeau, Maguenat,

Dinh Gilly, and Malatesta; while, among the new-comers, a very favourable impression was made by Marguerite Sheridan, a young Irish soprano, Thomas Burke, an English tenor, Ansseau, and Lappas, the former a French, the latter a Greek, tenor, both of fine accomplishment. The conductors were Beecham, Albert Coates, Mugnone, and Percy Pitt. The operas staged, with the number of performances (83 in all), were as follows: "Madame Butterfly, 5; "Aïda, 7; "Bohème," 9; "Un Ballo in Maschera," 2; "Il Barbiere di Seviglia," 3; "Faust," 6; "L'Heure Espagnole," 3; "Iris," 3; "Louise," 4; "Manon," 5; "Naïl," 2; "Prince Igor," 1; "Romeo et Juliette," 3; "Pagliacci," 6; "Rigoletto," 4; "Il Segreto di Susanna," 3; "Traviata," 3; "Tosca," 7; Thérèse, 2; "Thaïs," 5.

At Drury Lane there was a season of opera in English by the Thomas Beecham Company from March 19 to May 3, and highly successful it proved. The performances, which enlisted the services of the singers who had appeared in previous seasons under the same auspices, were of an admirable all-round standard, the works given including "The Magic Flute," "Marriage of Figaro," "The Seraglio," "Boris Godounov," "Khovantchina," "Ivan the Terrible," "The Boatswain's Mate," "Coq d'Or," "Aïda," "Tristan and Isolde," "Tannhäuser," "La Bohème," "Manon Lescaut," "Madame Butterfly," "Louise," "Samson and Delilah," and "Falstaff," of which masterpiece there was a belated, but very welcome, revival on the last night of the season. A few weeks later Beecham revived Lecocq's famous operetta, "La Fille de Madame Angot," in a new English version, for a limited number of performances. On Nov. 3 Beecham opened a two-months' season of opera in English at Covent Garden, a revival of "Parsifal" being among the features.

The Royal Carl Rosa Opera Company carried out a season of opera at popular prices at the Lyceum, opening on July 14. Crowded houses were the rule, and encouragement was given to native opera by the production of two novelties: Reginald Somerville's "Antoine," a melodious work with a fairly dramatic book, and Percy Coltson's "Pro Patria," a one-act opera which obtained a favourable reception.

Mention should be made here of an extraordinarily successful season of the Russian Ballet, which drew all London, as the phrase goes, to the Alhambra throughout the summer season. A delightfully whimsical ballet, "La Boutique Fantasque," wedded to melodies by Rossini, proved the most popular of the novelties, and Karsavina, Lopokova, and Leon Massine were the chief stars of the company. On Sept. 29 the Russian Ballet opened another season at the Empire. On the same evening began, with "The Gondoliers," a series of revivals of Gilbert—Sullivan operas at Prince's, under the management of Rupert D'Oyly Carte and Gilbert Miller. The advance bookings for the season constituted a record.

CONCERTS AND RECITALS

Of concerts, recitals, and the like the spring, summer, and autumn seasons brought an abundance. It must suffice to refer to some of the more important enterprises. At Queen's Hall the Royal Philharmonic Society held their 107th season, with, as conductors, Landon Ronald, Adrian C. Boult, and Geoffrey Toye. In addition to classical scores, and those in the more or less established modern repertory, the works performed comprised a new violin concerto by Delius, Gustav Holst's "The Planets," an extraordinarily clever and complex suite, Charles Stanford's second pianoforte concerto, which was new to London, and a very engaging and characteristic "Theme and Six Diversions," by Edward Germain. Elgar's "Falstaff" was a welcome addition to the Philharmonic repertory, and the season's soloists were Olga Haley,

George Baker, Robert Radford, Albert Sammons, Margaret Fairless, Myra Hess, and Moiseiwitsch.

The 23rd season of Symphony Concerts given at Queen's Hall by the New Queen's Hall Orchestra, under Sir Henry Wood, was marked by no little diversity and interest of programmes. A feature of particular interest was the appearance of Emma Calvé, who had not sung in London since the "old" Covent Garden days, and delighted all by the beauty and vitality of her style; while another very welcome return was that of the distinguished French pianist, Cortot. Interesting British novelties were Delius's Ballad for orchestra, "Eventyr," and a fine setting by Frank Bridge of Rupert Brooke's sonnet, "Blow out, you bugles," Gervase Elwes being the soloist. At other concerts of the series there appeared D'Alvarez, Muriel Foster, Carrie Tubb, Carmen Hill, Margaret Balfour, and, on the instrumental side, Myra Hess, Irene Scharrer, Leonard Borwick, A. de Greef, Moiseiwitsch, Lilia Kanevskaya, A. Sammons, Melsa, and Guilhermina Suggia.

From May 19 to 24 Robert Newman gave in the same hall a series of Beethoven Symphony Festival concerts to celebrate the 25th anniversary of his management of orchestral concerts. Henry Wood was the conductor. Under the latter's direction the annual season of Promenade Concerts was opened on Aug. 16, and continued for ten weeks.

Drawing upon the customary repertory, the Royal Choral Society held their 48th season at the Albert Hall, Sir Frederick Bridge conducting. Ruth Vincent, Carrie Tubb, Agnes Nicholls, Edna Thornton, Olga Haley, Phyllis Lett, Kirkby Lunn, Ben Davies, Gervase Elwes, Walter Hyde, Frank Mullings, Alfred Heather, Herbert Brown, Charles Tree, Norman Allin, Frederick Ranalow, Bertram Mills, Herbert Heyner, and Robert Radford were among the soloists. Other organisations that "carried on" effectively were the Alexandra Palace Choral Society, the Strolling Players Orchestral Society, the Bach Choir, and the Oriana Madrigal Society; while Hamilton Harty conducted several concerts of the London Symphony Orchestra, including a Sunday series at the Palladium. There were also Sunday concerts by the Queen', Hall Orchestra, and Landon Ronald's Orchestras the latter at the Royal Albert Hall, where also was given a series of special Sunday concerts, at which Melba, Clara Butt, Pachmann, and other "stars" appeared.

Chamber music was well to the fore, and owed much, notably, to the excellent work of the London String Quartet, the Classical Concert Society, the London Chamber Concert Society, the London Trio, the Philharmonic Quartet, the Harmonic Trio, the Catterall String Quartet, and the concerts of British music organised by Isidore de Lara.

Vocal recitals were given by, among other artists, Melba, Tetrazzini, Clara Butt, D'Alvarez, Muriel Foster, Donalda, Gladys Moger, Sylva van Dyck, Luia Juta, Ann Thursfield, Mrs. and Miss Kennedy-Fraser, John Coates, Vladimir Rosing, Plunket Greene, Murray Davey, Constantin Stroesco, Yves Tinayre, Hubert Eisdell, Mischa-Léon, Herbert Heyner, Gregory Stroud, and George Fergusson. Among pianists who came forward were Katharine Goodson, Adela Verne, Fanny Davies, Myra Hess, Hilda Saxe, Bertha Bert, Louie Basche, Lilias Mackinnon, Dorothy Howell, Frederic Lamond, Cortot, Victor Benham, Harold Samuel, Harry Field, Lloyd Powell, Moiseiwitsch, William Murdoch, Sydney Rosenbloom, and T. P. Fielden.

The list of violinists who gave recitals included Daisy Kennedy, May Harrison, Murray Lambert, Katie Goldsmith, Jessie Snow, A. Sammons, John Dunn, Anatol Melzak, Sascha Lasserson, Joseph Coleman (a young Russian of considerable accomplishment), Edith Abraham (another gifted newcomer), W. H. Reed (who introduced a new violin sonata by Elgar), and Michael Dore, a player of brilliant gifts. Violoncello recitals were given

by Beatrice Harrison, Suggia, May Mukle, Marie Dare, Cedric Sharpe, Georges Pitsch, and Livio Mannucci.

1920

Looking back upon the operatic side of musical activities in 1920 an impartial critic might easily arrive at the conclusion that its more important features were to be found not in the "grand" season at Covent Garden during the summer, but in the season of opera in English which preceded it there. Both ventures were given under the auspices of Sir Thomas Beecham, who, by virtue of arrangements entered into with the Grand Opera Syndicate, assumed entire direction of the second or "international" season, as it was called, thereby considerably enlarging the sphere of his operatic responsibilities. But, for reasons presently to be stated, that venture proved by no means epoch-making, and, as already said, there was really more of genuine interest for opera-lovers in the performances sung in the vernacular during the season that opened on Feb. 24 with a revival of "Parsifal." Albert Coates conducted the representations of that much-discussed work, and performances of conspicuous merit were those of Norman Allin as Gurnemanz and Gladys Ancrum as Kundry. Walter Hyde sang the title-part. On March 10 came the season's crowning event in a revival of another Wagner masterpiece, "The Mastersingers," the performance of which, having regard to the very considerable difficulties that had to be faced, reached a remarkably high standard, and showed that in Frederick Ranalow (the Hans Sachs), Webster Millar (Walter), Edmund Burke (Pogner), Herbert Langley (Beckmesser), Maurice D'Oisly (David), Miriam Licette (Eva), and Edith Clegg (Magdalene) we have British singers well able to hold their own against continental rivals. The orchestral reading of the score, under Beecham, was superlatively fine. Another interesting event of that English season, although one naturally appealing to a smaller section of the public, was a revival of a charming native work—Delius's "A Village Romeo and Juliet," which, originally staged at Covent Garden in 1910, had failed, largely because of its inherent dramatic weaknesses, to win for itself a place in the repertory. The two principal parts were sustained in the revival by Walter Hyde and Miriam Licette. Another opera by a British composer, Isidore de Lara's "Naïl," was also afforded a further hearing, with Rosina Buckman, Frank Mullings, and Percy Heming in the rôles they had filled in the production of that work in 1919. After the lapse of many years there was also a revival of Bizet's early little opera "Djamileh," while another early work of his, "The Fair Maid of Perth," was also given a place in the repertory. For Mozart-lovers there were performances of "The Magic Flute" and "Seraglio," while the season further brought in its course "Tristan and Isolde," Agnes Nicholls singing very finely in the latter rôle to the Tristan—often seen before —of Frank Mullings; "Tannhäuser" (with the artist last named and Elsa Stralia in the chief parts); "Faust," "Samson and Delilah" (Frederick Blamey and Edna Thornton as the protagonists), "Cavalleria" and "Pagliacci." The season ended on April 10.

As has been indicated, the "international" season held in the summer—May 10 to July 31—proved disappointing. The list of operas was insufficiently varied, and the general level of performance decidedly below that to which the habitués of Covent Garden had been accustomed. But for the appearance in the course of the summer of the famous Russian Ballet, headed by Karsavina and Massine, the season would have been voted singularly uneventful; yet, of evenings devoted exclusively or in part to the ballet there were so many that, had the purely operatic side of the venture been more in keeping with the traditions of the house, not a few opera-lovers might reasonably have complained of so much attention being given to another art-form. The opera season as such was chiefly remarkable for the introduction of the three one-act operas by Puccini which were originally staged in New York in 1918. Forming a trittico, these works, in the order of their representation, were " Il Tabarro," a piece of frank melodrama somewhat after the Grand Guignol pattern ; " Suor Angelica," of which the scene is a convent, all the dramatis personæ being women; and " Gianni Schicchi," a work in striking contrast to either of its companions by reason of its atmosphere of bustling humour. The whole spirit of that humour was found to be most faithfully and adroitly reflected in the music, the style and feeling of which bore some affinity to the Verdi of " Falstaff." But collectively the three operas proved rather too ample a feast, and on several occasions subsequent to their production one or another of them was given apart from the others.

A feature of the season that excited no little interest and curiosity was Dame Clara Butt's operatic debut—not counting her appearance in 1892 as a R.C.M. student—in Gluck's " Orphée." But, generally speaking, that revival was not of a distinguished order, a far higher level of achievement being reached, for example, in a revival of " Pelléas et Mélisande," with Edvina and Maguenat in the title-parts. The artist last named, a baritone, was among the most capable of the season's singers ; while another baritone, Ernesto Badini —excellent, more particularly, as Schicchi and in a revival of " Don Pasquale "—was, with Graziella Pareto (a coloratura artist who appeared in Bizet's " Pêcheurs de Perles "—sung in Italian —and " Traviata "), among the few newcomers that made any decided impression. The gifted Russian soprano, Maria Kousnezova, was heard at the beginning of the season as Mimi, but soon returned abroad ; and the company's tenors included Ansseau (a welcome recruit of the previous season), Riccardo Martin, Thomas Burke, Lappas, and Joseph Hislop. The latter, a young Scotsman, created a particularly favourable impression, while the invaluable Dinh Gilly rejoined the ranks of the baritones.

Reverting to the Diaghilev Ballet, it should be recorded that in addition to productions in which they had previously been seen, such as " Scheherazade," " Thamar," " La Boutique Fantasque," and " Le Tricorne," they presented, among novelties, an opera-ballet, Cimarosa's " Le Astuzie Femminili," a choreographic version of Stravinsky's " Le Chant du Rossignol," and " Pulcinella," a ballet-opera for which music by Pergolesi, as re-scored by Stravinsky, was used. The list of operas mounted during the season, with the number of performances accorded them, was as follows : " Pescatori di Perle " (4), " Louise " (6), " Pelléas et Mélisande " (3), " Don Pasquale " (2), " Orphée " (4), " Pagliacci " (4), " Thaïs " (2), " Manon Lescaut " (3), " La Bohème " (7), " Tosca " (6), " Madama Butterfly " (3), " Il Tabarro " (6), " Suor Angelica " (2), " Gianni Schicchi " (5), " L'Heure Espagnole " (4), " Traviata " (2), " Manon " (3). The principal conductors were Beecham, Bavagnoli, Coates, Percy Pitt, and—of the ballet—Ansermet.

Performances of ballet were not confined to Covent Garden, for at Drury Lane the distinguished Russian dancer, Pavlova, opened in April a season which continued for several weeks, and was transferred, when the theatre was required for other purposes, to Prince's.

It was not only over Covent Garden that the banner of opera floated. By way of widening the appeal of music-drama in the vernacular a season at popular prices was given in the early part of the year at the Surrey Theatre by Messrs. Fair-

bairn and Miln, the repertory ranging from " Faust " to " The Valkyrie," and including such classic examples as " Don Giovanni " and Gluck's " Orpheus." As an encouragement to native opera there were produced two works, both of them novelties, and both based upon plays of Shakespeare. J. E. Barkworth's " Romeo and Juliet," an opera cast in a mould of simple melodiousness, was the one ; Nicholas Gatty's " Tempest " the other, the latter exhibiting a more advanced and complex style. At the Lyceum the popular Carl Rosa Company held a summer season, adding to their repertory of standard operas Wolf-Ferrari's " Jewels of the Madonna," and Alick Maclean's " Quentin Durward," a native work which had not a little to commend it in the way of direct and unaffected melody set off by musicianship. In the autumn the Carl Rosa forces had a season at Covent Garden.

But the " surprise " of the year in operatic—or quasi-operatic—domains was the immense success that attended a revival, on June 5, as far afield as the Lyric, Hammersmith, of Gay's two-century-old " Beggar's Opera." Probably the quaintness of this production, its utter dissimilarity from any recognised form of opera, and the simple charm of its setting had as much to do with its unlooked-for success as anything else. The performance was mainly in the hands of singers who had served their stage apprenticeship with Sir Thomas Beecham—Sylvia Nelis, Frederick Ranalow, Alfred Heather, and Frederic Austin among them.

CONCERTS AND RECITALS

The activities of the concert season—or rather seasons, as musical events are by no means restricted nowadays to any particular period of the year—were hardly less manifold than usual. Among orchestral organisations pride of place, if only by reason of its age, must go again to the Royal Philharmonic Society, which held its 108th season (Queen's Hall) from Nov. 20 (1919) to May 20, the conductors being Albert Coates, Geoffrey Toye, Adrian C. Boult, Landon Ronald, and C. Kennedy Scott, the last-named taking charge of the newly formed Philharmonic Choir, whose appearances were a noteworthy feature of the series. The choir produced two native novelties, Delius's " Song of the High Hills," and Gustav Holst's " Hymn of Jesus," the latter a work of very considerable importance, and remarkable for its combination of simplicity and modern complexity. Foreign novelties brought to a hearing were Debussy's " Fantaisie " for piano and orchestra and Malipiero's " Le Pause del Silenzio "—an example of uncompromising modernity. Additions to the Society's repertory included Rimsky-Korsakov's " Battle of Kersjémetz," Holbrooke's " Ulalume," Scriabin's " Divine Poem " and Piano Concerto in F sharp minor, Percy Grainger's " Morning Song in the Jungle " and " Father and Daughter " (choral pieces), and Lalo's Violoncello Concerto. The solo singers who appeared were Carrie Tubb, Marguerite Nielka, Olga Haley, Carmen Hill, Margaret Balfour, Hubert Eisdell, and Murray Davey, the solo instrumentalists being Alfred Cortot, William Murdoch, Albert Sammons, Guilhermina Suggia, and Goss Custard (organ).

On Jan. 10, following the Christmas lull, the New Queen's Hall Symphony Orchestra resumed their twenty-fourth season of symphony concerts, under Sir Henry J. Wood. The symphonies performed in the course of the season, which ended on April 17, were Schubert in C major and B minor, Brahms in C minor and F major, Dvorák in E minor, Sibelius in A minor, and Chausson in B flat. Strauss's tone-poem, " Don Juan," was restored to the repertory, and among native works heard were Granville Bantock's Hebridean sea-poem, " The Sea Reivers," Delius's Violoncello Concerto, and Julius Harrison's " Worcestershire Pieces "—these three works being novelties ; Geo

Butterworth's " A Shropshire Lad," Vaughan Williams's " Norfolk Rhapsody " (No. 1), Geo. Dyson's " Siena," and the prelude to Act 2 of Ethel Smyth's " The Wreckers." First performances were given of Debussy's " Berceuse Heroique " and Roger Ducasse's " Suite " for small orchestra. The vocalists heard during the season were Calvé, Rosina Buckman, Félice Lyne, Kirkby Lunn, Margaret Balfour, and Gervase Elwes, and the solo instrumentalists Lamond, A. de Greef, Myra Hess, Melsa, May Harrison, Beatrice Harrison, and Suggia. On Aug. 14 the usual season of Promenade Concerts was opened at Queen's Hall under the conductorship of Henry Wood. Among other orchestral concerts of note were those given sporadically by the London Symphony Orchestra, the conductors including Beecham, Albert Coates, and Adrian Boult, and those also by the Royal Albert Hall Orchestra, which, under the command of Landon Ronald, gave a special Elgar concert at Queen's Hall. An interesting event was a visit from the New York Symphony Orchestra, whose performances under Walter Damrosch attracted a considerable amount of attention, and were remarkable for their flawless technical proficiency.

Chief among the year's choral doings was the revival of the historic Handel Festival at the Crystal Palace, beginning on June 19. Some fine performances of familiar masterpieces were given by the huge forces massed under Sir Frederic H. Cowen. The soloists engaged were Agnes Nicholls, Carrie Tubb, Esta d'Argo, Phyllis Lett, Kirkby Lunn, Ben Davis, Frank Mullings, Walter Hyde, F. Ranalow, Robert Radford, and Norman Allin. At the Albert Hall the Royal Choral Society held their 49th season, under Sir Frederick Bridge's direction, the repertory being on traditional lines, and including " Messiah," " Elijah," " Hiawatha," and " Gerontius," as well as smaller works by Parry, Stanford, Coleridge Taylor (" A Tale of Old Japan "), Balfour Gardiner, Hamilton Harty, Percy Fletcher, and Hubert Bath. Interesting features of the season were performances given at Queen's Hall by the Ukranian National Choir (conductor, Alex. Kochitz), Guldberg's Academic Choir from Norway, and the Newport Choral Society ; while the London Choral Society, under Arthur Fagge, re-emerged after the lapse of some years. An entirely new body, the Westminster Choral Society, gave a series of concerts at the Central Hall, Vincent Thomas being the conductor. In the domain of chamber music a good deal of activity was displayed in one direction and another, among the leading native organisations that obtained support for their ventures being the London String Quartet, London Chamber Concert Society, British String Quartet, Henkel Pianoforte Quartet, Edith Robinson Quartet ; while distinguished visitors were the Bohemian String Quartet (whose programmes included works by Elgar and Arnold Bax), and the famous Flonzaley Quartet. A concert at Wigmore Hall devoted to the chamber works of Stravinsky excited considerable interest because of the strangeness of the composer's idiom.

An unaccustomed feature of the summer season took the form of what came to be spoken of as the " American invasion," the allusion being to the number of artists who came across the Atlantic to give recitals in London. The singers in this category included Anna Case, Mabel Garrison, Sophie Braslau, Marcia van Dresser, Lambert Murphy, Cecil Fanning, and Reginald Werrenrath, the latter a remarkably fine baritone. Among other vocalists who gave recitals were Melba, Tetrazzini, Calvé, d'Alvarez, Mignon Nevada, Olga Haley, Flora Woodman, Clara Butt, Megan Foster, Dora Gibson, Dorothy Robson, Ursula Greville, Gina Sadero, Dorothy Silk, Diana Lawrence, John Coates, Tom Burke, Vladimir Rosing, Ronald Hayes (a Negro tenor), Gerald Cooper, Mischa-Léon (whose recital of German songs in the original text, given at the Aeolian Hall on March 13, was not allowed to proceed until there had been an anti-German demonstration), W. Johnstone-Douglas, Georgio Corrado, Mark Raphael, and Douglas Marshall. Pianists who came forward included Busoni, Lamond, Arthur Shattuck (American), W. Morse Rummel, Montariol-Tarres, Anderson Tyrer, Jan Herman, William Murdoch, Boyden Monteith, Claud Biggs, Howard-Jones, York Bowen, Leo Livens, Edwin S. Mitchell (the last-named specialising in Scriabin, as also did Lilias Mackinnon and Eyridice Draconi), Fanny Davies, Isabel Gray, Harriet Cohen, and Chilton-Griffin. Of the many violinists who were heard none created a greater " sensation " than Jascha Heifetz, a young Russian, whose playing, if it disappointed many of his hearers on the interpretative side of his art, astonished all by its flawless and brilliant technique. The list of violinists further included Jelly and Adila d'Aranyi, Albert Sammons, Isolde Menges, Margaret Fairless, Sybil Eaton, Murray Lambert, Michael Doré, Zacharewitsch, Dushkin, Joseph Coleman, Louis Godowsky, Achille Rivarde, and Yovanovitch-Bratza, a wonderfully gifted Serbian youth.

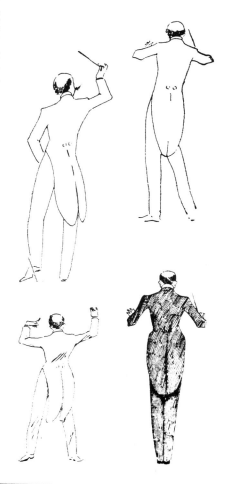

Mr Boult conducting (sketches by F B Craig).

INDEX